**Studia Fennica**
Historica 22

The Finnish Literature Society (SKS) was founded in 1831 and has, from the very beginning, engaged in publishing operations. It nowadays publishes literature in the fields of ethnology and folkloristics, linguistics, literary research and cultural history.

The first volume of the Studia Fennica series appeared in 1933. Since 1992, the series has been divided into three thematic subseries: Ethnologica, Folkloristica and Linguistica. Two additional subseries were formed in 2002, Historica and Litteraria. The subseries Anthropologica was formed in 2007.

In addition to its publishing activities, the Finnish Literature Society maintains research activities and infrastructures, an archive containing folklore and literary collections, a research library and promotes Finnish literature abroad.

Studia Fennica Editorial Board
Editors-in-chief
Pasi Ihalainen, Professor, University of Jyväskylä, Finland
Timo Kallinen, University Lecturer, University of Helsinki, Finland
Taru Nordlund, Professor, University of Helsinki, Finland
Riikka Rossi, Title of Docent, University Researcher, University of Helsinki, Finland
Katriina Siivonen, Title of Docent, University Teacher, University of Turku, Finland
Lotte Tarkka, Professor, University of Helsinki, Finland

Deputy editors-in-chief
Anne Heimo, Title of Docent, University of Turku, Finland
Saija Isomaa, Professor, University of Tampere, Finland
Sari Katajala-Peltomaa, Title of Docent, Researcher, University of Tampere, Finland
Eerika Koskinen-Koivisto, Postdoctoral Researcher, Dr. Phil., University of Helsinki, Finland
Laura Visapää, Title of Docent, University Lecturer, University of Helsinki, Finland

Tuomas M. S. Lehtonen, Secretary General, Dr. Phil., Finnish Literature Society, Finland
Tero Norkola, Publishing Director, Finnish Literature Society, Finland
Virve Mertanen, Secretary of the Board, Finnish Literature Society, Finland

oa.finlit.fi

Editorial Office
SKS
P.O. Box 259
FI-00171 Helsinki
www.finlit.fi

# Continued Violence and Troublesome Pasts

Post-war Europe between the Victors after the Second World War

Edited by Ville Kivimäki and Petri Karonen

Finnish Literature Society • SKS • Helsinki • 2017

**STUDIA FENNICA HISTORICA 22**

The publication has undergone a peer review.

The open access publication of this volume has received part funding via Helsinki University Library.

© 2017 Ville Kivimäki, Petri Karonen and SKS
License CC-BY-NC-ND 4.0. International

Cover Design: Timo Numminen
EPUB: Tero Salmén

ISBN 978-952-222-857-4 (Print)
ISBN 978-952-222-904-5 (PDF)
ISBN 978-952-222-903-8 (EPUB)

ISSN 0085-6835 (Studia Fennica)
ISSN 1458-526X (Studia Fennica Historica)

DOI: http://dx.doi.org/10.21435/sfh.22

This work is licensed under a Creative Commons CC-BY-NC-ND 4.0. International License.
To view a copy of the license, please visit http://creativecommons.org/licenses/by-nc-nd/4.0/

 A free open access version of the book is available at http://dx.doi.org/10.21435/sfh.22 or by scanning this QR code with your mobile device.

BoD – Books on Demand, Norderstedt, Saksa 2017

# Contents

PETRI KARONEN & VILLE KIVIMÄKI
Suffering, Surviving and Coping: Experiences of Violence and Defeat in Post-War Europe 7

## I Continued Violence: Estonia and Poland

ANU MAI KÕLL
Between Germany and Russia: Settling Scores from the Occupations in Post-War Estonia (1945–1950) 29

MARTA KURKOWSKA-BUDZAN
'Coming Out of the Woods': How Partisans of the Polish Anti-Communist Underground Adapted to Civilian Life 44

## II Reorienting and Taking Distance: Germany and Austria

MARIANNE ZEPP
Redefining Germany: Women's Politics in the Post-War US Occupation Zone 63

MARIA FRITSCHE
Austrian Men 'Do Everything with Feeling!': Representations of Masculinity in Post-War Austrian Cinema (1946–1955) 85

## III Gendered Memories: Finland and Hungary

Tiina Kinnunen
Fallen Angels, Fallen Nation?: Representations of Patriotic Women and Images of a Nation in Finland's Post-War Memory 109

Andrea Pető
Silencing and Unsilencing Sexual Violence in Hungary 132

List of Authors 145

Abstract 148

Index 149

Petri Karonen
ⓘ http://orcid.org/0000-0001-6090-5504

Ville Kivimäki

# Suffering, Surviving and Coping: Experiences of Violence and Defeat in Post-War Europe

Seventy years after the end of the Second World War (WWII) and over twenty years after the collapse of the Soviet Union, historical studies on both the 'short' and the 'long' post-war eras in Europe are flourishing. The perspectives and topics in this field are wide-ranging. At least from the early 2000s onwards, the emphasis has been shifting from the much-studied subjects of Cold War politics and the economic and social history of reconstruction toward cultural historical studies on individual and collective experiences and memory.[1]

A key reason for this change is well expressed by Frank Biess, who has approached the post-war period in Germany from a cultural and social-historical angle, noting that 'postwar societies needed to face more than just the classical tasks of reintegrating returning soldiers or even of converting a wartime to a peacetime economy.' There was also the massive effort needed to 'come to terms with the legacies' of unprecedented ethnic cleansing and genocide.[2] Understanding and discussing – as well as willfully neglecting – these legacies have been fundamental elements of post-war European identities and politics. In this respect, it is still relevant today to study the after-effects of war in Europe. One crucial task is to map the different spheres and dimensions of the transition from war to peace and to try to find intranational, as well as international connections between them – if there are any – thus slowly gaining a fuller picture of the 'European aftermath' from 1945 to the 1990s.[3]

Nevertheless, the socio-cultural impacts of WWII have so far not yet attracted the same amount of scholarship as the impacts of the First World War. According to Pieter Lagrou, this is partly due to the broadly shared European experience of violence in 1914–1918, whereas the memories of violence in 1939–1945 were more varied, divisive and contested in different parts of Europe.[4] Furthermore, right up until the end of the 1980s and early 1990s, Europe remained very much a post-war continent, scarred as it was by the Iron Curtain. This prolonged acuteness of the aftermath may have made it difficult to write a closing chapter to the era. Finally, sixty years after 1945, the late Tony Judt published his magisterial *Postwar: A History of Europe since 1945*, which is so far the most comprehensive account of the long post-war period. This is largely due to Judt's skill and insight in including the oft-forgotten histories of Central and Eastern European countries in his narrative. Judt powerfully demonstrates the burdens and suffering of the civilian populations and the massive destruction of cities and infrastructure especially in German-occupied countries,[5] where, east of the Elbe, the liberation from the Germans in 1944–1945 brought first the merciless maelstrom of war and then a new form of totalitarian regime under the Soviets. In this area between Berlin and Moscow, which had already suffered the worst of both the Stalinist terror and the Holocaust, the Anglo-American narrative of a 'good war' in 1939–1945 could hardly have been more inappropriate.[6]

## 'Zero Hour' and the Continuation of Violence

It is partly against this background that the popular concept of 'zero hour' (*die Stunde Null*) should perhaps be criticised. The term has been used to refer to Germany's total defeat and setting the clock back to zero, so that May 1945 would mark a fresh start and a decisive break from the past. There was a dire need to forget the horrors of the past decades and to start a whole new era, both politically and individually. Morally, too, the idea of a 'zero hour' helped to distance the post-war Germans from the Nazi regime and all its crimes. In this sense, the concept captures an essential (German) experience and sentiment at the end of the war.[7] However, Mark Mazower among others has challenged the 'old idea that 1945 had been a kind of Year Zero'.[8] For many in Central and Eastern Europe, the capitulation of Germany did not mean an end to violence and totalitarianism, but its continuation; and the direct consequences of war could not simply be pushed aside. In Germany itself, despite the denazification and re-education programs, many of the former Nazi officials and authorities retained their positions.[9]

After the war, the legitimacy of official authorities was weak everywhere in continental Europe. The reasons for this are obvious in the defeated countries. But also in those countries that had been occupied by Germany during the war, many of the local office-holders had served the occupiers in one way or another. In the Soviet-controlled areas, there was a strong pressure to purge fascist or allegedly fascist-affiliated functionaries.[10] In addition to such systematic campaigns, spontaneous acts of revenge and cleansings by outraged people were also widespread. Tens of thousands of Europeans continued to be killed in this way, just as they had before the end of hostilities; while in Western Europe, too, death sentences were a common occurrence.[11]

The continuation of wartime atrocities, expulsions, and purges well into the post-war period is now a widely recognised aspect of the human history of the aftermath, and there is a growing amount of research on these traumatic topics. The staggering number of refugees and displaced people in Europe threatened further human disaster and required huge and immediate relief efforts. In the area of the former Third Reich, there were over 10 million foreign slave labourers and concentration camp victims that needed to either return to homes that had been destroyed or find new ones.[12] After the war, as many as 20 million people suffered forced migration and ethnic cleansing; around 13 million of these were Germans from Central Eastern Europe now moved to the new, smaller Germany.[13] The situation of displaced and often also orphaned children was especially grave.[14] In the final stages of the war and in its immediate wake, it has become clear that hundreds of thousands if not over a million girls and women were raped by Soviet soldiers in German areas or in countries allied to Germany.[15] This violent mayhem, which Hitler's murderous regime had brought upon the German people as a whole, is still a source of the troublesome politics of memory and victimisation.[16] Immediately after the war, Germans tended to downplay their concentration and extermination camps as no worse than the Soviet gulags. Frank Biess has categorised the narratives of victimisation in East and West Germany into Christian, social-democratic, and communist: in the West, 'the most influential promoters of narratives of victimisation were the Christian churches'.[17]

At the end of WWII, millions of men were either in military service or in foreign captivity. In Europe, the demobilisation of vast armies in different countries is still a relatively little-studied subject.[18] In the United States, on the other hand, the homecoming of 'the greatest generation' and the Servicemen's Readjustment Act of 1944 (the G.I. Bill of Rights) has gained more attention. Michael D. Gambone has called this act 'arguably the greatest social-welfare program in U.S. history'.[19] After the G.I. Bill, the educational status of American veterans improved greatly, and the number of university students soared – as it did in many European countries, too.[20] In the Soviet Union the demobilisation of over 8.5 million Red Army soldiers posed a gigantic task. All in all, the effort lasted until the end of 1948, and despite the positive tone of the official propaganda, there were serious shortcomings and much corruption involved in providing proper housing and jobs for the veterans.[21]

The brutal treatment of close to six million Soviet prisoners of war by the Germans in 1941–1945 had resulted in over three million deaths, and subsequently those who survived often had to face harsh treatment as 'traitors' from their own Soviet regime.[22] In the case of Germany, the return of approximately two million prisoners of war from Soviet captivity lasted until the 1950s.[23] Of the former German allies, Italy, Finland, Rumania and Bulgaria had changed sides in 1943–1944 and turned their armies against the Germans. Hungary, by contrast, was occupied by Germany in March 1944 and was then made to follow the Nazi regime into the abyss of its final defeat. As a consequence, over half a million Hungarian soldiers and civilians were taken prisoner by the Red Army. Their return to Hungary continued until 1956, while an estimated 100,000–150,000 Hungarians perished in Soviet captivity.[24]

## Gendered Experiences of Reintegration

So far, according to David A. Gerber, the history of those left disabled by the war has not received enough attention. Their post-war situation was especially troublesome in defeated or occupied countries.[25] In Austria, for instance, the mere presence of war invalids was an unwelcome reminder of the Nazi past, clashing with the cherished myth of Austria as 'the first victim of National Socialism'.[26] Thus, the soldiers' homecoming did not just mean bringing celebrated heroes back into society; indeed, especially where defeated nations, prisoners of war, and serious physical and mental traumas were concerned. Rather, their return could be perceived as a crisis of masculinity;[27] in terms of the concrete wounds in men's bodies and the symbolic wounds in the image of military men. This image had been closely linked to the national identity, had now raised the question of redefining the ideals of manliness. In his fine study of prisoners of war in both Germanies, Frank Biess has studied the figure of a physically and mentally exhausted POW coming home from Soviet captivity and described how this figure contrasted so sharply with the previous wartime image of heroic, martial, and aggressive German soldiers. Especially in West Germany, homecomers were encouraged 'to win back their masculinity' by taking on a strong, even authoritarian, position in their families and becoming the breadwinners, thus allowing (or forcing) women to return to more traditional roles.[28] In the analysis of post-war masculinities and gender roles, the concept of 'remasculinisation' has been used to describe this social, cultural, and political process; one where manly subjectivity and authority is reclaimed in a post-war society and simultaneously regenerates a national self-image of coherence and strength.[29]

Practically all war veteran surveys in different countries have shown that the veterans did not want to share their experiences with anyone else than their former military comrades.[30] For instance, General George S. Patton noted in his diary in the summer of 1945, '[n]one of them [civilians] realizes that one cannot fight for two and a half years and be the same';[31] and there were many young war veterans who had fought much longer. During the past fifteen years, the terms 'shell shock' and 'trauma' have become focal keywords in studies on WWI.[32] This vein of research is now also becoming visible in research on WWII and its aftermath, although the image of a mentally broken soldier is not so iconic here as for 1914–18.[33] There have been attempts to apply the present-day psychiatric diagnosis of post-traumatic stress disorder (PTSD) in interpreting the psychological consequences of WWII, but such an approach poses some serious problems. Born in the wake of the Vietnam War (and thus in a particular societal and cultural context) PTSD as a medical category is perhaps not the best-suited concept for understanding the trauma of war in a historical context.[34]

For a long time now, the study of women and war has been an active field in women's history. Among the key issues has been the question of the significance of war for the women's movement and female emancipation. As a consequence of total mobilisation in both world wars, vast numbers of women entered formerly 'male-only spheres' of employment – e.g., farm work, various public services, schools, and military auxiliary work. Many contemporary feminists consider the years 1914–1918 and 1939–1945 to have represented periods that saw the greatest progress in women's self-confidence and the women's movement. On the other hand, as many scholars have stressed, this emancipatory progress seems to have been quite short-lived: on the level of cultural norms and values, war could also reinforce traditional gender roles and attitudes, and the wartime deployment of women to 'male tasks' was commonly followed by a post-war backlash in which women were pushed back into the 'female sphere' of the home and marriage.[35]

Indeed, reuniting families and re-establishing homes became one of the major tasks in post-war Europe. Naturally, the urge to return to the normalcy and safety of 'how it used to be' was felt deeply by the majority of post-war populations; this is easy to understand socially and psychologically. However, the return was also a political project that aimed at stabilising and bolstering shattered societies. Usually this stability was conceived on the basis of a conservative view of the family. Our image of the 1950s as a decade of stability, homogeneity and traditional family values may be partly a cliché, but as a stereotype it certainly reflects the *zeitgeist* to some extent.[36] In Europe of the 1940s and 1950s, the shattering effects of war also gave birth to a moral panic about the 'immoral' attitudes and behaviour of post-war youth. With a future that looked dim and uncertain, it was commonplace to project these fears and insecurities onto the alleged moral depravity and deviance of adolescents.[37]

## Politics of Remembrance and Victimhood

The study of memories, remembrance, and memory politics has been one of the most flourishing fields in the cultural history of war.[38] This is especially true with regard to the memory culture of WWI, which has produced a rich body of literature.[39] The Second World War created a haunting memory of completely new dimensions, especially because of the Holocaust, the massive human costs of total war and forced migration, and the advent of the atomic age. Nevertheless, and despite the immediate post-war revelations and trials of war crimes, Western Europe in the 1950s was much more concerned with economic reconstruction and social stabilisation than making any critical evaluation of the recent past. It may be surprising to see how late in the 1960s and 1970s the testimonies of the Holocaust and the war of annihilation in the East made their way into European – and especially German – memory culture. Although not forgotten, this genocidal past had not occupied a central place in remembering the war. Today, this remembrance of perpetration seems to be contested by memory discourses which again emphasise the victimhood of the Germans produced by the Allied strategic bombing campaign and the expulsion of the civilian population from the East.[40]

In the countries east of the Iron Curtain, the post-war memory culture was to a great extent dominated by an endeavour to legitimise the new Stalinist rule and to build up a cult of the glorious Red Army. As a result, the memory of non-communist victims and opponents of the Nazi regime was officially ignored, as was Stalinist responsibility for the war and any cruelties committed by the liberating Red Army. These harsh memories have nevertheless survived well in the form of personal and family remembrance in Eastern and Central Europe. As the historian Krisztián Ungváry has said of the Hungarian memory culture of the war, one of the tragic consequences of the Red Army's brutalities against the civilian population in 1944–1945 was that the Hungarians were thus allowed to escape from confronting their own responsibility for the war and the Holocaust: among the memories of the war, it was the suffering of one's own kin and people that remained in the foreground.[41] After the collapse of the Soviet system there is now finally public space for the open contemplation of historical responsibilities and forgotten victims – but unfortunately also for revanchist and chauvinistic reinterpretations of the past.

The horrific legacy of 1939–1945 has made it quite difficult to remember WWII with much glory. Despite the Anglo-American memory narrative of saving democracy from totalitarianism and the Soviet epic of the Great Patriotic War, the fundamental experience of war for so many Europeans was that of immense personal losses and often meaningless hardships. Of the victorious European nations, only Great Britain (though greatly weakened) and the Soviet Union avoided total collapse and occupation. This means that overall, the memory culture of WWII in Europe is very much one of defeat.[42] One of the central themes in research has thus been the memory and remembrance of the fallen, but here, too, most of the studies have focused on the victims of the First World War. However, the 'memory boom' of the past twenty years is clearly visible in studies dealing with WWII and its aftermath as well.[43] Instead of national or collective memory cultures, many recent studies have shown the fragmentation, diversity, and controversial nature of memories among different groups and individuals. Jay Winter, who is critical of the concept collective memory, prefers to use the term historical remembrance, which 'overlaps with personal or family remembrance on the one hand and religious remembrance, so central to sacred practices, on the other'. Historical remembrance may be seen as an interpretation of the past, which includes both history and memory.[44] Even now, seventy years after the end of WWII, our historical understanding of 1939–1945 is closely bound up with the active cultures of remembrance of those who have direct experiences of those years. In the aftermath of the seventieth anniversary of 1945, it is still too early to regard the post-war period as mere history; at the time of writing these lines, the memory politics and rhetoric of WWII and its aftermath are again being used, and perhaps abused, to serve contemporary power politics in Eastern Europe.

## Between Victors: This Volume

The following six chapters will offer case studies that concretise many of the issues described above. This anthology brings into focus some of the lesser known histories of the aftermath; in addition to Germany, the studies discuss the different aspects of the post-1945 situations in Estonia, Poland, Austria, Finland, and Hungary. The rationale of the book is to study the aftermath of WWII from three overlapping angles: defeat, gender, and the countries between the victors. It is very important to pay attention to these countries that have escaped the standard Western and Soviet narratives of liberation and post-war development as they produce a more nuanced and often ambiguous picture of that troubled period. This is what makes the study of Hungarian, Austrian, Polish, Estonian, Finnish, and German cases interesting.

During WWII, the Baltic countries were subject to successive occupations by the Soviet Union and Germany. **Anu Mai Kõll** writes about the situation in Estonia at the end of the war. Estonia had to deal with a foreign occupying power yet again, and a new political regime. Establishing a new political order in Estonia meant vetting the population in order to find trustworthy citizens as well as possible traitors and threats to the new rulers. Thus, for the Estonian people, reorientation meant understanding and complying with the requirements of the new regime. The Estonian case shows how people survived a difficult new situation by adapting in one locality (Viljandimaa). As Kõll points out, the success of the repressive Soviet policies was possible because local Estonian people agreed to cooperate. Cooperation could be, for instance, either a survival strategy, an opportunity for social mobility, or a means of settling scores. There is no one single story to explain post-war reorientation in Estonia.

**Marta Kurkowska-Budzan** examines Polish post-war experiences in a country that was forced to become a part of the communist bloc. Her chapter's focus is on anti-communist partisans in Poland and how they afterwards explained their decision to join and then to leave the anti-communist resistance. Kurkowska-Budzan presents the perceptions of the people themselves, the recollections of 'ordinary' soldiers, and especially of those who at some point ceased to pursue the anti-communist struggle and tried to adapt to civilian life. Those who did not do so, either died in fighting or vanished in prisons. The former soldiers interviewed by Kurkowska-Budzan between 2003 and 2008 give us a glimpse into a kind of lost post-war history, which was subsequently vindicated after the collapse of communism. However, the life histories of former anti-communist partisans are less tales of unfaltering heroism, and more often of survival and adaptation to usually undesirable circumstances.

Unlike in 1918, the German defeat of 1945 was total and unconditional. With millions of working-age men in foreign captivity and the country in ruins, the immediate post-war era in Germany has been called the hour of the woman. **Marianne Zepp** studies those West German women activists, who early on rose to the task of drawing inevitable conclusions about the bankruptcy of Nazism and who were ready and able to seek out a new path towards a democratic, liberal and more gender-equal Germany. Their efforts ran in parallel with the re-education policies of the western powers, the aim of which was to eradicate Nazism and totalitarianism. At the onset of the Cold War, this anti-totalitarianism was increasingly meant to counter the spread of communism, too, and so in this emerging, polarised context of the 1950s, public and non-partisan women's activism then had to give way to party-centred and largely male-dominated politics.

**Maria Fritsche** looks at the processes of normalisation and the redefinition of masculinities in post-war Austrian film culture. In her discussion of three distinct film genres, Fritsche demonstrates how the construction of a national identity is intertwined with the construction of masculinities: 'real' Austrian males were depicted as sensitive, peace-loving and cheerful – thus distancing both Austrian men and the Austrian nation from the common past with Nazi Germany. Although this new masculinity enabled 'softer' versions of manliness and more equal gender relations, it did not mean giving up the traditional, patriarchal hierarchy altogether. Fritsche's analysis reminds us how cultural identities and a changing society are mutually constitutive and how constructions of gender have a crucial significance in this process.

The memory of war is tightly connected to a nation's self-image and collective imagination. **Tiina Kinnunen** analyses Finnish memory culture of war from the 1950s to 2005 through a discussion of public representations of war that point to important changes in the social, cultural and political frameworks that shape public remembrance. The image of the Finnish woman in wartime played a crucial role in the 'memory wars' after 1945. Representations of wartime women as pure and innocent have maintained the patriotic values of the nation, whereas the image of an immoral, sexually active women has been used to depict the wretchedness of war and the decay of pre-war and wartime conservative patriotism. During the 1990s, as Kinnunen shows, the dutiful sacrifice and suffering of Finnish women came to symbolise the victimhood of a small nation defending itself against a huge aggressive Soviet neighbour. In the midst of these national redefinitions and contested memory politics, the vast variety of women's personal memory narratives is easily forgotten, instrumentalised, and sometimes silenced.

In Eastern and Central Europe, the end of WWII did not mean the end of violence. Together with ethnic cleansing and deportations in 1945 and the years immediately after, the question of sexual violence has perhaps been the most difficult and painful to address. **Andrea Pető** investigates here the ways in which the rapes committed by Red Army soldiers in Hungary could be studied and made visible; but there are two problems. First, the 'ethnicisation' of rape crimes blurs the gendered nature of this violence in a wider military culture, and neglects the fact that Hungarian soldiers also committed rapes in the Soviet Union when they were the occupying force. Second, a study into this topic should respect the dignity and agency of the women who suffered sexual violence, instead of forcing them to remain eternal victims. The images of raped women are also very strong and can draw attention away from the women's own voices. Thus, the real sufferings from the past may become political instruments in constructing collective victim identities, and projecting the perpetrator status on specific targets.

The six chapters in the current volume offer useful points of departure for examining this history between victors. Regarding the experience of defeat, the case of Germany is quite clear – the total war ended with a total defeat. But the national cases of Hungary, Estonia, Poland, Austria, and Finland all also present defeats of various sorts: they had either fought the war on the German side at one point, or suffered occupation and vast-scale destruction, or lost part or all of their national sovereignty. Linked to these different levels of defeat, the processing of war experiences had to adapt to the victorious war narratives in one way or another. This meant the downplaying of former cooperation with Germany and/or the presence of domestic Fascism, while in the Soviet sphere of influence it more usually meant the outright silencing of those experiences, in contrast to the glib narrative of the liberating Red Army. This straitjacket of remembrance was stripped off when communism collapsed, but the effects were not simply emancipatory. Over the past decades, much of Eastern and Central European memory politics of WWII comes across as a bizarre competition for 'real victimhood', so much so that the uniqueness of the Holocaust has been in danger of being subjected to historical relativism. Yet the history of those countries in 1944–1945 and after cannot be reduced to mere identity politics but must be studied in all its complexity. As we see, this is the only means to overcome the continuous, ethnicity-based split to collective victims and perpetrating 'others'. And this is one main reason why the questions of remembrance and memory also have a strong presence in the current volume.

In addition to the various aftermaths of defeat, a second theme brings together most of the chapters here: the ultimate importance of gender in studying post-war histories. This may be a universal phenomenon, connected to the issues of establishing and reintegrating families after years of separation. Yet gender seems to have particular relevance in the context of lost wars. On the level of concrete experiences, an occupation and/or defeat had several gender-specific ramifications: the absence of men and the collapse of male authority, women's high responsibility in keeping the families together, their role in communal matters and in establishing new relations, and the sexual violence of foreign soldiers. On the level of collective ideals and identities, one must add the highly gendered representations of defeat, victimhood and violence. As the chapters here show, both masculinity and femininity were often renegotiated in a post-war situation and their redefinitions were an important vehicle in constructing new national self-images. On both levels – subjective experiences and collective identities – the analysis of gender is most useful in understanding the societal ruptures and coping strategies at the end of the war and in deconstructing national historiographies.

The third key theme of the book is to challenge the streamlined narratives of the post-war era. Even though Hungary, Estonia, Poland, Austria, Finland, and Germany each present here national cases, the chapters' topics underline the asynchronous transition to peace in individual experiences, when compared to the smooth timelines of national and international historiographies. Furthermore, it is important to note that instead of a linear chronology, both personal and collective histories tend to return back to the moments of violence and loss, thus forming continuous cycles of remembrance and forgetting. Several of the authors also pay specific attention to the constructed and contested nature of national histories in these cycles. The role of these 'in-between' countries – and even more their peoples' multifaceted experiences – will add to the widening European history of the aftermath, thereby challenging the conventional dichotomies (Allied vs. Nazis) and periodisations (e.g., the 'Zero Hour' and the end of war, violence, and occupation in May 1945). An anthology with six case studies can only touch on some particular issues; yet we hope that the change of perspective will renew the focus on the Europe that lay between the victors.

## Notes

1. See L. Kettenacker and T. Riotte, '"Old Europe" and the Legacy of Two World Wars', in *The Legacies of Two World Wars: European Societies in the Twentieth Century*, L. Kettenacker and T. Riotte (eds) (Oxford: Berghahn, 2011), 3; also T. Farrell, 'Memory, Imagination and War', *History* 87, no. 285 (2002), 62–63; R. Bessel and D. Schumann, 'Introduction: Violence, Normality, and the Construction of Postwar Europe', in *Life after Death: Approaches to a Cultural and Social History of Europe during the 1940s and 1950s*, R. Bessel and D. Schumann (eds) (Cambridge: CUP, 2003), e.g. 7–8. For two further extensive anthologies with a strong cultural and social historical focus, see F. Biess and R.G. Moeller (eds), *Histories of the Aftermath: The Legacies of the Second World War in Europe* (New York: Berghahn, 2010); K. Naumann ed.), *Nachkrieg in Deutschland* (Hamburg: Hamburger Edition, 2001).
2. F. Biess, *Homecomings: Returning POWs and the Legacies of Defeat in Postwar Germany* (Princeton, NJ: Princeton UP, 2006), 8.
3. For an overview of post-war transition challenges and state-level coping strategies from the long-term Finnish and Swedish perspectives, see P. Karonen, 'Coping with Peace after a Debacle: The Crisis of the Transition to Peace in Sweden after the Great Northern War (1700–1721)', *Scandinavian Journal of History* 33, no. 3 (2008); P. Karonen and A. Holmila, 'La guerra y la paz en la historia de Finlandia: 1590–1950', *Istor* 12, no. 48 (2012).
4. P. Lagrou, 'The Nationalization of Victimhood: Selective Violence and National Grief in Western Europe, 1940–1960', in Bessel and Schumann (eds), *Life after Death*, 243–245, 252–253.
5. T. Judt, *Postwar: A History of Europe since 1945* (New York: Penguin, 2005), 13–17; see also J. Reinisch, 'Introduction: Relief in the Aftermath of War', *Journal of Contemporary History* 43, no. 3 (2008), theme issue 'Relief in the Aftermath of War', 372–374.
6. For an idea of the geographical concentration of violence in 1933–45, see T. Snyder, *Bloodlands: Europe between Hitler and Stalin* (New York: Basic Books, 2010); for the continuation of violence in Central and Eastern Europe after 1945, see A. Applebaum, *Iron Curtain: The Crushing of Eastern Europe 1944–56* (London: Allen Lane, 2012). For a grim overall account, see also K. Lowe, *Savage Continent: Europe in the Aftermath of World War II* (London: Viking, 2012).
7. R. Bessel, *Germany 1945: From War to Peace* (London: Simon & Schuster, 2009), 384, 390, 394–396. For a comprehensive account of the final stages of the Third

Reich, see I. Kershaw, *The End: Hitler's Germany, 1944-45* (London: Allen Lane, 2011). For the inclusion of the Asian perspective, see also I. Buruma, *Year Zero: A History of 1945* (New York: Penguin, 2013); J.W. Dower, *Embracing Defeat: Japan in the Wake of World War II* (New York: W.W. Norton, 1999).

8   Cit. M. Mazower, 'Reconstruction: The Historiographical Issues', *Past & Present* 210, theme issue 'Postwar Reconstruction in Europe', Suppl. 6 (2011), 22; R. Bessel, 'Establishing Order in Post-war Eastern Germany', 143 and note 14, ibidem; Judt, *Postwar*, 4; Biess, *Homecomings*, 43; G. Macdonogh, *After the Reich: The Brutal History of the Allied Occupation* (New York: Basic Books, 2007); D. Stone, 'Editor's Introduction: Postwar Europe as History', in *The Oxford Handbook of Postwar European History*, ed. D. Stone (Oxford: OUP, 2012), 7; see also R. Overy, 'Interwar, War, Postwar: Was There a Zero Hour in 1945?', in D. Stone (ed.), The Oxford Handbook of Postwar European History (Oxford: OUP, 2012), 60; F. Taylor, *Exorcising Hitler: The Occupation and Denazification of Germany* (New York: Bloomsbury, 2011), Ch. 4.

9   Taylor, *Exorcising Hitler*; K. H. Jarausch, *After Hitler: Recivilizing Germans, 1945-1995* (Oxford: OUP, 2006); N. Frei, *Adenauer's Germany and the Nazi Past: The Politics of Amnesty and Integration*, trans. J. Golb (New York: Columbia UP, 2002).

10  Judt, *Postwar*, 39, 43–44, 132; M. Mazower, 'Introduction', in *After the War Was Over: Reconstructing the Family, Nation and State in Greece, 1943-1960*, ed. M. Mazower (Princeton, NJ: Princeton UP, 2000), 10; P. Ballinger, 'At the Borders of Force: Violence, Refugees, and the Reconfiguration of the Yugoslav and Italian States', *Past & Present* 210, Suppl. 6 (2011), 158–176; Kettenacker and Riotte, '"Old Europe" and the Legacy', 9; Overy, 'Interwar, War, Postwar', 63; F. Tsilaga, '"The Mountain Laboured and Brought Forth a Mouse": UNRRA's Operations in the Cyclades Islands, c. 1945-46', *Journal of Contemporary History* 43, no. 3 (2008), 527–528.

11  Judt, *Postwar*, 42, 44–53; Stone, 'Editor's Introduction', 4; Overy, 'Interwar, War, Postwar', 73. For more on the Soviet Union and Ukraine, see A. Weiner, *Making Sense of War: The Second World War and the Fate of the Bolshevik Revolution* (Princeton, NJ: Princeton UP, 2001), e.g. 176–179.

12  B. Shephard, *The Long Road Home: The Aftermath of the Second World War* (London: Bodley Head, 2010); see also the theme issue 'Relief in the Aftermath of War' in the *Journal of Contemporary History* 43, no. 3 (2008); as well as a critical commentary by S. Gemie and L. Humbert, 'Writing History in the Aftermath of "Relief": Some Comments on "Relief in the Aftermath of War"', *Journal of Contemporary History* 44, no. 2 (2009), 309–318.

13  Judt, *Postwar*, 22–26; P. Ther, 'Ethnic Cleansing', in Stone (ed,), *Oxford Handbook*, 157; C. Vollnhans, 'Disillusionment, Pragmatism, Indifference: German Society after the "Catastrophe"', in Kettenacker and Riotte (eds), *Legacies of Two World Wars*, 188; see also *People on the Move: Forced Population Movements in Europe in the Second World War and Its Aftermath*, P. Ahonen et al. (eds) (Oxford: Berg, 2008); J. Reinisch, E. White (eds), *Disentanglement of Populations: Migration, Expulsion and Displacement in Postwar Europe, 1944-49* (London: Palgrave Macmillan 2011).

14  T. Zahra, *The Lost Children: Reconstructing Europe's Families after World War II* (Cambridge, MA: Harvard UP, 2011); M. Mouton, 'Missing, Lost, and Displaced Children in Postwar Germany: The Great Struggle to Provide for the War's Youngest Victims', *Central European History* 48, no.1 (2015): 53–78. The problem was also acute in Finland: during the war, over 60,000 children had been evacuated to neutral Sweden.

15  For descriptions and estimates of the Soviet atrocities, see Judt, *Postwar*, 20; Macdonogh, *After the Reich*, 25–26; A. Petö, 'Memory and the Narrative of Rape in Budapest and Vienna 1945', in Bessel and Schumann (eds), *Life after Death*; K. Ungváry, *The Siege of Budapest: 100 Days in World War II*, trans. L. Löb (New

Haven, CT: Yale University Press, 2005), 339–357; Vollnhans, 'Disillusionment, Pragmatism, Indifference', 189; Taylor, *Exorcising Hitler*, 49–50.

16 Judt, *Postwar*, Ch. I 'The Legacy of War' summarises this issue. See also S. Behrenbeck, 'Between Pain and Silence: Remembering the Victims of Violence in Germany after 1949', in Bessel and Schumann (eds), *Life after Death*; Bessel, 'Establishing Order'; Ther, 'Ethnic Cleansing', 155, 157; E. Glassheim, 'Ethnic Cleansing, Communism, and Environmental Devastation in Czechoslovakia's Borderlands, 1945–1989', *The Journal of Modern History* 78, no. 1 (2006), esp. 68.

17 Biess, *Homecomings*, 52, 56, 63. See also R.G. Moeller, '"The Last Soldiers of the Great War" and Tales of Family Reunions in the Federal Republic of Germany', *Signs* 24, no. 1 (1998), 132; R.G. Moeller, 'What Has "Coming to Terms with the Past" Meant in Post-World War II Germany? From History to Memory to the "History of Memory"', *Central European History* 35, no. 2 (2002), 226, 239; Judt, *Postwar*, 57; A. Grossman, 'Trauma, Memory, and Motherhood: Germans and Jewish Persons in Post-Nazi Germany, 1945–1949', in Bessel and Schumann (eds), *Life after Death*; J.K. Olick, *In the House of the Hangman: The Agonies of German Defeat, 1943–1949* (Chicago: Chicago UP, 2005); F. Slaveski, *The Soviet occupation of Germany: hunger, mass violence and the struggle for peace, 1945–1947* (Cambridge: Cambridge University Press, 2013).

18 For an in-depth and 'street-level' analysis of demobilisation, see L. McEnaney, 'Nightmares on Elm Street: Demobilizing in Chicago, 1945–1953', *The Journal of American History* 92, no. 4 (2006), 1265–1291; see also P. Karonen, 'Johdanto: Kun rauha tuo omat ongelmansa', in Karonen P. and Tarjamo K. (eds), *Kun sota on ohi: Sodista selviytymisen ongelmia ja niiden ratkaisumalleja 1900-luvulla* (Helsinki: SKS, 2006), 14–15, the sources mentioned in notes 6–7; B. Schneider, 'From Demilitarization to Democratization: Demobilized Soldiers Between the American Occupation and the German and Japanese States, 1945–1955', *Militärgeschichtliche Zeitschrift* 70, no. 2 (2011), 329–362.

19 M.D. Gambone, *The Greatest Generation Comes Home: The Veteran in American Society* (College Station: Texas A&M UP, 2005), 10–11. See also S. Mettler, *Soldiers to Citizens: The G.I. Bill and the Making of the The Greatest Generation* (Oxford: OUP, 2005); K. D. Rose, *Myth and the Greatest Generation: A Social History of Americans in World War II* (New York: Routledge, 2008), Ch. 10.

20 Gambone, *The Greatest Generation*, 68–69; the reform of the education system was an important subject in post-war Germany, as in other defeated countries, although this debate was rather short-lived: B. M. Puaca, 'Navigating the Waves of Change: Political Education and Democratic School Reform in Postwar West Berlin', *History of Education Quarterly* 48, no. 2 (2008), 244–264.

21 R. Dale, 'Rats and Resentment: The Demobilization of the Red Army in Postwar Leningrad, 1945–50', *Journal of Contemporary History* 45, no. 1 (2010), 114–115, 120, 124, 126; M. Edele, *Soviet Veterans of the Second World War: A Popular Movement in an Authoritarian Society, 1941–1991* (Oxford: OUP, 2008), esp. 22–23. For a case study on the city of Rostov, see J. W. Jones, *Everyday Life and the 'Reconstruction' of Soviet Russia during and after the Great Patriotic War, 1943–1948* (Bloomington: Indiana UP, 2008).

22 C. Merridale, *Ivan's War: The Red Army 1939–45* (London: Faber & Faber, 2005), 122–124, 251–252, 303–304.

23 Biess, *Homecomings*, 50–51, 62, 70–71, 75–76, 87–88, 91–94, 126; Moeller, 'The Last Soldiers of the Great War', 136–138, 141. For the return of the Austrian prisoners of war, see E. Hornung, 'The Myth of Penelope and Odysseus: An Austrian Married Couple Narrate Their Wartime and Post-War Experiences', in Duchen C. and Bandhauer-Schöffmann I. (eds), *When The War Was Over: Women, War and Peace in Europe, 1940–1956* (London: Leicester UP, 2000), 44; G. Weeks, 'Fifty Years of Pain: The History of Austrian Disabled Veterans after 1945', in *Disabled Veterans*

in *History*, ed. D.A. Gerber, enlarged and rev. ed. (Ann Arbor: Michigan UP, 2012), 243. On the post-war German veteran culture, see T. Kühne, *Kameradschaft: Die Soldaten des nationalsozialistischen Krieges und das 20. Jahrhundert* (Göttingen: Vandenhoeck & Ruprecht, 2006), Chs. VI and VII.

24 K. Ungváry, 'Kriegsschauplatz Ungarn' in *Das Deutsche Reich und der Zweite Weltkrieg*, Vol. 8: *Die Ostfront 1943/44*, ed. K.-H. Frieser, 2nd ed. (München: DVA, 2011), 955–956: quite amazingly, the last Hungarian prisoner-of-war was not repatriated to Hungary until 2001.

25 D. A. Gerber, 'Preface: The Continuing Relevance of the Study of Disabled Veterans', in Gerber (ed.), *Disabled Veterans*, x, xii; D. A. Gerber, 'Introduction: Finding Disabled Veterans in History', 1, in Gerber (ed.), *Disabled Veterans*; Gambone, *The Greatest Generation*, Ch. 2 discusses the G. I. Bill and American war invalids. For the Soviet case, see Edele, *Soviet Veterans*, Ch. 4; E. Dunn, 'Disabled Russian War Veterans: Surviving the Collapse of the Soviet Union', in Gerber (ed.), *Disabled Veterans*. For a comparative analysis of the British and German WWI invalid policies, see also D. Cohen, *The War Come Home: Disabled Veterans in Britain and Germany, 1914–1939* (Berkeley: California UP, 2001), 4–5, 189–190.

26 Weeks, *Fifty Years of Pain*, 229, 234.

27 On the cultural history of wounded male bodies and their position in post-First World War society, see J. Bourke, *Dismembering the Male: Men's Bodies, Britain and the Great War* (London: Reaktion, 1996); S. Kienitz, *Beschädigte Helden: Kriegsinvalidität und Körperbilder 1914–1923* (Paderborn: Schöningh, 2008).

28 Biess, *Homecomings*; see also F. Biess, 'Men of Reconstruction – The Reconstruction of Men: Returning POWs in East and West Germany, 1945–1955', in Hagemann, K. and Schüler-Springorum, S. (eds), *Home/Front: The Military, War and Gender in Twentieth-Century Germany* (Oxford: Berg, 2002).

29 On the concept of remasculinisation, see S. Jeffords, *The Remasculinization of America: Gender and the Vietnam War* (Bloomington: Indiana UP, 1989); on the German case of the 1950s, see the remasculinisation theme issue of *Signs* 24, no. 1 (1998) and also R.G. Moeller, 'Heimkehr ins Vaterland: Die Remaskulinisierung Westdeutschlands in den fünfziger Jahren', *Militärgeschichtliche Zeitschrift* 60, no. 2 (2001), 403–36.

30 Hornung, 'The Myth of Penelope', 45, 47, 52; Moeller, 'What Has', 253; K. Tarjamo and P. Karonen, 'Kun sota on ohi: Loppusanat', in Karonen and Tarjamo (eds), *Kun sota on ohi*, 390–394; T. Haggith, 'Great Britain: Remembering a Just War (1945–1950)', in Kettenacker and Riotte, *Legacies of Two World Wars*, 236; J. Shay, 'Afterword: A Challenge to Historians', in Gerber (ed.), *Disabled Veterans*, 379. More generally on war and silence, see also Ben-Ze'ev, E., Ginio, R. and Winter, J. (eds), *Shadows of War: A Social History of Silence in the Twentieth Century* (Cambridge: CUP, 2010).

31 Cited in Gambone, *The Greatest Generation*, 86, on the silence of veterans, see also 87.

32 For more on shell shock, see the theme issue, *Journal of Contemporary History* 35, no. 1 (2000); P. Leese, *Shell Shock: Traumatic Neurosis and the British Soldiers of the First World War* (Basingstoke: Palgrave, 2002); L.V. Smith, *The Embattled Self: French Soldiers' Testimony of the Great War* (Ithaca, NY: Cornell UP, 2007); M.S. Micale and P. Lerner (eds), *Traumatic Pasts: History, Psychiatry, and Trauma in the Modern Age, 1870–1930* (Cambridge: CUP, 2001); P. Lerner, *Hysterical Men: War, Psychiatry, and the Politics of Trauma in Germany, 1890–1930* (Ithaca, NY: Cornell UP, 2003); F. Reid, *Broken Men: Shell Shock, Treatment and Recovery in Britain 1914–30* (London: Continuum, 2010).

33 For studies on trauma and WWII, see Biess, *Homecomings*, esp. Ch. 3; S. Goltermann, *Die Gesellscahft der Überlebenden: Deutsche Kriegsheimkehrer und ihre Gewalterfahrungen im Zweiten Weltkrieg* (München: DVA, 2009); B. Shephard,

A War of Nerves: Soldiers and Psychiatrists 1914–1994 (London: Pimlico, 2002); V. Kivimäki, Battled Nerves: Finnish Soldiers' War Experience, Trauma, and Military Psychiatry, 1941–44 (PhD thesis: Åbo Akademi, 2013).

34 For attempts to use PTSD to analyse the traumatic experiences of WWII, see A. Förster and B. Beck, 'Post-Traumatic Stress Disorder and World War II: Can a Psychiatric Concept Help Us Understand Postwar Society?', in Bessel and Schumann (eds), Life after Death, 16–18; N. Birbaumer and D. Langewiesche, 'Neuropsychologie und Historie – Versuch einer empirischen Annäherung: Posttraumatische Belastungsstörung (PTSD) und Soziopathie in Österreich nach 1945', Geschichte und Gesellschaft 32, no. 2 (2006). For critical remarks, see e.g. Goltermann, Gesellschaft der Überlebenden, 18–22; Biess, Homecomings, 73–74; Kivimäki, Battled Nerves, 60–66.

35 For an overview of the various consequences of war for women and gender relations, see the articles on gender and post-war experiences in the following anthologies: Higonnet, M. R. et al. (eds), Behind the Lines: Gender and the Two World Wars (New Haven, CT: Yale UP, 1987); Braybon, G. and Summerfield, P. (eds), Out of the Cage: Women's Experience in Two World Wars (London: Pandora, 1987); Wingfield, N. M. and Bucur, M. (eds), Gender and War in Twentieth-Century Eastern Europe (Bloomington: Indiana UP, 2006); Duchen and Bandhauer-Schöffmann (eds), When the War Was Over; Hagemann and Schüler-Springorum (eds), Home/Front.

36 On the case of German post-war 'normalisation' and family politics, see D. Herzog, Sex after Fascism: Memory and Morality in Twentieth-Century Germany (Princeton, NJ: Princeton UP, 2005), esp. Ch. 3; V. Neumann, Nicht der Rede wert: Die Privatisierung der Kriegsfolgen in der frühen Bundesrepublik; Lebensgeschichtliche Erinnerungen (Münster: Westfälisches Dampfboot, 1999).

37 See e.g., E. Avdela, '"Corrupting and Uncontrollable Activities": Moral Panic about Youth in Post-Civil-War Greece', Journal of Contemporary History 43, no. 1 (2008); F. Biess, 'Moral Panic in Postwar Germany: The Abduction of Young Germans into the Foreign Legion and French Colonialism in the 1950s', Journal of Modern History 84, no. 4 (2012). For the situation in Finland, see also K. Tarjamo, 'Kansakunnan tulevaisuutta pelastamassa: Viranomaisten keskustelu rikollisuudesta 1940- ja 1950-luvun Suomessa', in Karonen and Tarjamo (eds), Kun sota on ohi.

38 For an overview of this field of study, see the following anthologies: Winter, J. and Sivan, E. (eds), War and Remembrance in the Twentieth Century (Cambridge: CUP, 1999); Ashplant, T.G., Dawson, G. and Roper, M. (eds), Commemorating War: The Politics of Memory (New Brunswick, NJ: Transaction, 2004); Berding, H., Heller, K. and Speitkamp, W. (eds), Krieg und Erinnerung: Fallstudien zum 19. und 20. Jahrhundert (Göttingen: Vandenhoeck & Ruprecht, 2000); Müller, J.-W. (ed.), Memory and Power in Post-War Europe: Studies in the Presence of the Past (Cambridge: CUP, 2002); Lingen, K. von (ed.), Kriegserfahrung und nationale Identität in Europa nach 1945: Erinnerung, Säuberungsprozesse und nationales Gedächtnis (Paderborn: Schöningh, 2009); Echternkamp, J. and Martens, S. (eds), Experience and Memory: The Second World War in Europe (New York: Berghahn, 2010); Stenius, H., Österberg, M. and Östling, J. (eds), Nordic Narratives of the Second World War: National Historiographies Revisited (Lund: Nordic Academic Press, 2011).

39 From this vast literature, see e.g. P. Fussell, The Great War and Modern Memory (Oxford: OUP, 1975); J. Winter, Sites of Memory, Sites of Mourning: The Great War in European Cultural History (Cambridge: CUP, 1995); J. Winter, Remembering War: The Great War Between Memory and History in the Twentieth Century (New Haven, CT: Yale UP, 2006); G. L. Mosse, Fallen Soldiers: Reshaping the Memory of the World Wars (Oxford: OUP, 1990); S. Audoin-Rouzeau and A. Becker, 14–18: Understanding the Great War, trans. C. Temerson (New York: Hill & Wang, 2002).

40 N. Frei, *Vergangenheitspolitik: Die Anfänge der Bundesrepublik und die NS-Vergangenheit* (Munich: C. H. Beck, 1996); R. G. Moeller, *War Stories: The Search for a Usable Past in the Federal Republic of Germany* (Berkeley: California UP, 2001); for an overview on the various aspects of the discourse on German victimhood, see also Niven, B. (ed.), *Germans as Victims: Remembering the Past in Contemporary Germany* (Basingstoke: Palgrave Macmillan, 2006).

41 Ungváry, *Siege of Budapest*, 357.

42 See Macleod, J. (ed.), *Defeat and Memory: Cultural Histories of Military Defeat in the Modern Era* (Basingstoke: Palgrave Macmillan, 2008); Carl, H. et al. (ed.), *Kriegsniederlagen: Erfahrungen und Erinnerungen* (Berlin: Akademie, 2004); for the French memory culture of WWII, see H. Rousso, *The Vichy Syndrome: History and Memory in France Since 1944* (Cambridge, MA: Harvard UP, 1994).

43 On the 'memory boom', see Winter, *Remembering War*, 1; also G. L. Mosse, 'Two World Wars and the Myth of the War Experience', *Journal of Contemporary History* 21, no. 4 (1986). On the fallen soldiers, see M. Sledge, *Soldier Dead: How We Recover, Identify, Bury & Honor Our Military Fallen* (New York: Columbia UP, 2005); L. Capdevila and D. Voldman, *War Dead: Western Societies and the Casualties of War*, trans. R. Veasey (Edinburgh: Edinburg UP, 2006).

44 Winter, *Remembering War*, 4–5, 9; also, e.g. Farrell, 'Memory, Imagination and War'; Haggith, 'Great Britain', 243–245.

# Bibliography

Ahonen, P. et al. (eds), *People on the Move: Forced Population Movements in Europe in the Second World War and Its Aftermath*. Oxford: Berg, 2008.

Applebaum, A., *Iron Curtain: The Crushing of Eastern Europe 1944–56*. London: Allen Lane, 2012.

Ashplant, T.G., Dawson G. and Roper M. (eds), *Commemorating War: The Politics of Memory*. New Brunswick, NJ: Transaction, 2004.

Audoin-Rouzeau, S. and Becker, A., *14–18: Understanding the Great War*, trans. C. Temerson. New York: Hill & Wang, 2002.

Avdela, E., '"Corrupting and Uncontrollable Activities": Moral Panic about Youth in Post-Civil-War Greece', *Journal of Contemporary History* 43, no. 1 (2008).

Ballinger, P., 'At the Borders of Force: Violence, Refugees, and the Reconfiguration of the Yugoslav and Italian States', *Past & Present* 210, Suppl. 6 (2011).

Behrenbeck, S., 'Between Pain and Silence: Remembering the Victims of Violence in Germany after 1949', in Bessel and Schumann (eds), *Life after Death*.

Ben-Ze'ev, E., Ginio, R. and Winter, J. (eds), *Shadows of War: A Social History of Silence in the Twentieth Century*. Cambridge: CUP, 2010.

Berding, H., Heller, K. and Speitkamp, W. (eds), *Krieg und Erinnerung: Fallstudien zum 19. und 20. Jahrhundert*. Göttingen: Vandenhoeck & Ruprecht, 2000.

Bessel, R., *Germany 1945: From War to Peace*. London: Simon & Schuster, 2009.

Bessel, R. and Schumann, D., 'Introduction: Violence, Normality, and the Construction of Postwar Europe', in *Life after Death: Approaches to a Cultural and Social History of Europe during the 1940s and 1950s*, R. Bessel and D. Schumann (eds). Cambridge: CUP, 2003.

Biess, F., 'Men of Reconstruction – The Reconstruction of Men: Returning POWs in East and West Germany, 1945–1955', in Hagemann, K. and Schüler-Springorum, S. (eds), *Home/Front: The Military, War and Gender in Twentieth-Century Germany*. Oxford: Berg, 2002.

Biess, F., *Homecomings: Returning POWs and the Legacies of Defeat in Postwar Germany.* Princeton, NJ: Princeton UP, 2006.

Biess, F., 'Moral Panic in Postwar Germany: The Abduction of Young Germans into the Foreign Legion and French Colonialism in the 1950s', *Journal of Modern History* 84, no. 4 (2012).

Biess, F. and Moeller, R.G. (eds), *Histories of the Aftermath: The Legacies of the Second World War in Europe.* New York: Berghahn, 2010.

Birbaumer, N. and Langewiesche, D., 'Neuropsychologie und Historie – Versuch einer empirischen Annäherung: Posttraumatische Belastungsstörung (PTSD) und Soziopathie in Österreich nach 1945', *Geschichte und Gesellschaft* 32, no. 2 (2006).

Bourke, J., *Dismembering the Male: Men's Bodies, Britain and the Great War.* London: Reaktion, 1996.

Braybon, G. and Summerfield, P. (eds), *Out of the Cage: Women's Experience in Two World Wars.* London: Pandora, 1987.

Buruma, I., *Year Zero: A History of 1945.* New York: Penguin, 2013.

Capdevila, L. and Voldman, D., *War Dead: Western Societies and the Casualties of War*, trans. R. Veasey. Edinburgh: Edinburg UP, 2006.

Carl, H. et al. (eds), *Kriegsniederlagen: Erfahrungen und Erinnerungen.* Berlin: Akademie, 2004.

Cohen, D., *The War Come Home: Disabled Veterans in Britain and Germany, 1914–1939.* Berkeley: California UP, 2001.

Dale, R., 'Rats and Resentment: The Demobilization of the Red Army in Postwar Leningrad, 1945–50', *Journal of Contemporary History* 45, no. 1 (2010).

Dower, J.W., *Embracing Defeat: Japan in the Wake of World War II.* New York: W.W. Norton, 1999.

Dunn, E., 'Disabled Russian War Veterans: Surviving the Collapse of the Soviet Union', in Gerber (ed.), *Disabled Veterans.*

Echternkamp J. and Martens, S. (eds), *Experience and Memory: The Second World War in Europe.* New York: Berghahn, 2010.

Edele, M., *Soviet Veterans of the Second World War: A Popular Movement in an Authoritarian Society, 1941–1991.* Oxford: OUP, 2008.

Farrell, T., 'Memory, Imagination and War', *History* 87, no. 285 (2002).

Frei, N., *Vergangenheitspolitik: Die Anfänge der Bundesrepublik und die NS-Vergangenheit.* Munich: C. H. Beck, 1996.

Frei, N., *Adenauer's Germany and the Nazi Past: The Politics of Amnesty and Integration*, trans. J. Golb. New York: Columbia UP, 2002.

Fussell, P., *The Great War and Modern Memory.* Oxford: OUP, 1975.

Förster A., and Beck, B., 'Post-Traumatic Stress Disorder and World War II: Can a Psychiatric Concept Help Us Understand Postwar Society?', in Bessel and Schumann (eds), *Life after Death.*

Gambone, M.D., *The Greatest Generation Comes Home: The Veteran in American Society.* College Station: Texas A&M UP, 2005.

Gemie, S., Humbert, L., 'Writing History in the Aftermath of "Relief": Some Comments on "Relief in the Aftermath of War"', *Journal of Contemporary History* 44, no. 2 (2009).

Gerber, D. A., 'Preface: The Continuing Relevance of the Study of Disabled Veterans', in *Disabled Veterans in History*, ed. D.A. Gerber, enlarged and rev. ed. Ann Arbor: Michigan UP, 2012.

Gerber, D. A., 'Introduction: Finding Disabled Veterans in History', in *Disabled Veterans in History*, ed. D.A. Gerber, enlarged and rev. ed. Ann Arbor: Michigan UP, 2012.

Glassheim, E., 'Ethnic Cleansing, Communism, and Environmental Devastation in Czechoslovakia's Borderlands, 1945–1989', *The Journal of Modern History* 78, no. 1 (2006).

Goltermann, S., *Die Gesellscahft der Überlebenden: Deutsche Kriegsheimkehrer und ihre Gewalterfahrungen im Zweiten Weltkrieg*. München: DVA, 2009.

Grossman, A., 'Trauma, Memory, and Motherhood: Germans and Jewish Persons in Post-Nazi Germany, 1945–1949', in Bessel and Schumann (eds), *Life after Death*.

Haggith, T., 'Great Britain: Remembering a Just War (1945–1950)', in Kettenacker and Riotte (eds), *Legacies of Two World Wars*.

Herzog, D., *Sex after Fascism: Memory and Morality in Twentieth-Century Germany*. Princeton, NJ: Princeton UP, 2005.

Higonnet, M. R. et al. (eds), *Behind the Lines: Gender and the Two World Wars*. New Haven, CT: Yale UP, 1987.

Hornung, E., 'The Myth of Penelope and Odysseus: An Austrian Married Couple Narrate Their Wartime and Post-War Experiences', in Duchen C. and Bandhauer-Schöffmann I. (eds), *When The War Was Over: Women, War and Peace in Europe, 1940–1956*. London: Leicester UP, 2000.

Jarausch, K. H., *After Hitler: Recivilizing Germans, 1945–1995*. Oxford: OUP, 2006.

Jeffords, S., *The Remasculinization of America: Gender and the Vietnam War*. Bloomington: Indiana UP, 1989.

Jones, J. W., *Everyday Life and the 'Reconstruction' of Soviet Russia during and after the Great Patriotic War, 1943–1948*. Bloomington: Indiana UP, 2008.

*Journal of Contemporary History* 35, no. 1 (2000).

Judt, T., *Postwar: A History of Europe since 1945*. New York: Penguin, 2005.

Karonen, P., 'Coping with Peace after a Debacle: The Crisis of the Transition to Peace in Sweden after the Great Northern War (1700–1721)', *Scandinavian Journal of History* 33, no. 3 (2008).

Karonen, P., 'Johdanto: Kun rauha tuo omat ongelmansa', in Karonen and Tarjamo, (eds), *Kun sota on ohi*.

Karonen, P. and Tarjamo, K. (eds), *Kun sota on ohi: Sodista selviytymisen ongelmia ja niiden ratkaisumalleja 1900-luvulla*. Helsinki: SKS, 2006.

Karonen, P. and Holmila, A. 'La guerra y la paz en la historia de Finlandia: 1590–1950', *Istor* 12, no. 48 (2012).

Kershaw, I., *The End: Hitler's Germany, 1944–45*. London: Allen Lane, 2011.

Ketternacker, L. and Riotte, T., '"Old Europe" and the Legacy of Two World Wars', in *The Legacies of Two World Wars: European Societies in the Twentieth Century*, L. Kettenacker and T. Riotte (eds). Oxford: Berghahn, 2011.

Kienitz, S., *Beschädigte Helden: Kriegsinvalidität und Körperbilder 1914–1923*. Paderborn: Schöningh, 2008.

Kivimäki, V., *Battled Nerves: Finnish Soldiers' War Experience, Trauma, and Military Psychiatry, 1941–44* (PhD thesis: Åbo Akademi, 2013).

Kühne, T., *Kameradschaft: Die Soldaten des nationalsozialistischen Krieges und das 20. Jahrhundert*. Göttingen: Vandenhoeck & Ruprecht, 2006.

Lagrou, P., 'The Nationalization of Victimhood: Selective Violence and National Grief in Western Europe, 1940–1960', in Bessel and Schumann (eds), *Life after Death*.

Leese, P., *Shell Shock: Traumatic Neurosis and the British Soldiers of the First World War*. Basingstoke: Palgrave, 2002.

Lerner, P., *Hysterical Men: War, Psychiatry, and the Politics of Trauma in Germany, 1890–1930*. Ithaca, NY: Cornell UP, 2003.

Lingen, K. von (ed.), *Kriegserfahrung und nationale Identität in Europa nach 1945: Erinnerung, Säuberungsprozesse und nationales Gedächtnis*. Paderborn: Schöningh, 2009.

Lowe, K., *Savage Continent: Europe in the Aftermath of World War II*. London: Viking, 2012.

Macdonogh, G. *After the Reich: The Brutal History of the Allied Occupation*. New York: Basic Books, 2007.

Macleod, J. (ed.), *Defeat and Memory: Cultural Histories of Military Defeat in the Modern Era*. Basingstoke: Palgrave Macmillan, 2008.

Mazower, M., 'Introduction', in *After the War Was Over: Reconstructing the Family, Nation and State in Greece, 1943–1960*, ed. M. Mazower. Princeton, NJ: Princeton UP, 2000.

Mazower, M. 'Reconstruction: The Historiographical Issues', *Past & Present* 210, theme issue 'Postwar Reconstruction in Europe', Suppl. 6 (2011).

McEnaney, L., 'Nightmares on Elm Street: Demobilizing in Chicago, 1945–1953', *The Journal of American History* 92, no. 4 (2006).

Merridale, C., *Ivan's War: The Red Army 1939–45*. London: Faber & Faber, 2005.

Mettler, S., *Soldiers to Citizens: The G.I. Bill and the Making of the the Greatest Generation*. Oxford: OUP, 2005.

Micale, M.S. and Lerner, P. (eds), *Traumatic Pasts: History, Psychiatry, and Trauma in the Modern Age, 1870–1930*. Cambridge: CUP, 2001.

Moeller, R.G., '"The Last Soldiers of the Great War" and Tales of Family Reunions in the Federal Republic of Germany', *Signs* 24, no. 1 (1998).

Moeller, R.G., 'Heimkehr ins Vaterland: Die Remaskulinisierung Westdeutschlands in den fünfziger Jahren', *Militärgeschichtliche Zeitschrift* 60, no. 2 (2001).

Moeller, R.G., *War Stories: The Search for a Usable Past in the Federal Republic of Germany*. Berkeley: California UP, 2001.

Moeller, R.G., 'What Has "Coming to Terms with the Past" Meant in Post-World War II Germany? From History to Memory to the "History of Memory"', *Central European History* 35, no. 2 (2002).

Mosse, G.L., 'Two World Wars and the Myth of the War Experience', *Journal of Contemporary History* 21, no. 4 (1986).

Mosse, G.L., *Fallen Soldiers: Reshaping the Memory of the World Wars*. Oxford: OUP, 1990.

Mouton, M., 'Missing, Lost, and Displaced Children in Postwar Germany: The Great Struggle to Provide for the War's Youngest Victims', *Central European History* 48, no.1 (2015).

Müller, J.-W. (ed.), *Memory and Power in Post-War Europe: Studies in the Presence of the Past*. Cambridge: CUP, 2002.

Naumann, K. (ed.), *Nachkrieg in Deutschland*. Hamburg: Hamburger Edition, 2001.

Neumann, V., *Nicht der Rede wert: Die Privatisierung der Kriegsfolgen in der frühen Bundesrepublik; Lebensgeschichtliche Erinnerungen*. Münster: Westfälisches Dampfboot, 1999.

Niven, B. (ed.), *Germans as Victims: Remembering the Past in Contemporary Germany*. Basingstoke: Palgrave Macmillan, 2006.

Olick, J.K., *In the House of the Hangman: The Agonies of German Defeat, 1943–1949*. Chicago: Chicago UP, 2005.

Overy, R., 'Interwar, War, Postwar: Was There a Zero Hour in 1945?', in D. Stone (ed.), *The Oxford Handbook of Postwar European History*, ed. D. Stone. Oxford: OUP, 2012.

Pető, A., 'Memory and the Narrative of Rape in Budapest and Vienna 1945', in Bessel and Schumann (eds), *Life after Death*.

Puaca, B.M., 'Navigating the Waves of Change: Political Education and Democratic School Reform in Postwar West Berlin', *History of Education Quarterly* 48, no. 2 (2008).

Reid, F., *Broken Men: Shell Shock, Treatment and Recovery in Britain 1914–30*. London: Continuum, 2010.

Reinisch, J., 'Introduction: Relief in the Aftermath of War', *Journal of Contemporary History* 43, no. 3 (2008).

Reinisch, J. and White, E. (eds), *Disentanglement of Populations: Migration, Expulsion and Displacement in Postwar Europe, 1944–49*. London: Palgrave Macmillan 2011.

Rose, K.D., *Myth and the Greatest Generation: A Social History of Americans in World War II*. New York: Routledge, 2008.

Rousso, H., *The Vichy Syndrome: History and Memory in France Since 1944*. Cambridge, MA: Harvard UP, 1994.

Schneider, B., 'From Demilitarization to Democratization: Demobilized Soldiers Between the American Occupation and the German and Japanese States, 1945–1955', *Militärgeschichtliche Zeitshrift* 70, no. 2 (2011).

Shay, J., 'Afterword: A Challenge to Historians', in Gerber (ed.), *Disabled Veterans*.

Shephard, B., *A War of Nerves: Soldiers and Psychiatrists 1914–1994*. London: Pimlico, 2002.

Shephard, B., *The Long Road Home: The Aftermath of the Second World War*. London: Bodley Head, 2010.

Slaveski, F., *The Soviet occupation of Germany: hunger, mass violence and the struggle for peace, 1945–1947*. Cambridge: Cambridge University Press, 2013.

Sledge, M., *Soldier Dead: How We Recover, Identify, Bury & Honor Our Military Fallen*. New York: Columbia UP, 2005.

Smith, L.V., *The Embattled Self: French Soldiers' Testimony of the Great War*. Ithaca, NY: Cornell UP, 2007.

Snyder, T., *Bloodlands: Europe between Hitler and Stalin*. New York: Basic Books, 2010

Stenius, H., Österberg, M. and Östling, J. (eds), *Nordic Narratives of the Second World War: National Historiographies Revisited*. Lund: Nordic Academic Press, 2011.

Stone, D., 'Editor's Introduction: Postwar Europe as History', in *The Oxford Handbook of Postwar European History*, ed. D. Stone. Oxford: OUP, 2012.

Tarjamo, K., 'Kansakunnan tulevaisuutta pelastamassa: Viranomaisten keskustelu rikollisuudesta 1940- ja 1950-luvun Suomessa', in Karonen and Tarjamo (eds), *Kun sota on ohi*.

Tarjamo, K. and Karonen, P., 'Kun sota on ohi: Loppusanat', in Karonen and Tarjamo (eds.), *Kun sota on ohi*.

Taylor, F., *Exorcising Hitler: The Occupation and Denazification of Germany*. New York: Bloomsbury, 2011.

Thematic issue on remasculinisation in *Signs* 24, no. 1 (1998).

Thematic issue 'Relief in the Aftermath of War' in the *Journal of Contemporary History* 43, no. 3 (2008).

Ther, P., 'Ethnic Cleansing', in *The Oxford Handbook of Postwar European History*, ed. D. Stone. Oxford: OUP, 2012.

Tsilaga, F., '"The Mountain Laboured and Brought Forth a Mouse": UNRRA's Operations in the Cyclades Islands, c. 1945–46', *Journal of Contemporary History* 43, no. 3 (2008).

Ungváry, K., *The Siege of Budapest: 100 Days in World War II*, trans. L. Löb. New Haven, CT: Yale University Press, 2005.

Ungváry, K., 'Kriegsschauplatz Ungarn' in *Das Deutsche Reich und der Zweite Weltkrieg*, Vol. 8: *Die Ostfront 1943/44*, ed. K.-H. Frieser, 2nd ed. München: DVA, 2011.

Weeks, G., 'Fifty Years of Pain: The History of Austrian Disabled Veterans after 1945', in *Disabled Veterans in History*, ed. D. A. Gerber, enlarged and rev. ed. Ann Arbor: Michigan UP, 2012.

Weiner, A., *Making Sense of War: The Second World War and the Fate of the Bolshevik Revolution*. Princeton, NJ: Princeton UP, 2001.

Wingfield, N. M. and Bucur M. (eds), *Gender and War in Twentieth-Century Eastern Europe*. Bloomington: Indiana UP, 2006.

Winter, J., *Sites of Memory, Sites of Mourning: The Great War in European Cultural History*. Cambridge: CUP, 1995.

Winter, J., *Remembering War: The Great War Between Memory and History in the Twentieth Century*. New Haven, CT: Yale UP, 2006.

Winter, J. and Sivan, E. (eds) *War and Remembrance in the Twentieth Century.* Cambridge: CUP, 1999.

Vollnhans, C., 'Disillusionment, Pragmatism, Indifference: German Society after the "Catastrophe"', in Kettenacker and Riotte (eds), *Legacies of Two World Wars*

Zahra, T., *The Lost Children: Reconstructing Europe's Families after World War II.* Cambridge, MA: Harvard UP, 2011.

# Continued Violence: Estonia and Poland I

Anu Mai Kõll

# 1. Between Germany and Russia: Settling Scores from the Occupations in Post-War Estonia (1945–1950)

Conflicts of the peace in Eastern Europe included retaliations for collaboration with the German occupation, or what was considered as such, resistance and adjustment to the Soviet regime, including recruitment of local cadres, and the repressive measures towards enemy classes, such as so-called kulaks. Within Eastern Europe, the dividing line after World War II fell between the nominally independent People's Republics (e.g., Poland, Hungary, and Czechoslovakia), and those areas that had been subsumed into the Soviet Union (e.g., the Baltic states, Moldova, and the western parts of Belarus and Ukraine). In the case of the Baltic countries the submission was not considered legitimate and caused severe conflict among locals. My subject will be a local study, that is, a grass root level study of Estonia, Viljandimaa, in the 1940's. Viljandimaa was a rural district with good soil and relatively prosperous farms, cultivated with family labour. Historically it was a centre of national culture including education, temperance and peasant co-operation as well as journals, choirs, theatres constituting a nascent public sector.[1]

The war in Estonia started with Molotov and Ribbentrop signing a non-aggression pact between the USSR and Nazi Germany in August 1939, which officially placed Estonia (among other countries) under the Soviet sphere of influence, were there to be any 'territorial and political rearrangements' of these countries. Ultimatums were then issued demanding Soviet military bases in Lithuania, Latvia, Estonia and Finland. The Baltic governments decided they were not able to resist militarily and accepted the installation of Soviet bases.[2] The Finnish government was the only one to refuse and the result was the Winter War.

In Estonia, Soviet troops entered the country and kept to their bases for a year. But in June 1940, demands for a more 'friendly' government were issued from Moscow. A coup d'état against the mild but still authoritarian centre-right government in power (which was called fascist by Soviet standards) was staged with the help of Red Army soldiers, and President Konstantin Päts was forced to resign and arrested a few weeks later. In his place, a puppet government consisting of left-wing intellectuals rather than die-hard communists, was installed in cooperation with Soviet Politburo member Andrej Zhdanov who remained the *eminence grise* behind the scenes. This new government organised rigged elections, which resulted in a Chamber of Deputies, immediately applying to become a member republic of the Soviet Union. The 'annexation' was thus carried out according to a peculiarly legalistic procedure. However, this deceived few observers, particularly as the same procedure took place in Latvia and Lithuania at the same time.[3] Occupation would have been a more exact way to describe it, as that conveys its violent and unlawful character a bit more than annexation.

Sovietisation in the area was sudden and thorough. The new Soviet republics inherited the legislation and organisation of the Union and the police and administration were purged. In principle, Soviet law prevailed from this point on, even if transitional measures took longer.[4] But the Soviet government in Estonia lasted for less than a year. The Nazi attack on the USSR started in late June 1941, and the Nazi troops immediately crossed the border to the Lithuanian Soviet Republic and went northwards through Latvia to Estonia. A week before the attack, leading members of pre-Soviet Estonian society were deported to Siberia along with their families: employers, leaders of labour unions, policemen, officers and other pillars of society.[5] Approximately 10,000 were deported at this point, which means almost 1% of the total population of Estonia.[6] It sent a shock wave through the population, as practically every family knew some of the victims.

Representatives of the communist regime also evacuated eastwards before the Germans took over. A few battles took place, and in connection with the evacuation political prisoners were executed.[7] Moreover, the small Jewish population of around five thousand persons also chose to leave for the Soviet Union, for obvious reasons. The total number of evacuated persons has been estimated at 25,000 not counting the Estonians that were in the Red Army.[8]

The Baltic States were ruled by the German military until December 1941, when *Ostministerium* and *Reichskommissariat Ostland* took over responsibility. Formally, the occupied territories had the same status as the occupied parts of the USSR.[9] The German authorities set up a formal native self-government, or another puppet government, consisting of sympathisers of Estonian origin.

By early 1944, the Red Army were fighting large-scale battles in Estonia and slowly driving the Germans westwards. The German army did not give up immediately, but by the early autumn of that year, about 70,000 Estonians had chosen to leave the country. This was easier for those on the coast than those further inland, and it was just as well they did, as by later that same autumn the war in Estonia was over.

This background is important because occupations do not only mean foreign rulers being in charge for 3–50 years and then leaving. A long history of Russo-German conflict formed the background against which scores were settled in post-war Estonia, as we shall see in this chapter. The post-war conflicts have often been framed in terms of Estonians against Russians, but this is a simplification. To begin with, there was retaliation between locals who had been fighting on different sides. Another issue was the difficulty in finding reliable and loyal officials, as the Soviet authorities wanted to make sure that no one who had worked for the Germans remained in office, and yet because of the poverty and devastation left by war, it was impossible to buy allegiances, so that material needs came over other priorities. Soviet nationality policy was meant to solve the ethnic and linguistic differences between Russians and Estonians, and the liminal state of the country, having been occupied by both Germans and Soviets. However, the settling of scores went on for over five years and ended with the largest wave of repression after the war – the deportations prior to collectivisation, where most victims were chosen on the grounds of their real or alleged collaboration with the German occupiers previously. Finally in 1950, the repression turned in on itself, as the leading members of Estonia's Communist Party and Estonian officers in the Red Army were purged and deported.

## *Retaliation at the Local Level*

A letter sent to the local Communist Party office gives some idea of how retaliation was taking place at the local level in Viljandimaa. It conveys the troubled and sometimes violent situation immediately after the conquest of a country. There are other letters with similar content, so this is just one example. Still, the writer of this letter had expected something else, and these were clearly unusual or noteworthy incidents, that compelled an official to hand in a complaint.

> Laws are there to support them, but still shootings have been happening. When I was visiting the father of the revolutionary home guard P., I was shot at on my return to the local town of Mustla. Luckily they were too far away to hit us, as at the same time, comrade A. from the battalion was also shot at. We believe we know who it is but cannot be sure. The mood of the population has calmed down, but I have had to work at explaining to them, and the men of the battalion, that they can no longer gather like that. People have been coming out of the woods, except the old district leadership. They have disappeared led by the secretary, a few police constables, and some of the home guard leaders.

The letter shows how locals were also drawn into the conflict, and fought it out against each other; with the result that policies of retaliation followed on from this. The context of the letter above is that the writer, E. K., had supported the Soviet regime previously in 1940/41. When the Germans invaded, he was in charge of a destruction battalion at the rear of the Soviet troops. His group had been charged with killing the inmates of Viljandi prison before leaving for the USSR. In the final days before the Germans took over, the destruction battalions fought with former home guards from the days of independence. E. K. had escaped, whereas other locals collaborating or sympathising with the Soviets were killed or handed over to the German commanders by the home guard. He had been in the Soviet Union during the war, in the final years belonging to a small group planning to return to Estonia after Red Army victory. Now in charge of one part of the local administration, he had been recognised as such by the Forest Brothers ('bandits' in the letter) and became the target of an attack. This is one example of how the war was played out between locals as the settling of scores for deeds done under occupation.[10]

One could argue that this particular thread of settling of scores began in 1905, when locals attacked German manors in the countryside and were severely punished by the tsarist regime; this continued with the Russian revolutions of 1917, and the fighting between Bolsheviks and Nationalists backed by German forces in 1917 and 1919, when Estonia gained independence; and then the subsequent imprisonment of local communists during independence especially after 1924.

The procedure after gaining control of areas in Estonia was that everybody should be controlled before receiving their papers. This had to be done locally by the militia, the party and the local government. The leaders of these three organisations made up a troika that was to judge difficult cases. This vetting of the population was thorough and supposed to reach every grown-up person. The officials were searching for those who had collaborated with the Germans, and this seems to have happened on two levels. The first consisted of those who had 'blood on their hands', i.e., participated in the persecution of communists or Jews during the German occupation – these were usually sentenced to death. The second level consisted of people who had been members of organisations who were thought to have helped the Nazi occupiers but could not be directly linked to acts of violence. They had, for instance, worked in the local administration, been members of the home guard working under the Germans, or contributed to the organisation *Eesti Rahva Ühisabi* where women were also members.[11] These 'enemies of the people' were imprisoned and sent to the Gulag with long sentences; five years seems to have been usual. Their families were also punished, in the countryside by reducing their farmstead to seven hectares (often involving moving out to less valuable farmland) and reducing their herd of cattle to a single cow.[12] Few studies have been made about this particular period in the history of the occupation, and the numbers arrested are just estimates. The most recent estimate is that about 10,000 were arrested, of which about half died in the first two years of detention.[13] The families are to be added to these numbers. The Soviet state was rather vulnerable at this point. Instead of being powerful, it had to destroy the institutions of civil society in order to be able to rule. The individuals were left alone, without supporting structures, and were one by one integrated in the new structure that was created by the new power holders.

Members of the Communist Party were vetted in a special procedure. They had to present their party cards – which many had destroyed. They had to explain how they lost it, and month for month they had to report what they had been doing and have reliable witnesses to support them. Let us take the example of H. N., a local resident. He had worked in a sawmill during the interwar years, and adhered to the SR (Socialist Revolutionaries). After the communist coup in June 1940, he joined the red militia and a year later he was accepted as a member of the Communist Party. When the Germans were on the point of taking over Estonia, he was scheduled to be evacuated to the USSR; but this did not happen due to the general chaos of war. He lost his party membership card in the process, and when he asked to be reinstated after the war, a thorough investigation was made with many witnesses. He had ended up making his way to Viljandi municipality to flee the German troops, and because his own village was on fire. The Estonian home guard intercepted him and he was sent to concentration camp. Two years later he was in a labour camp in Harku outside Tallinn, working in a peat bog. From there he was transferred to the central prison of Patarei, where he made an unsuccessful attempt to escape. Further labour camps followed, until he finally escaped from a lumbering district in May 1944, with the Red Army not far away. According to one witness, he joined the communist sympathisers in the forest near his home and participated in an attack to sabotage local communications. Provided the investigation witnesses were truthful, his story seems to be one of making unusual efforts for the communist cause. And yet he was not accepted as a party member, for two reasons (according to the investigators). Firstly, circumstances notwithstanding, he had disobeyed orders to join the evacuation east to other republics in the Soviet Union. Secondly they were not sure about his record in jail.[14] From this we can see how hard it was to live up to the communist ideals of the mythological Red Army.

## *The Resistance of the Forest Brotherhood*

The armed resistance to Soviet rulers in the Baltic countries was strongest in Lithuania, where certain central coordination also existed.[15] During the turbulent war years it was not unusual for people to take to the forest when they expected armies or police forces to be after them. The Forest Brotherhood, or the guerrillas, consisted of people who had chosen to resist the Soviets, of draft resisters who sometimes had been fleeing from both German and Soviet recruitment. Moreover, there were those who had participated in the German auxiliary police or as soldiers in the final German effort to contain the Red Army at the border, and who knew they would be shot if they were caught. The boundaries between these groups could sometimes be thin. Ironically, in the Soviet sources, the forest brothers were used to refer to the communist forest fighters during the German occupation, and bandits referred to what others called the Forest Brotherhood.

The main targets for the resistance were requisition agents and local leaders, belonging to the administration or Communist Party. The actions were mostly directed towards local Estonians working in the new administration. The main task of the internal security, NKVD/MGB, was to fight the guerrillas, or 'bandits' as they called them. In the Estonian countryside, the guerrillas were most active in 1944–1945. After that activities diminished following amnesties by the regime and greater efficiency of the internal security as local forces were increasingly participating in their work. When the deportations connected to collectivisation took place in March 1949, a final large-scale effort was made to disturb the repressive forces, needless to say, without success.[16]

This resistance is important as it demonstrated the unwillingness to accept the new regime. Still, the heroic accounts of their activities appearing in the early 1990s have had to be somewhat revised. There were serious groups and targeted actions, but there were also instances where armed groups mostly used their arms in order to find food, and outright thefts did occur.[17]

## Soviet Nationality Policy

The difficulties recruiting locals on all levels were a failure of the official nationality policy of the USSR, adopted in the early years. The Soviet nationality policy was to allow local languages for instance in schools, to have local communists at the highest posts in government and man the administration with people from the local community.[18] Behind the scenes, certainly, there were representatives of the central power institutions, like the Supreme Soviet, the Central Committee and Politburo of the Communist Party of the Soviet Union (CPSU) controlling and directing local policies. The most important of these was in the long run the Estonian Bureau of the CPSU. Responsibility for the policies and repressive methods undoubtedly lay at the central level, but local people were taking these orders in visible positions.

With the close relationship to Russia since russification in the late nineteenth century, the nuances of national ties were several. There were ethnic Estonians whose families had migrated to Russia in the nineteenth century and who hardly knew any Estonian. There were also Estonians who had evacuated with the revolutionary forces in 1918 and had lived in the Soviet Union for two decades, and so at this time they were called 'Yestonians' because of their heavy Russian accent. There were also ethnic Russians who had belonged to a national minority in Estonia for decades, and Russians who had fled during the revolution to Estonia. Yet another group consisted of hunger migrants from the border areas, coming to the Baltic countries in periods of hardship such as the collectivisation years 1929–32 or the Second World War. Finally, there were Russians who, more or less voluntarily, had been brought in as labourers in the process of shock industrialisation in Estonia after the war.

The leadership favoured ethnic Estonians in the 1940s, whereas the process of purges and retaliation after the war resulted in the dominance of the 'Yestonians'. In fact, due to its international aspect, the communist system laid a lot of stress on the ethnic characteristics of the leadership,[19] and so Russians were consciously kept in the background.

The policy of promoting a national elite with communist convictions should, however, not obscure the fact that important decisions for starting a campaign of repression were taken at the central level – it was the execution of orders that was left to the local leadership. In the early years, the Estonian leadership believed they had more room for manoeuvre than was actually the case; and in the 1950 purge of the Estonian Communist Party the leadership was accused of being nationalistic. A more probable reason might have been that they simply adhered to another faction within the CPSU leadership – the part that lost Stalin's trust.[20]

## Recruiting New Cadres

As the power shifted over time, it became increasingly difficult for new rulers to assess the loyalty of local leaders. From the point of view of the central Soviet government the situation after the war was simple. Since the annexation in 1940, the Baltic countries were now part of the USSR, and they had simply been won back from the Germans. For the Baltic population, however, this was not so clear. They did not consider the Soviet occupation as something permanent. Many had sided with the German forces, probably in the same non-committed way as in Finland, because they had the Soviet Union as a common enemy. The Soviets locally experienced that they were not welcome, and considered the Baltic republics as a border population not to be trusted, in the same sense as all the western territories that had previously been occupied by the Germans were.[21]

The first task of the new administration (but the third time this had happened during the war) was to recruit cadres to get society up and running again. The local Estonian activists they brought with them after evacuation were few and thinly dispersed. There were about twenty to thirty people to run a whole county, a number including both party and local government officials and security forces. These people could only cover the most strategic offices, and on the municipality and village level they had to find local supporters.[22] There was a shortage of personnel to fulfil all tasks. The number of communist sympathisers had been reduced in the first year of communist rule as a consequence of the 1941 deportations, and communists had also been persecuted during the German occupation. A central recommendation was to try and find people who had suffered under the Germans, and so would appreciate having a position of power to make up for this.[23] Rural municipal leaders had to take the responsibility for fulfilling state assignments. The implementation of unpopular decisions made their situation awkward. Instability was the main characteristic of the rural cadres directly after the war. The executive committee chairmen of rural areas were replaced at an average rate of once a year and local Party organisers were replaced only slightly less frequently.[24] These were turbulent years, and many administrators lost their jobs within the first year.[25]

The allegiance of the locals could not be bought with privileges, in the situation of dire need that prevailed. The local cadres could not trust the militia or the security forces, charged with keeping order. This can be illustrated with a letter from late December 1944. The writer was a woman member of the Communist Party. She had been in Leningrad in early 1944, preparing the takeover of Viljandimaa county. Now she had local responsibilities in the Executive Committee, and was complaining about the post-war anarchy:

> We will use as examples following impermissible incident: On the 26th of December, the office of the District Executive Committee was visited by an interpreter from the NKGB. He demanded that the Executive Committee should give permission to the NKGB men to take a certain amount of foodstuffs from the local Tuksi farm. The Executive Committee could not give such a permission,

so they phoned to the Executive Committee chairman in Viljandi, comrade Piip, who categorically said no, that would be against the law.

Later on, we heard that these men anyway had gone to Tuksi farm and taken what they wanted.

And today, on the 28th, a group of activists were sent to the Tuksi farm, to make an inventory of the property there, but there were people already there, in Red Army uniforms who chased them away and said they would take care of the property of the farm.

We went there together with the war commissar of Viljandimaa, comrade O., to investigate what was happening, and it turned out that two lambs and some poultry had been taken from the farm.

What is going on here? We are speechless!

Those employed by the militia have started to act the same way; if they are asked to make inventories of the belongings of those who have been arrested, they are taking objects which are then not reported to the militia organisation.[26]

The NKGB, the branch of security forces dealing with external threats was at that moment staffed almost exclusively with Russian-speaking agents. They did not know the area and had difficulties speaking with the locals, and were also thus rather inefficient. Still, the Soviet regime seemed to prefer them to the local inhabitants. The militia and internal security forces NKVD/MGB consisted of somewhat more Estonians. Archives were destroyed or taken to Russia, but from those party cell protocols available in Viljandimaa, it is obvious that both the internal and external security forces consisted predominantly of Russian speakers during the first years – meaning Ukrainians, Belarusians, and other Soviet nationalities, as well as Russians. The local recruitment started through the Young Communist League (*Komsomol*), but the militia's equipment was deficient and they often protested about the poor living conditions.[27] It seems the authorities simply did not have the resources to buy people through privileges.

## Estonians in the Red Army

The cadre problem was eventually solved by recruiting demobilised Red Army soldiers. After the war they were sent to so-called 'screening camps' and returned only in 1946–1947. In the camps, some received education for administrative work and were thus officially socialised into the Soviet system; they had not had the possibility to collaborate with the German occupational forces. Another argument in favour of their recruitment was the prestige of the Red Army after victory.

The war marked a watershed for the USSR. The image of the glorious October Revolution had been tarnished in people's minds with violence, repression and the first losses in war. Now, the war victory, which also brought international recognition and internal support, became the main icon of success in the propaganda. The Red Army was vital to the Soviet Union's public discourse. Being a soldier and risking one's life for the 'Soviet Motherland' became the most important sign of revolutionary loyalty. The Red Army, according to the myth, consisted of faultless heroes, and this consequently set a tough standard to match. All kinds of collaboration with the enemy – even just getting on with your job under a new ruler – were regarded as treachery. It seems as if the only way to irrevocably show allegiance would have been to die for the USSR. American historian Amir Weiner has noticed the same phenomenon occurring in the reconstruction process in Nazi-occupied Ukraine.[28] If somebody had been rude to a Red Army prisoner of war, it was considered a war crime.

Estonian recruits in the Red Army had been evacuated to the Soviet Union in 1941. Their fate during the war was difficult. To begin with, some of them were dispersed in collective farms and industries all over the country, depending on the need for labour. New recruits were largely dispatched to labour battalions for hard work. Even though they shared the fate of local Russians, the conditions were extremely hard. Survivors of the labour battalions describe the conditions as near starvation and really not that different from the Gulag, so those who had hoped a better life would await them in the USSR were deceived.[29] In 1942, Estonian units were formed inside the Red Army, assembling Estonians from the work battalions. The national Estonian Red Army unit was deployed on the Western front where the main goal was to come to the rescue of Leningrad. At the same time, some units went towards Estonia. Memoirs of these soldiers tell how they were encouraged to carry on by the message, conveyed by their officers, that they were on their way home.[30] Their first battles, for instance that of Velikije Luki, were extremely difficult with enormous losses. Later they were engaged in battles with other Estonian soldiers fighting in German uniforms. It is generally believed that a large number of desertions took place in such situations. For instance, according to a recent estimation about 5,000 out of a total of 70,000 Estonians in the Red Army defected to the other side.[31]

With demobilisation in 1946–1947, those Red Army soldiers of Estonian origin were able to get the best positions. They had, after all, belonged to the most prestigious of all Soviet institutions, the victorious Red Army, and could thus be trusted. They had had no contacts with the German occupation and therefore they could not be collaborators. Secondly, they had been socialised into the Soviet system for four to five years already, so they were used to it and knew how it worked. Thirdly, they were also vetted in the screening camps, which was a kind of debriefing after the war, where they were trained as, for instance, local administrators. When they were released from screening camps, many wartime local Executive Committee chairmen were immediately 'released' and replaced with former Red Army soldiers. According to my material, the soldiers were often posted back 'home', in the municipalities where they had been living before the war. This happened mostly in 1947, and improved local government from being very unstable to at least a crudely functioning system.[32]

## Transition through Collectivisation and Dekulakization

Formal institutions in the countryside were destroyed as a consequence of occupation. However, informal structures in villages and municipalities held on in the countryside for some time, as they were tried and trusted by the inhabitants. It was these informal institutions at the heart of local communities that had grown around the existing system of agriculture (decreed by the CPSU to be run by 'tight fisted' farmers, or *kulaki*) that seem to have been the real target of the 'dekulakisation' and collectivisation of agriculture in 1947–49 in the conquered area. Collectivisation would destroy the power of kulaks through harnessing the participation of many local inhabitants in the process.

The persecution was set up to create a social pressure, so that locals were obliged to participate in the 'class struggle'. It was carried through in bureaucratic processes where individual initiatives were not necessary, functionaries were simply required to provide victims, sometimes even the number of victims required was issued from above. In most countries, it is usual for the state to monopolise violence through the police and the army; but in the Soviet Union, this monopoly was literally 'given to the people', but in effect it meant they were expected to carry out this violence on behalf of the state.[33]

In dekulakisation, the task was formally to uncover kulaks, seen as the rich farmers who exploited the landless population. But as there were few farming families that could afford to use wage labourers, it was difficult to find exploitation according to normal criteria. In the war years, there was a lack of able-bodied men in the countryside. The German administration made it possible for local farmers in Estonia to make use of Soviet prisoners of war (POWs) as farm labourers. This would be in particular the old, the ill and single women whose husbands had left for the war. As part of the vicious circle of post-war retaliation, this use of POWs soon became the most frequently used frame of reference for accusing farmers of being exploiters and kulaks.

The uncovering of kulaks was made according to a bureaucratic procedure. The local Executive committees were asked to send in lists of kulaks in their district to the county administration. Those who had accepted to perform administrative duties could hardly have suspected that they would be participating in such repressive measures. The committee was to fill in a form for each family on the list, specifying the exploitation the kulaks were accused of, the size of the farm, its implements etc. Often a political comment was also penciled in the margins. Then the accused family was informed and simultaneously demanded to pay a much higher tax. The family had a possibility to protest the accusation, which most of them did. Their case was then discussed in a special 'court' and they could be acquitted or remain in the kulak register. All documents regarding the process were held in family files with the local Executive committee.

In small villages most people probably knew the histories of their neighbours and were well-informed about their doings during the German occupation. Still, they did not denounce them until the repressive policies had provoked serious enough conflicts at the local level. Among the files regarding kulak families to be investigated in Viljandimaa, there were denunciation letters included in one family file of approximately twenty. This suggests that denunciations were not a crucial part of the penal system; rather the kulaks were selected on the basis of the administrative procedure, set in motion by the central authorities.

On the contrary, many of the neighbours participated in protest against the accusations of kulaks. The files of kulak families to be investigated contained many letters in support of the accused family. They typically agreed that kulaks should be eliminated, but with regard to that particular family a mistake must have occurred, they were not kulaks. Most rural people, including party members and officials signed such support letters. This was done in spite of the risk that policemen or judges could go back to the files, find the letters and accuse those signing them of having supported a kulak family.[34]

The letters of support was an important form of protest in a situation where locals were expected to perform tasks normally given to the security police. The administrative form of repression, using archives, screenings and unsuspecting local leaders, was a main factor in compelling the subdued peoples to participate in the procedures leading to deportations and arrests, from the onset of the 'kulak campaign' in 1947 to the large-scale deportations in March 1949.

The extensive use of ordinary people in purges and 'class struggles' was a feature of the Soviet system that only lately has been discussed in historiography.[35] Threats and fear were obviously the main factors leading people to comply with the system. Other contributing factors have been mentioned in the literature. An explanation used in Russian historiography may apply here too. When repressive measures had already removed large parts of the previous elite in society, there were now ample opportunities for social mobility. This upcoming group or class is widely considered to have been the mainstay of Stalin's USSR.[36] Another explanation is that, to escape revenge and punishment, some of the original elite under the Nazi regime became some of the most zealous pro-Soviets to safeguard themselves and their families. There are enough cases in the archives, where such people were found out and arrested, to show that this was not an unreasonable course to take for those already guilty of 'war crimes'.

Finally, propaganda could have contributed. The vice secretaries of both central and local Communist Party units were responsible for propaganda, which indicates the importance attached to the issue. And indeed propaganda was everywhere in the newly occupied area. Propaganda groups made regular reports on the number of public meetings and private talks they held with local people; and these make impressive reading as the numbers in the meetings are often greater than the actual number of inhabitants in the area. Obviously the statistics are forged, but what is most clear from this is that it indicates just how important propaganda must have been for this forging to even be necessary. Distributing newspapers was one of the main tasks of communists, and the propaganda probably did not convince people; they listened and read just to know what the regime thought they should be thinking.

## Consequences of Being Occupied Twice

For the locals of Viljandimaa, and Estonia as a whole, living between the USSR and Nazi Germany meant not just being occupied once, but twice, with each occupying regime going through the process of punishing the collaborators with the former regime and recruiting new loyal citizens into their own administration. People were forced to take sides, and after 1944 the Soviet Union also aimed at control on the individual or family level. Screenings and extensive reports on the class and previous record of the individual were demanded when applying for a job, higher education, or passports. This process went through several phases. To begin with there were general assessments. Later people already in office were vetted again and found to be lacking in some respect. The whole rural population was enrolled in the anti-kulak struggle, even if they often participated in an unexpected way, protesting the accusations. When the countryside was eventually purged of kulaks, it was usually more because the kulaks had German contacts than were actually exploiters of the poor.

Thus, being geographically situated between Germany and Russia and occupied by both, the Baltic peoples were punished repeatedly. Still the most widespread and longest punishment took place under the Stalin regime of isolation in the years after the war. This process of retaliation and retribution went on for the first five years of the post-war period.

The final purge of this period happened in 1950, and concerned the Communist Party and the local government. But that is another story, since it was nationalism rather than collaboration with the Germans that was the main issue of that purge.

### Notes

1. See A. M. Kõll, *The Village and the Class War. Anti-kulak Campaign in Estonia* (Budapest: Central European University Press, 2013).
2. See M. Ilmjärv, *Silent Submission* (Stockholm: Studia Baltica Stockholmiensia, 2004), in particular pages 464–477 for a detailed account of this process.
3. For the general history of Estonia in English, see T. Raun, *Estonia and the Estonians* (Stanford: The Hoover Press, 1991; new editions and a revision also available). Pages 139–146 give an account that has since been accepted in the post-Soviet period.
4. Exiled Estonians have given accounts of their experiences in *Eesti riik ja rahvas teises maailmasõjas* [The Estonian State and People in the Second World War], vols. I–X (Stockholm: EMP, 1954–1962).
5. J. Ant, *Eesti 1939–41: Rahvast, valitsemisest, saatustest* [Estonia 1939–41: the People, the Governance, the Destiny] (Tallinn: Rahvusarhiiv, 1999), 167–170.
6. A. Rahi-Tamm, 'Human losses', in *The White Book: Losses Inflicted on the Estonian Nation by Occupation Regimes 1940–1991* (Tallinn: Estonian Encyclopedia Publishers, 2005), 27.
7. M. Laar and J. Tross, *Punane terror* [Red Terror] (Stockholm: Välis-Eesti EMP, 1996), 7.
8. Rahi-Tamm, 'Human losses', 38.

9  S. Myllyniemi, *Die Neuordnung der Baltischen Ländern 1941-1944* (Helsinki: Suomen Historiallinen Seura, 1973), 87.
10 Eesti Rahvusarhiivi Filiaal (ERAF) 19-13-11, 59; basically the Communist Party archive.
11 *Ühisabi* was an official aid organisation, established in the German period instead of the neutral Red Cross.
12 According to Decree no. 380. E. Laasi, *Eesti NSV talumajapidamiste kollektiviseerimise ettevalmistus ja selle seostamine (1944-49)* [Preparation for Collectivization of Farms in the Estonian SSR in 1944-49 and Its Causes: a Case Study of Võru County] (Tallinn: manuscript, 1966), 53; Ruusmann, A., *Põllumajanduse taastamine ja kollektiviseerimine Eesti NSV-s aastail 1944-1950: dissertatsioon ajalooteaduste kandidaadi teadusliku kraadi taotlemiseks* (Eesti NSV Teaduste Akadeemia, Ajaloo Instituut, 1967), 343.
13 Rahi-Tamm, 'Human losses', 31.
14 ERAF 19-2-30, p 4-9.
15 See A. Anušauskas (ed.), *The Anti-Soviet Resistance in the Baltic States* (Vilnius, 1999).
16 M. Laar, '1949. aasta märtsiküüditamine ja relvastatud vastupanuliikumine [March Deportations of 1949 and the Armed Resistance Movement]', in E. Andresen et al. (eds), *Eestlaste küüditamine: Mineviku varjud tänases päevas* [The Deportation of Estonians: Yesterday's Shadows Today] (Tartu: Korp!Filiae Patriae, 2004), 65-69.
17 See, for instance, A. Mäesalu et al., *Eesti ajalugu* [Estonian History], Part II (Tallinn: Avita, 1995), a relatively recent textbook for students.
18 D. Feest, *Zwangskollektivierung im Baltikum: Die Sowjetisierung des estnischen Dorfes 1944-1953* (Vienna: Böhlau, 2007), 32-38, 68-69.
19 Feest, *Zwangskollektivierung im Baltikum*, 57-58.
20 Feest, *Zwangskollektivierung im Baltikum*, 441.
21 Feest, *Zwangskollektivierung im Baltikum*, 478-480.
22 ERAF 811-1-7; Laasi, *Eesti NSV*, 10.
23 Laasi, *Eesti NSV*, 10-12; E. Kivimaa, 'Eesti NSV Põllumajanduse kollektiviseerimine 1947-1950 [Collectivization of Agriculture in the Estonian SSR in 1947-1950]', in Tõnurist, E. (ed.), *Sotsialistliku põllumajanduse areng Nõukogude Eestis* [Development of Socialist Agriculture in Soviet Estonia] (Tallinn: Valgus, 1976), 70.
24 I. Paavle *Kohaliku halduse sovetiseerimine Eestis 1940-1950* [Sovietisation of local administration in Estonia 1940-1950], dissertation Tartu 2009, 286-287.
25 Laasi, *Eesti NSV*, 10; Ruusmann, *Põllumajanduse taastamine*, 337-339.
26 ERAF 19-3-11, 63.
27 The archive of the security forces is not available in Estonia, probably it has been destroyed. Minutes oft he party cell of the local internal security are accessible, ERAF, F 408, Op 2.
28 A. Weiner, *Making Sense of War: The Second World War and the Fate of the Bolshevik Revolution* (Princeton, NJ: Princeton University Press, 2001), 160-162.
29 H. Ojalo et al., (eds), *Korpusepoisid* (Tallinn: Sentinel, 2007), 5; *Velikije Luki, Tehumardi, Kuramaa* [A Soviet-time Commemorative Book] (Tallinn: Eesti Raamat, 1974), 113f.; R. Hinrikus, ed., *Eesti rahva elulood. 1 osa, Sajandi sada elulugu kahes osas*. 2. trükk (Tallinn: Tänapäev, 2003), 134.
30 *Velikije Luki*, 14.
31 Ojalo et al., *Korpusepoisid*, 125.
32 Paavle, *Kohaliku halduse sovetiseerimine*, 174-175
33 This has been demonstrated by Jan T. Gross in *Revolution from Abroad: The Soviet Conquest of Poland's Western Ukraine and Western Belorussia* (Princeton, NJ: Princeton University Press, 1988), 231-233.

34 Kõll, *The Village and the Class War*, 92.
35 For an in-depth argument, on which the following is based, see Kõll, *The Village and the Class War*, 231–248.
36 The explanation was originally developed in 1979 by Sheila Fitzpatrick in *Education and Social Mobility in the Soviet Union 1921–1943* (Cambridge: Cambridge University Press). It has since then been widely accepted and used in other works.

# Sources and Bibliography

## Archival sources

Eesti Rahvusarhiivi Filiaal (ERAF) (basically the Communist Party archive)
F 408, Op 2
19-2-30; 19-13-11; 811-1-7

## Printed sources

*Eesti riik ja rahvas teises maailmasõjas* [The Estonian State and People in the Second World War], vols. I–X. Stockholm: EMP, 1954–1962.
*Velikije Luki, Tehumardi, Kuramaa* [A Soviet-time Commemorative Book]. Tallinn: Eesti Raamat, 1974.

## Literature

Ant, J., *Eesti 1939–41: Rahvast, valitsemisest, saatustest* [Estonia 1939–41: the People, the Governance, the Destiny]. Tallinn: Rahvusarhiiv, 1999.
Anušauskas, A. (ed.), *The Anti-Soviet Resistance in the Baltic States*. Vilnius, 1999.
Feest, D., *Zwangskollektivierung im Baltikum: Die Sowjetisierung des estnischen Dorfes 1944–1953*. Vienna: Böhlau, 2007.
Fitzpatrick, S., *Education and Social Mobility in the Soviet Union 1921–1943*. Cambridge: Cambridge University Press, 1979.
Gross, J. T., *Revolution from Abroad: The Soviet Conquest of Poland's Western Ukraine and Western Belorussia*. Princeton, NJ: Princeton University Press, 1988.
Hinrikus, R., ed., *Eesti rahva elulood. 1 osa, Sajandi sada elulugu kahes osas*. 2. trükk. Tallinn: Tänapäev, 2003.
Ilmjärv, M., *Silent Submission*. Stockholm: Studia Baltica Stockholmiensia, 2004.
Kivimaa, E., 'Eesti NSV Põllumajanduse kollektiviseerimine 1947–1950 [Collectivization of Agriculture in the Estonian SSR in 1947–1950]', in Tõnurist E. (ed.), *Sotsialistliku põllumajanduse areng Nõukogude Eestis* [Development of Socialist Agriculture in Soviet Estonia]. Tallinn: Valgus, 1976.
Kõll, A. M., *The Village and the Class War. Anti-kulak Campaign in Estonia*. Budapest: Central European University Press, 2013.
Laar, M., '1949. aasta märtsiküüditamine ja relvastatud vastupanuliikumine [March Deportations of 1949 and the Armed Resistance Movement]', in Andresen, E. et al. (eds), *Eestlaste küüditamine: Mineviku varjud tänases päevas* [The Deportation of Estonians: Yesterday's Shadows Today]. Tartu: Korp!Filiae Patriae, 2004.
Laar M. and Tross, J., *Punane terror* [Red Terror]. Stockholm: Välis-Eesti EMP, 1996.

Laasi, E., *Eesti NSV talumajapidamiste kollektiviseerimise ettevalmistus ja selle seostamine (1944-49)* [Preparation for Collectivization of Farms in the Estonian SSR in 1944-49 and Its Causes: a Case Study of Võru County]. Tallinn: manuscript, 1966.

Myllyniemi, S., *Die Neuordnung der Baltischen Ländern 1941-1944*. Helsinki: Suomen Historiallinen Seura, 1973.

Mäesalu, A. et al., *Eesti ajalugu* [Estonian History], Part II. Tallinn: Avita, 1995.

Ojalo, H. et al., (eds), *Korpusepoisid*. Tallinn: Sentinel, 2007.

Paavle, I., *Kohaliku halduse sovetiseerimine Eestis 1940-1950* [Sovietisation of local administration in Estonia 1940-1950], dissertation Tartu 2009.

Rahi-Tamm, A., 'Human losses', in *The White Book: Losses Inflicted on the Estonian Nation by Occupation Regimes 1940-1991*. Tallinn: Estonian Encyclopedia Publishers, 2005.

Raun, T., *Estonia and the Estonians*. Stanford: The Hoover Press, 1991.

Ruusmann, A., *Põllumajanduse taastamine ja kollektiviseerimine Eesti NSV-s aastail 1944-1950: dissertatsioon ajalooteaduste kandidaadi teadusliku kraadi taotlemiseks*. Eesti NSV Teaduste Akadeemia, Ajaloo Instituut, 1967.

Weiner, A., *Making Sense of War: The Second World War and the Fate of the Bolshevik Revolution*. Princeton, NJ: Princeton University Press, 2001.

Marta Kurkowska-Budzan

## 2. 'Coming Out of the Woods': How Partisans of the Polish Anti-Communist Underground Adapted to Civilian Life

In Poland, the Second World War neither ended in the year 1944, when most of its territory was 'liberated' from German occupation by the Red Army, nor on 8 May 1945, when the Nazis signed the act of capitulation in Berlin. In January 1945, despite the Home Army (AK) of the Polish Underground State being officially disbanded, some of the soldiers decided not to lay down their arms, deciding instead to fight the newly formed regime. The war lasted until at least 1947, which is commonly accepted to be the year the communist system was finally 'installed' in Poland, and when the authorities proclaimed an amnesty for the partisans providing they would 'come out of the woods', lay down their arms, and disclose their identities. Until then, everyday life for all Poles, not just partisans, remained under war conditions.[1]

The history of the anti-communist armed underground was complex, and it was understandably little explored in the subsequent decades of socialism in Poland. The history of this period was effectively suppressed both in the public domain and in local areas where the resistance was most active (albeit for different reasons). With the political transformations of the 1980s and 1990s, and the collapse of socialism in Europe, the imminent revision of this part of Polish history was obvious. Indeed, as evidenced by the numerous publications that have appeared, particularly in the last decade, the anti-communist underground has been the subject of a large number of historical studies and is gaining more and more interest among the younger generation of historians in Poland. Perhaps the most spectacular publication is the *Atlas of the Independence Underground in Poland*, which summarises a number of detailed historical studies, and was issued by the Institute of National Remembrance in 2007.[2] In addition to a cartographic visualisation of where the centres of resistance and key events took place, this extensive publication contains expanded descriptions and illustrations on the period 1944–1956. Research into the anti-communist armed underground has been very much influenced by the changing political climate in Poland and, at the same time, the growing number of publications reinforce current political and public discourse. One sign of this is the fact that in 2011, the Polish parliament established a new national day to be celebrated on March 1 called 'the Day of Remembrance of the Cursed Soldiers'.

## Research and Methodology

For the last few years, Polish historians have written at length about the political context and historical facts of the anti-communist underground after the war.[3] However, it usually remains silent about the individual fates of the partisans. That is why in 2006, as part of one project entitled 'The National Armed Underground in the Białystok Region (1942–1957): Memory Discourses', I adopted the biographical research methodology of Fritz Schütze to interview, among others, veterans of the anti-communist underground.[4] The aim of my research was not so much to reveal new historical and political details and facts; nor to either judge the people of the past or heap tributes on them. I was simply interested in people's various stories and the meanings that these create nowadays, in the current social and political situation. Do they support the prevailing public discourse or are they against it? This is the question that does not seem to have been raised by Polish historians to date, who have been exploring the subject of anti-communist resistance in the country.

Methodologically the project belongs to the field of oral history, which today is no longer just a research method but also a separate branch altogether of historiography. It is not about bringing facts unknown to the written documents to light, nor about comparing oral accounts with 'more reliable' sources. The stories of these interlocutors do not perform the same function as a classical historical source. Oral history is co-created, as a matter of fact, in dialogue with a historian. I am interested in the human experience which, in Reinhart Koselleck's definition, is 'a contemporary past, whose events are internalised and which can be recollected.'[5] In oral history I move within a frame of recollection that depends on the construction of an oral narrative and its rhetoric. Starting from my initial question, 'tell me about your life, please', I move on to then question the narrator more precisely in an interview situation to get more details about the content, form, and context of the recorded account. My aim is to discover what influences a given narration about the past, and in what way? How do these interlocutors give a sense of meaning to their life in a specific story? What concepts and terms do they use in relation to history, and why?

The subject of this chapter is about the process of adapting to civilian life in a communist system. Therefore, the main focus is on those partisans who, at some point gave up any further fighting. I would like to emphasise that I have not interviewed people who were high up in the hierarchy of anti-communist armed organisations. My interlocutors are residents of small towns and villages, simple soldiers, and that is how I intended my research to be, so as to gain a perspective 'from below'. I was driven by a humanistic interest in ordinary resistance movement members, in as much as this could provide a good enough historical raison d'être for my research.

Those veterans who were in positions of command or were acting in regional or national headquarters of the resistance have already been the main characters of historical books for more than a decade. Some of them have even written their own memoirs for publication.[6] Among them, there were and still are many with special intellectual predispositions, and they hold prominent positions in Polish academia or political elites. These people and their biographies must surely therefore be taken as exceptional when compared to the background of thousands of other resistance movement members.

Those who did not lay down arms died, either in direct fights with the state security or in prison. We will never know their personal accounts, having only the information left in the official records, interrogation protocols and biographies that are stored in the archives of the Institute of National Remembrance. Today, relatives, friends, and witnesses speak of events on behalf of those who did not give up and suffered death, as 'unwavering till the end'. Equally, the partisan troop commanders are being mythologised once more; but this time it is a heroic myth, contingent upon what their death means from the perspective of the present-day political situation, whereas under the communist regime they were treated as 'bandits from the woods' and a 'fascist reactionary underground'. Breaking up the anti-communist underground was only half the success of the 'people's authorities'. Equally important for them was to be able to banish the very idea that these partisans had stood for any kind of liberation in the people's consciousness.

The authorities used historiography, propaganda in press and radio campaigns, and even literature and film to these ends. For example, in 1956, which was already the period of political thaw in Poland, in the popular social drama and thriller, *Cień* (Shadow), directed by Jerzy Kawalerowicz, bandits from the National Armed Forces appear, and with the support of the kulaks, they oppress the poor, defenceless peasants and cruelly murder soldiers of the *Korpus Bezpieczeństwa Wewnętrznego* (Internal Security Corps).[7]

But it was the first years of the communist regime when there was the most extensive and aggressive propaganda of all, and this must have influenced not only the general perceptions of the resistance, but also the personal recollections of former partisans, obliged to recreate pictures of their own 'me in the current of history'. That is why this chapter attempts to answer the questions which follow. How do veterans construct their 'life stories' in the specific political situation of today (in this case 'today' was 2003–2008)? How do they narrate the motives for disclosing their true identities, or for joining the underground (in many cases these were young people) after the end of official war activities? How did they perceive their future after having 'come out of the woods'; and what was the 'return to normality' like? Did they see it as such, and do they see it as such now? Indeed, what happened to them after 'coming out of the woods'? How did they adapt to life, and the political and social system that was being introduced in Poland after the war? How do they evaluate their life decisions today?

In my project, I focused on gathering and recording interviews with individuals looking back over the post-war years in the region of Białystok, and specifically the Łomża province. During my visits and longer stays in the town of Łomża and the surrounding area in 2003, and then between 2006 and 2008, I conducted in-depth narrative interviews with thirty-two people. In addition, my students from the Jagiellonian University interviewed eight people as part of their fieldwork practice. Most narrations are biographical in nature, with the exception of group interviews in which it was more difficult to maintain the focus on each narrator's individual biography.

I reached my interlocutors in various ways, but primarily through using the snowball method. This 'snowball' originated in the Łomża branch of the 'Association of Soldiers of the National Armed Forces' (*Związek Żołnierzy Narodowych Sił Zbrojnych*). There I met five veterans who had been active within the nationalist underground as soldiers or as members of a conspiratorial network. I also spoke with former soldiers of the Home Army. My students interviewed three active members of the Association of Combatants of the Republic of Poland and former political prisoners, who had been wartime members of the Home Army. All the interlocutors were people aged between 73 and 94 years old (in the period 2003–2008). Between 1944 and 1957 they had performed various functions, had numerous occupations, and represented a variety of social and political perspectives.

## *Timeline for the Anti-Communist Underground Organisations*

It happens that the region in Northeastern Poland where groups of the anti-communist underground acted for the longest, and with the greatest intensity, was the province of Łomża. Historians agree that this is likely to be due to the specific historical experience of the people living in this region.[8] However, whereas some scholars assume that it was the traumatic experience of the Soviet occupation in the years 1939–1941 that catalysed post-war resistance, others put more emphasis on the extensive influence of nationalist ideology[9] in the area. Either way, it is a fact that in this period, the region back then harboured other organisations besides the 'post-AK underground' (a prolongation of the disbanded Home Army).[10]

There were strong partisan factions, on the one hand invoking the ideology of the pre-war National Democrats (*endecja*), and on the other the National Radical Camp (*Obóz Narodowo-Radykalny*). The latter group was known to have fascist tendencies, and it had indeed been outlawed for these tendencies already in the 1930s. Defining themselves as nationalists (*narodówka*), they had also been a part of the National Armed Forces (NSZ) from 1942.[11] There was much antagonism between the democrat and nationalist factions of anti-communist resistance, which often resulted in armed fights. The conflict was exacerbated in politically significant moments demanding final declarations and decisions, such as the referendum of 30 June 1947, elections to the Polish parliament (*Sejm*), and the 'disclosure action' in 1947 – which allowed partisans amnesty if they revealed themselves.

It seems understandable that people associated with the Home Army, and other national organisations, would continue their underground activity even after the end of the Second World War. The Polish Committee of National Liberation (*Polski Komitet Wyzwolenia Narodowego*), which was supported by the Soviet Union, came to power and was a symbol of national betrayal to both the democratic and nationalist groups. The former was counting on fast and democratic parliamentary elections, which they saw as the only chance to remove the communists from power; while the latter sought to deter the outbreak of the Third World War.

The following periods can be distinguished in the timeline of post-war resistance activity in the territory of northeastern Poland:

I. January 1945–November 1945
General Leopold Okulicki orders the Home Army to disband, with the result that new structures of the post-AK underground begin to form, while national organisations merge to form the National Military Union (NZW).

II. November 1945–February 1947
The NZW begins an intensive armed struggle with the communist authorities. Meanwhile, partisan troops of the former AK are disbanded to be replaced by the newly established Freedom and Sovereignty organisation (*Wolność i Niezawisłość*), whose activities focus on propaganda campaigns aimed at the civilian population.

III. February 1947–April 1947
The amnesty enacted by the Polish parliament in February 1947, which was supposed to encourage the disbanding of the underground and laying down of arms, was a turning point in the biographies of many participants in the resistance movement. The resulting disclosure action, conducted in the spring of 1947, put an end to the post-AK underground's activity, as numerous soldiers of the NZW took advantage of the action.

IV. April 1947–1957
However, not all the partisans trusted the communist authorities and stayed 'in the woods' without revealing their identities for another few years. The secret police fought with them ruthlessly until the last of them had been liquidated in 1957. Some of them, like Jan Tabortowski, aka *Bruzda*, had not lain down their arms since 1939, while others had joined the partisans either during the German occupation or after the Red Army had taken over. The years 1947–1957 were therefore a period of activity for small groups of partisans conducting a struggle for their own survival in the face of increasing pressure from the Office of Security (UB or *Urząd Bezpieczeństwa*).

## *Motives for Joining the Anticommunist Underground*

Rafał Wnuk, until now the only Polish historian to have taken up an extensive analysis of the individual fates of anti-communist underground activists, claims that the people who chose the path of illegal resistance after the liberation were guided in their decisions by two groups of factors – systemic and individual. By systemic factors he means those circumstances to which an individual had little or no option but to react in a certain way. An example of this would be those activists who joined the ranks of underground organisations because of the repressions they had suffered at the hands of occupying troops or the communist state. Another was if they were at risk of being drafted or had deserted from the army. Indeed, as a result of international politics and the post-war fate of Eastern Europe, the ranks of the underground were swollen by refugees from the territories that had now fallen under the aegis of the Soviet Union after the Second World War.

By individual factors Wnuk means personal motivations, such as feelings of responsibility, in the case of command corps' members who felt responsible for their subordinates; or an individual's belief and values, in the case of people who had consciously decided to fight the communist system because it was hostile and alien to them. Another factor might also have been disappointment, in the case of active individuals with left-wing views, who felt let down by the new regime. These people may have initially been favourably inclined towards the new authorities but then they experienced disappointment because of the course of events and returned to the underground. In contrast, another factor was that the younger generation may have felt motivated by enthusiasm to fight, having missed out on the 'glory' of the anti-German underground. One other motivating factor could also have been the inability of a large group of men who had been 'infected by war' and could not find their place in any other reality than warfare. Finally, another main reason was simply because they were following the common paths of behaviour ('everybody else joined the partisans, so I did too'). This phenomenon was extremely widespread in so-called 'partisan villages'. The last factor was a personal experience connected with the Soviet reality (1939–1941) or during deportations to the East.[12]

In my research I also ask about the motives behind key decisions made after the war – about when people joined the underground, remained in it, or gave oneself up (disclosure). However, I did not directly question the interviewees about this, but addressed them within the context of their autobiographical narration. The answers thus depend on the type of narration, which I have divided into two groups: stories that the author places in the context of the greater historical narrative; and more immediate stories located in the interlocutors' individual everyday environment.

## *Life Stories Deeply Rooted in the Greater Historical Narrative*

People who present their life stories as part of a greater narrative usually begin by emphasising family traditions, including the decision to join the underground. The biographical narration begins with an introduction to the exceptional religiousness of the parents or their involvement in the pre-war *endecja* (see footnote 9), and the patriotism instilled in them in their youth.

> My parents were very religious; they had such needs that they even fasted on the first day of Easter and the first day of Christmas. My father had always been with the nationalists. He would always sing this hymn and had that tie with this [sword] of Chrobry on it.[13] My father always said that Poles should develop economically, and that trade […] should flourish because of Poles and not the Jews.[14]

> My parents were nationalists, my father was in Haller's army[15] and my mother was a teacher [...] I myself have never been a member of the AK. Not because I'm opposed to it [...] but anyone could join the AK – a Jew, pagan, [...] and a traitor to the country – they were taking everyone, whoever came [...] but in NSZ they did not accept everyone. They accepted only 100% Poles, patriots.[16]

> My mum and dad were true Catholics, well [...] true Poles. We would always go to the cathedral to church, and the sons, that is us, were altar boys. Mum was a saintly woman, I can tell you. And a true patriot.[17]

In the historiography and journalism of the period of the communist regime in Poland, the National Armed Forces, whose members were authors of the abovementioned statements, had the grim reputation of being 'fascists' and 'bandits'. While the Home Army's veterans were socially rehabilitated fairly soon – at the end of the 1950s – and the eager ones even went on to join the official Union of Fighters for Freedom and Democracy (ZBoWiD – *Związek Bojowników o Wolność i Demokrację*), the nationalists remained on the margins of veteran associations until as late as 1990. This resulted in a lack of access to various privileges and social rights that ZBoWiD veterans enjoyed.

New veteran associations, including the Union of the National Armed Forces Soldiers (ZZNSZ – *Związek Żołnierzy Narodowych Sił Zbrojnych*), began to appear in the 1990s; but the public discourse regarding the political profile of the NSZ and their activities did not notably change. But more recently, with the changing political atmosphere, this is happening. The three interlocutors, whose statements were quoted above, have become activists in the local ZZNSZ and are aware of the new historical policy of the Polish authorities. In their narrations they emphasise their unbeaten and indomitable attitude towards life, 'remaining at [their] post' in spite of all the political adversities, persecutions, and suffering that they were forced to live through in the communist period. When I came to interview them, which was conducted as a group, out of necessity, and to which I was, so to speak, 'lured' by them, my interlocutors greeted me at the door with a joyful declaration, 'we're all family here – all nationalists; always to the right, never to the left.'[18]

## *Life Stories Deeply Rooted in the Immediate Everyday Environment*

Mr. Teofil L. comes from a rich farming family. He was already enrolled in the ZWZ (later the AK) in November 1939, when a friend from the village came to him with a proposal.

> 'You have to be with us, 'cause here where you live [outside the village] it will be easy for us to do everything... all kinds of exercises.' A moment later he gave some of those pseudonyms to us and everything... Well, you know, how could I refuse? I was afraid of nothing back then.[19]

Shortly after this incident, however, he was sent with all his family to Kazakhstan. He returned in the spring of 1946 and was immediately involved in the anti-communist resistance. However, according to his words, this was not according to his free will. Suddenly he found himself in a situation where he 'couldn't say no' to lodging armed partisans on his farm. From that point on the NSZ groups of Jastrzębski (pseudonym *Zbych*) and Żebrowski (pseudonym *Bąk*) had a hideaway in his barn.[20] Teofil L. illustrated this with an anecdote in the interview. 'Zbych asks me, "how was it in that Siberia?" So I say that "if it wasn't for the hope that I would eventually come back, I would have probably hanged myself." At this point, Zbych called all his friends in and asked Teofil to repeat the same story to them all "so that they [knew] what they [were] fighting for!"'

In 1949, during the UB manhunt for Teofil L.'s farm, the pre-war leader of a local *endecja* was killed. The death of *Bąk* (mentioned in Teofil's narrative above) and of his son is one of those tales mythicised by historians and politicians alike about the indomitability and righteousness of the last of the 'cursed soldiers'.[21] Teofil L. is one of the last people still alive who knew *Bąk* personally, and he spoke candidly about him in our interview, and in practical terms.

> That Bąk was a decent guy, and had a nice farm. But when communism came, he gave it up. They were going to deport him to Russia and so he ran away. They would have deported his son too, but the women covered him with a blanket and they didn't find him. Then the son kept being pestered by the UB with questions like 'where's your father? ...where's your father?' So his father took him with him [to the woods – MKB].[22]

Teofil L. builds his life story around such anecdotes, which emphasise his ironic attitude to what happened to him, his practical perspective, and his ability to deal with the most difficult moments in life. His participation in underground activities certainly involved the latter ability. But because he was also the leader of a local branch of the ZZNSZ at the time of the interview, he tried to convey some moral values too, by lightly joking as these anecdotes are told.

## *Disclosure and Its Consequences*

The disclosure action in the spring of 1947 consisted in the authorities preparing points in the bigger towns, where partisans, either as troops or individually, could lay down their arms and sign up on a list in an organised way in return for amnesty. By this means, the UB gained all the necessary information about former partisans and 'enemies of the state'.

An analysis of the underground activists' biographical entries shows that the vast majority immediately after disclosure (and some earlier, such as AK members that had disbanded in January 1945) attempted to start a new life with new conditions in a new place. Usually they chose the 'Recovered Territories' that had formerly been in the east of Germany (Pomerania, East Prussia, and Silesia) where there was a chance to study or be given an industrial job and a farm or a house that had formerly been German property. In the case of people who wanted to study, they chose large, distant cities like Łódź, Warsaw, or Wrocław.[23]

Those who disclosed themselves immediately after the amnesty – and they were the vast majority – rationalised their decision by referring to two different factors. The first factor referred to the general course of history; while the second factor had to do with more personal matters (like getting married). These are illustrated, respectively, by the two quotes below.

> We didn't want to be involved in the struggle anymore because we knew it was impossible in Poland, against such a powerful Soviet army, to stage any kind of properly organised [coup]. [...] Unfortunately, me and my cousin had already decided to do a runner to the Recovered Territories, just to get away from it all, 'cause there were no prospects. [...] My father would say, 'two of you are already dead. Do you want to be too?'[24]

> [I] already had a fiancée... with this fiancée it had been for quite a long time... They said amnesty – so then I realised it was gonna be alright! In April I disclosed myself and in November there was a wedding. Just after that we went to Wrocław.[25]

It was characteristic that even though they officially handed their arms over, a lot of men still kept some kind of firearms (like a pistol or rifle) at home.

> During the first years after the war, people came to school with guns [...] One day a teacher was pestering someone in the Polish lesson, so the guy put his piece on the table [...][26]

Firearms were more frequently kept in villages than in cities as it was easier to hide them there. And they were not kept because the person was necessarily involved in an underground struggle against the system; it was done 'just in case' simply because 'the times were uncertain', as some interviewees put it.

Since not all the underground activists disclosed their identities, the UB started to keep under surveillance those former activists who had a link with those remaining 'in the woods'. The UB was counting on intimidating them and forcing them to cooperate in getting rid of the anti-communist underground. They were thus often imprisoned without sentence, interrogated and tortured; and the families of those who were in hiding suffered the same fate.

Some broke down and agreed to fully cooperate with the UB; and they returned to the partisan troops as agents for the UB.[27] In the autobiographical narratives of the NSZ veterans, one of the recurring themes is when they contrast themselves to some of these legendary traitors. It seems that imprisonment, even for a short time, was at the same time the most important period in the life history of these people who, as nationalists, gained veteran status only a relatively short time ago.

Consequently, not everyone started a new life. As Zygmunt M. was leaving his partisan troop, *Róg*, the commander told him: 'you'll regret that you've disclosed yourself'. Indeed, he was arrested two years later, judged guilty of being a member of an 'illegal organisation' and sentenced to fifteen years of imprisonment. Meanwhile, his former commander died in 1952 in a skirmish with the UB.

There were others, however, who did not have any trouble reintegrating after disclosure.

> On 7 March 1947 (my birthday), I went to the UB for this so-called 'disclosure'. And during those first years (1947–48), there was no animosity after all, none [...] not with the teachers, or with the university authorities [...] With the lecturers, in the majority of cases, when they discovered I was a former AK member that was even a plus! And what lecturers I had! The dean was a lecturer from Lvov. The history of common architecture lecturer was a professor from Stefan Batory University in Vilnius. I was studying in the period when most of the teachers were *Kresowiacy*.[28]

## *Professional Career and Adaptation to the New System*

> When I started the job they saw me as a 'spitting dwarf' (*zapluty karzeł*) [laughter].[29]

According to the biographical entries of the resistance movement members, those who after disclosure were not imprisoned usually did not have any problems getting a job in the Recovered Territories in any field, even the public services, because in Poland these would include, and still do, for example, forestry and railway jobs.[30] It was more difficult for people who decided to disclose their identities after the spring of 1947 or had a previous sentence for involvement in the underground. Mrs. Halina, whose husband was hiding until 1949, bitterly recollects that her husband

> [...] never had a permanent job. We wanted to go to the Recovered Territories. My husband applied in Pisz to the deputy manager of the Agricultural Department for a farm, but they didn't want to give us a farm. 'There are no farms for bandits,' they said, 'let them starve!'[31]

Mr. Henryk, who was released from prison after five years had a similar story to tell.

> I wrote to the MKB Committee [Polish United Workers' Party] and they replied to say that there was neither school nor job in Łomża Province for me or my brother, and there never would be. We were at a loss then.[32]

But some, such as Mrs. Halina (who eventually became a teacher) finally managed to 'straighten out their lives' and achieve some professional success.

> I used to get these awards from the ministry, because they had nothing to accuse me of, and I worked honestly. I wasn't working for communism or anybody, just for my children, so that they could read, and write, and so they knew those patriotic poems. It was not to appeal to the communists.[33]

There is a common belief in Poland that in order to make a professional career in communist times, one had to join the Communist Party and that everyone was put under pressure to join. Almost all of my interlocutors – in line with the current tendency to boast about having nonconformist attitudes during the communist regime – were eager to talk about unsuccessful attempts that had been made to persuade them to join the party.[34]

> Later I started to teach – because you have to do something, right? And then complaints started being made about me being nationalist [...]; so I was constantly called in by the Party, and asked why I wasn't a member of the Party [...]. So I say that I have different views, that I can't be in the Party. 'Then, comrade, you can't work for us', they replied. When I'd been married for a while and had two little children, without anything to live on, then I went to join that Party, 'cause the Party rules everything, and I say – why have you deprived me of this job? – I have two children, I have to raise and feed them. And they say, 'we give jobs only to our people, and you, citizen, are against us, so we can't give you a job.' They said that there was no work for me, and so I said '[...] thank you, I'm glad that you've shown me what you really are [...] Even if you took out my eyes, I would still see you for what you are through my ass, and I wouldn't come to you again!' [laughter][35]

Regardless of their initial problems, however, the majority of former activists of the anti-communist resistance that I interviewed seemed to adjust well to life in socialist Poland – some of them even went on to carry out important functions in public administration or in the state's industrial plants. Among my interlocutors, both those who admit to an accidental involvement in history as well as those who place their lives squarely within the framework of a greater historical narrative emphasising ideological values (national, pro-independence, Catholic), none of them took part in democratic opposition – either in the 1970s or even in the era of Solidarity (1980–1981).

A fairly clear and simple explanation can be given for their stories. The bitter lesson of history, which they were given in their youth, determined their later attitude. The interlocutors themselves rarely resorted to an explicit explanation of their choices or to a moral justification of them. I had the impression that they silently assumed on my behalf that I would make this interpretation myself. It should be remembered that these stories were told me in a specific social and political situation, and at certain moments of the narrators' lives. On the one hand, at their age they did not expect to perform any further function in the current social and political system, but on the other hand, they were aware that they could now finally evaluate life choices made in the period of communism in public without fear of recrimination. One former AK soldier, an architect by profession, re-examined his life in the following way: 'I was trying not to interfere in politics, as not to be locked up and, luckily, I somehow managed it. Stay closer to the hearth – you'll be better off for it.'[36]

This conclusion, though made by an educated man, is a symbolic expression of a general folk attitude. In other words, the most important thing was to save one's own life and maintain the biological continuity of one's own family. Its justification stated by the above interlocutor sounds somewhat ironic, a joke, but a similar attitude seemed to prevail among all former members of the anti-communist underground that I talked to, although such direct expressions were rare during the interviews. As I have mentioned before, the group of interlocutors participating in this research were not particularly representative due to some factors that I had no control over, and which certainly seem to be significant. For instance, commanders and ideological leaders of the resistance movement died in direct fights or at the hands of the secret police (NKVD or UB); and the 50 odd years since 1957, when the last partisan in Łomża fell, means that the older participants in the resistance were unavoidably excluded. These older participants may have decided to join the ranks of the anti-communists for quite different reasons than the former teenagers I interviewed. I talked to the generation that spent their childhood under German occupation and their everyday life in war conditions had been the only one they had known up to that point. Operation 'Tempest'[37], which started on 4 January 1944 and was aimed at conducting armed diversionary actions against German in the face of the approaching Red Army, even provided some of this younger generation with the opportunity to take part in the struggle that their parents had fought in 1939 and after.

Historians analysing official and/or written documents of that period (e.g. orders, proclamations, leaflets, judgements, and sentences) either omit the aspect of individual motives and conditions of participating in the partisan underground or attribute the collective political, ideological and even social context of a given region to them. In the case of the Łomża region there are the strong nationalist (*endecja*) influences from the 1930s, the great influence of the Catholic Church, and the historical experience of persecution by the Soviet occupying forces in 1939–1941.[38] In the works of historians specialising in the history of the anti-communist underground there is an important element of the analysis which presents a particular social profile for the partisans, who were mostly selected from among young villagers. In the literature these recruits in the Łomża region were either from peasant stock or impoverished nobles; and conservatism, together with affection for national and religious values are attributed to both these groups.

In my research such motives also appeared in those autobiographical stories where the authors incorporated their lives into the fate of the nation as a whole. However, not all of them referred to their origins, although interviewees who incorporated their biographies into their immediate everyday environment at the same time mentioned if they 'came from the nobility.' Thus, at least as far as the narrators saw it, the decision to join the anti-communist underground was not due to the world view traditionally attributed to their origins. While talking about it, some of the interlocutors admit that they were attracted by 'an adventure' and belonging to a peer group. 'All of my friends were in the underground', said Mrs. Stanisława.[39] 'It was the kind of village where at night they could be partisans in the woods and during the day, if it was necessary, they ploughed.'[40] In interviews there is also reference to a certain partisan way of doing things: for example, dance parties where people arrived in horse carts commandeered from the village;

and specific ways of dressing, like shoes decorated with white paint.[41] It gives the impression that being a partisan was more than just a political statement, or taking up arms, it was also a way of life. Apologists for the 'national, anti-communist uprising' write about a widespread participation in the struggle against communism, motivated by the idea of protecting specific, national values and ideas.[42] In the oral sources too, it appears to have been a common experience for the whole generation, but it was perhaps less secretive and less attached to lofty ideals than some historians would like us to think.

Due to a series of events which led to a clash of interests between the Polish underground and the Soviet Union, ordinary members of the Polish underground were forced to take further decisions, crucial to their individual existence at the beginning of Operation Tempest: whether to continue the fight, this time against the Red Army, NKVD, and a new regime or to 'come out of the woods'. It was always difficult to know whether offers of amnesty were genuine or not, so the onus fell on individual partisans whether they would reveal themselves or not. The anti-communist underground, especially in the region discussed here, was decentralised, had poor communication networks, and sometimes the troops even fought against each other. Their members had no view of the broader political situation even in their region. Soldiers, who were often no more than 16–20 years of age, were often given the right to make their own choice, and so it was a decision *par excellence* 'about life'. Coming out of the woods later on was seen as being more risky, because it involved consequences difficult to predict back in the civilian world.

If we go beyond the sphere of traditional symbolism and the interpretation present in both the public discourse about the anti-communist underground and Polish historiography, and look more closely at the everyday (economic) context of village life in the Łomża region immediately following the Second World War, then we should take into account a number of important contextual points about those interviewed here.

Although these accounts differ in many important respects, the narrators all come from the same region, and share the same religious faith and ethnicity. Also they had a similarly hard social upbringing (in wartime), in similar families and local communities. Even before the Second World War, this part of the country was described as 'Poland B', with a relatively backward economy in relation to the territory west of the Vistula River. On top of this, there was also a great civilisational disparity between urban centres and villages. My interlocutors, were all brought up in the villages of the Białystok and Łomża regions, and were shaped by values handed down by generations of experience from ancestors in the Polish peasantry whose everyday concern was a struggle for their own and their children's physical survival. Personal success was assessed with this basic measure. Thus, it is not altogether surprising that regardless of whether their autobiographical narration is replete with ideological motives or it focuses on the practical side of life, at the crucial moment of 'coming out of the woods', the authors do not discuss the issue of defeat in the battle with communism, but instead move on to the next chapter of their lives, which is successfully adapting to new conditions. Getting an education, job, social position, accommodation, bringing up children, and providing them with an education, and doing this all under the auspices of a new political system, is an embodiment of the great Polish archetype – the cunning peasant who deceived the Devil.

## *Conclusion*

About five years have passed since this study was concluded (some brief excerpts of which are above), and at roughly the same time, the Day of Remembrance of the 'Cursed Soldiers' was established, officially approving the mythologised version of the heroic underground. It is reflected not only in commemorative public rituals, in museum and exhibition activity, in pop-culture (music), but also in everyday purchases. There is a great demand for so-called 'patriotic clothing', with dominant graphics of the 'cursed soldiers' and symbolism connected (or associated) with this, and even tattoos. I am writing about it, because the great significance of every autobiographical narration is the social and political situation in which the narration appears, even if it is 'only' an oral story. A few years ago the some of my interlocutors talked about their lives being overtaken by the fate of the nation and homeland. For the vast majority of others they put it down to more personal motivations. The question I am left asking is how many of the former partisans of the anti-communist underground would nowadays narrate the same story about how they stayed 'close the hearth' in socialist Poland.[43]

### NOTES

1. It was not only in Poland that communists faced an active, armed social resistance. Other nations occupied during the years 1939–1940. Lithuanians, Latvians, Ukrainians, and Estonians were also fighting against the Soviet system in a more or less active way. However, the underground structures in neighbouring countries did not necessarily cooperate with each other because of conflicts that had arisen as part of the Second World War. According to the Lithuanian historian Anušauskas, it is the places where the highest number of victims fell (i.e., in Lithuania and Western Ukraine) which indicate where the most powerful centres of anti-communist resistance were in Eastern Europe. See A. Anušauskas, 'The Resistance Movement in Lithuania and its Methods of Activity in years 1944–1956', in P. Niwiński (ed.), *Repressive Apparatus and the Social Resistance Against the Communist System in Poland and in Lithuania in years 1944–1956* (Warszawa: Instytut Pamięci Narodowej, 2005), 45–56.
2. The Institute of National Remembrance – Commission for the Prosecution of Crimes against the Polish Nation (IPN) was established on 18 December 1998 by an Act of Parliament. The IPN is at one and the same time: state and justice administration, archives, an academic institute, an education centre, and (since 2007) a body which which vets proceedings.
3. Apart from the mainstream IPN publications coming out in Poland, consisting of detailed articles, monographs of armed resistance in specific regions and biographies of 'cursed soldiers', there are works of a more general nature, like the book by Polish-British historian Anita Prażmowska called *Civil War in Poland, 1942–1948*

(Palgrave Macmillan 2004/2013). However, according to most IPN authors, there was no 'civil war' in Poland; only a war against the Soviets who had imposed their rule on Poland by installing the communist regime. There are also a few historians who have used the term 'anti-communist uprising'. This appears to be the dominant discourse in contemporary Polish historiography of this subject.

4  See for example: F. Schütze, 'Kognitive Figuren des autobiographischen Stegreiferzählens', in M. Kohli & G. Robert (eds), *Biographie und soziale Wirklichkeit* (Stuttgart: Metzler, 1984); 'Presja i wina: doświadczenia młodego żołnierza niemieckiego w czasie drugiej wojny światowej i ich implikacje biograficzne', in J. Włodarek & M. Ziółkowski (eds), *Metoda biograficzna w socjologii* (Warszawa: PWN, 1990).

5  R. Koselleck, '"Przestrzeń doświadczenia" i "horyzont oczekiwań" – dwie historyczne kategorie', in R. Koselleck (ed.), *Semantyka historyczna* (Poznań: Wydawnictwo Poznańskie, 2001), 365.

6  For instance, R. Czaplińska, *Z archiwum pamięci... 3653 więzienne dni* (Warsaw: Institute of National Remembrance, 2005).

7  *Cień*, motion picture, directed by Jerzy Kawalerowicz, script by A. Ścibor-Rylski (Poland: Studio Filmowe Kadr, 1956).

8  See the bibliography in S. Poleszak, *Podziemie antykomunistyczne w łomżyńskim i grajewskim, 1944–1957* (Warsaw: Volumen, 2004).

9  It was personified by Roman Dmowski (1864–1939), who died in the vicinity of Łomża, and who had been the creator and leader of the National Democrats, (*Narodowa Demokracja* or '*endecja*') – a nationalistic, right-wing party active from the late 19th century.

10  The Home Army (*Armia Krajowa*, AK) was the army of the Polish underground state, the head of which was the Polish government n exile in London.

11  The National Armed Forces came into being as the result of a split in the NOW ('National Military Organisation' in operation since 1939) and was, along with the Home Army, subordinate to the government in exile. In 1942 it was decided to merge the NOW with the AK, to which some of the 'nationalists' did not agree. In September 1942, along with the 'Lizard Union' (*Związek Jaszczurczy*) – who were associated with the National Radical Camp – they established the National Armed Forces, which in 1945 became the National Military Union.

12  R. Wnuk, 'Dylematy żołnierzy podziemia antykomunistycznego w latach 1944–1947', in *Polska 1944/1945–1989: Studia i materiały*, vol. 2 (Warsaw: Polska Akademia, 1997), 63–65.

13  Lapel pin of the sword of Poland's first king Bolesław Chrobry (967–1025), adorned with the Polish flag. This symbol was first used during the period of 1926–1933 as the symbol of the OWP (*Oboz Wielkiej Polski*) a nationalistic political party and later by *endecja* supporters

14  Mrs. Ch., born in 1928, interviewed in Łomża, 8 May 2007, M. Kurkowska-Budzan's private archive (MKB).

15  Polish military contingent created in France during the latter stages of the First World War.

16  Mrs. Halina, born in 1927, interviewed in Łomża, 8 May 2007, MKB.

17  Mr. Henryk K., born in 1925, interviewed in Łomża, 8 May 2007, MKB.

18  Mrs. Ch. and Mrs. Halina, 8 May 2007, MKB.

19  Mr. Teofil L., born in 1923, interviewed in Śniadowo, 12 May 2007, MKB.

20  Many of today's veterans in the Union of the National Armed Forces Soldiers were farmers who were helping the partisans – the so-called 'net'. They were persecuted by the UB for this support and equally by the partisans for withholding it (on suspicion of collaborating with the communists).

21 See G. Wąsowski and L. Żebrowski (eds), *Żołnierze wyklęci: Antykomunistyczne podziemie zbrojne po 1944 roku* (Warsaw: Volumen, 1993); also the documentary 'Cursed Soldiers' (*Żołnierze wyklęci*), directed by Wincenty Ronisz (Poland: Fundacja Filmowa Armii Krajowej, 2006).
22 Mr. Teofil L., 12 May 2007, MKB.
23 Cf. Poleszak, *Podziemie antykomunistyczne*.
24 Mr. Józef Łojewski, born in 1925, interviewed in Łomża, 10 May 2007, MKB.
25 Mr. Zygmunt M., born in 1923, interviewed in Kolno, 20 September 2006, MKB.
26 Mr. Mieczysław M., born in 1930, interviewed in Łomża, 9 May 2007, MKB.
27 See Poleszak, *Podziemie antykomunistyczne*.
28 Mr. Jerzy W., born in 1924, interviewed in Łomża, 10 May 2007, MKB; *Kresowiacy* describes the displaced ethnic Poles coming from *Kresy* a territory in the eastern borderlands of pre-war Poland. After the treaties in Yalta and Potsdam it had become part of the Soviet Union.
29 Mr. Jerzy W., born in 1924, interviewed in Łomża, 10 May 2007, MKB; the term 'spitting dwarf' refers to AK soldiers and comes from a socialist propaganda poster 'The Giant and the Reactionary Spitting Dwarf' by Włodzimierz Zakrzewski.
30 See Poleszak, *Podziemie antykomunistyczne*.
31 Mrs. Halina, 8 May 2007, MKB.
32 Mr. Henryk K., 8 May 2007, MKB.
33 Mrs. Halina, 8 May 2007, MKB.
34 Contrary to popular opinion, the Polish United Workers' Party was not a mass organisation: it had 1.4 million members (1949), 1.1 million in 1951, 1.4 million in 1957, and 1 million in 1959, with the population of Poland being 23.6 million in 1946 and 25 million in 1950. The party tried to avoid recruiting 'ideologically uncertain' members like former activists of the anti-communist underground.
35 Mrs. Halina, 8 May 2007, MKB.
36 Mr. Jerzy W., 10 May 2007, MKB.
37 'Operation Tempest' was aimed at seizing control of cities and areas occupied by the Germans while they were preparing their defences against the advancing Soviet Red Army.
38 See for example: Poleszak, *Podziemie antykomunistyczne*; S. Poleszak, *Jeden z wyklętych. Major Jan Tabortowski 'Bruzda'* (Warszawa, 1998); J. Kułak, *Pierwszy rok sowieckiej okupacji: Białystok 1944–1945*, t. 1 (Białystok, 1996); Wąsowski and Żebrowski (eds), *Żołnierze wyklęci*.
39 Mr. Stanisława H., born in 1933, interviewed in Łomża-Konarzyce, 15 January 2008, MKB.
40 Mr Zenon Z., born in 1932, interviewed in Łady Borowe, 02 September 2007, MKB.
41 Mr. Zenon Z. 02.09.2007; Łukasz W. and Bolesława W., interviewed in Łady Borowe, 22 August 2007, MKB.
42 for example Marek Jan Chodakiewicz, Leszek Żebrowski, Rafał Sierchuła.
43 Considerable part of this article was published in Polish in J. Barański, M.Golonka-Czajkowska and A. Niedźwiedź (eds), *W krainie metarefleksji* (Kraków: Wydawnictwo Uniwersytetu Jagiellońskiego, 2015), 196–209.

# Sources and Bibliography

## Archival sources

M. Kurkowska-Budzan's private archive (MKB)
Interviews by Marta Kurkowska-Budzan

## Audiovisual material

*Cień*, motion picture directed by Jerzy Kawalerowicz, script by A. Ścibor-Rylski (Poland: Studio Filmowe Kadr, 1956).
'Cursed Soldiers' (*Żołnierze wyklęci*), documentary directed by Wincenty Ronisz (Poland: Fundacja Filmowa Armii Krajowej, 2006).

## Literature

Anušauskas, A., 'The Resistance Movement in Lithuania and its Methods of Activity in years 1944–1956', in Niwiński, P. (ed.), *Repressive Apparatus and the Social Resistance Against the Communist System in Poland and in Lithuania in years 1944–1956*. Warszawa: Instytut Pamięci Narodowej, 2005.
Barański, J., Golonka-Czajkowska, M. and Niedźwiedź, A. (eds), *W krainie metarefleksji*. Kraków: Wydawnictwo Uniwersytetu Jagiellońskiego, 2015.
Czaplińska, R., *Z archiwum pamięci... 3653 więzienne dni*. Warsaw: Institute of National Remembrance, 2005.
Koselleck, R., '"Przestrzeń doświadczenia" i "horyzont oczekiwań" – dwie historyczne kategorie', in Koselleck, R. (ed.), *Semantyka historyczna*. Poznań: Wydawnictwo Poznańskie, 2001 (German original '"Erfahungsraum" und "Erwartungshorizont" – zwei historische Kategorien', 1975).
Kułak, J., *Pierwszy rok sowieckiej okupacji: Bialystok 1944–1945*, t. 1, Białystok 1996.
Poleszak, S., *Jeden z wyklętych. Major Jan Tabortowski 'Bruzda'*. Warszawa 1998.
Poleszak, S., *Podziemie antykomunistyczne w łomżyńskim i grajewskim, 1944–1957*. Warsaw: Volumen, 2004.
Prażmowska, A., Civil War in Poland,1942–1948. Palgrave Macmillan 2004/2013.
Schütze, F., 'Kognitive Figuren des autobiographischen Stegreiferzählens', in M. Kohli & G. Robert (eds), *Biographie und soziale Wirklichkeit*. Stuttgart: Metzler, 1984;
Schütze, F., 'Presja i wina: doświadczenia młodego żołnierza niemieckiego w czasie drugiej wojny światowej i ich implikacje biograficzne', in J. Włodarek & M. Ziółkowski (eds), *Metoda biograficzna w socjologii*. Warszawa: PWN, 1990.
Wąsowski, G., Żebrowski. L. (eds), *Żołnierze wyklęci. Antykomunistyczne podziemie zbrojne po 1944 roku*, Warszawa 1999.
Wnuk, R., 'Dylematy żołnierzy podziemia antykomunistycznego w latach 1944–1947', in *Polska 1944/1945–1989: Studia i materiały*, vol. 2. Warsaw: Polska Akademia, 1997.

# Reorienting and Taking Distance: Germany and Austria

II

Marianne Zepp

# 3. Redefining Germany: Women's Politics in the Post-War US Occupation Zone[1]

In 1945, the German political elite was morally and politically discredited. Germany as a sovereign national state had practically ceased to exist. It had foreign troops on its territory and a reputation for being warmongering, militaristic, and unable to foster a democratic society. But with the occupying powers gradually stepping down from the political decision-making process, the Federal Republic of Germany was founded in May 1949 as a functioning democratic (though not yet sovereign) state. During the period of occupation, a group of male and female German intellectuals and politicians had, with the support of a number of military government officials, begun not only to justify the restoration of German statehood, but develop concepts of democratic participation that went beyond institutionalised party politics. These democratisation measures, partial as they were, and undertaken in the US zone of occupation, offered a brief opportunity for a grass-roots policy to flourish, based on ideas of individual responsibility and a concept of citizenship involving active participation. This approach was not fully realised in practice but it paved the way for a political culture based on civic procedures, representation, and a modern idea of citizenship. *Frauenpolitik*, women's politics, comprising both the discourses about and actions by women in the arena of public politics, is a prime example of the way German political elites started immediately after the war to legitimise and establish their participation in politics within the framework of a revived German state. It is also an example of one pragmatic way in which political activists seized the opportunities offered by the US military government in the immediate aftermath of war to support political and social reconstruction.[2]

This contribution focuses on women's politics in the US zone of occupation. It examines the arguments used by a group of prominent German women activists, many of whom had a background in the bourgeois women's movement of the Weimar Republic,[3] to justify a particular female contribution to post-war reconstruction. It also traces the development of their political practice from participation in local initiatives in the immediate aftermath of war to the building of larger structures across the US zone and across zonal boundaries within the Western Allies territory of occupation. It also asks how far the agenda and actions of German activists in this period were influenced by US military government officials, in particular via the Office for Women's Affairs.[4] This window of opportunity, initiated by the occupying powers in the immediate post-war era, had been opened to allow and support political and social reconstruction.

This chapter argues that women's political activism in the US zone underwent three distinct stages of development between 1945 and the establishment of the two German republics in 1949. Firstly, women's activism defined itself as a specific social interest group; secondly, the claim for political participation was legitimised; and finally an institutionalised framework for women's politics was set up. It also argues that the outlook of these activists was shaped by a mixture of political experience gained under the Weimar Republic, a pre-Nazi German democratic tradition, and adapting to the western occupying powers' ideas of re-education and democratic behaviour. At the same time, in line with the rest of the German political elite, this group of women politicians also showed a tendency towards denial and self-deception that characterised much of German society as a whole in this period in relation to the recent past and questions of guilt.

The women who entered the arena of public politics in all the major cities of the US zone of occupation were mostly academically educated, middle-aged, middle-class women. Some had been in the women's movement that existed before 1933, but many found themselves in the political limelight for the first time in their lives. An immediate prerequisite for any kind of public activism at this time was to distance oneself from National Socialism, both mentally and politically. Accordingly, this cohort of women began with a gendered analysis which argued that National Socialism had been a 'men's state' (*Männerstaat*). Highlighting the gulf between their ideals and Nazi ideology, they stressed the notion of self-empowerment, whereby women as a distinct social interest group would define their own needs, rights, and obligations.[5]

In a second step, German women's groups in 1945–1946 laid the groundwork for creating their own lobby groups, grass-roots organisations, and institutions. They introduced an idea of politics that was based on liberal democracy, defining constitutional proceedings, political and social rights, and access to resources as the prerequisites for a functioning democracy. At the same time they not only claimed equal rights but also expanded the idea of public politics as such. The difficult economic conditions meant that issues of supply were at the centre of public debate. Recalling the German women's movement's idea of expanding what would be regarded as a 'female sphere' within the realm of institutionalised politics they claimed that everything 'from needlework to the atomic bomb' is politics, as Agnes Zahn-Harnack, a pre-war member of the German women's movement phrased it.

This led to them embracing the idea that they had the moral responsibility to reclaim German society. However, this post-war German discourse was ambiguous; it also allowed them to turn the debate away from German guilt to a rhetoric of self-empowerment instead by stressing how the German people had suffered and should go about righting these wrongs themselves.[6]

In a third step, they embraced the proceedings of a new institutionalised political system by referring to the western liberal idea of citizenship, *Staatsbürgerschaft*. This meant not only setting up training courses for women to learn how parliamentary systems worked, and developing the proper tools for democratic participation, but also helping to build up women's organisations and institutions at a national level after the founding of the Federal Republic of Germany. They deployed the concept of citizenship to engage with the emerging democratic institutions of West Germany. As the Cold War began, women's politics became part of the contradictions and ideological rifts between the east and west.

## *'Operation on the German Mind' Starts*

In 1945, the occupying powers and the Germans viewed each other with a mixture of mutual aversion, distrust, but at the same time a willingness to cooperate. In her study on post-war Frankfurt am Main, Donna Harsh has described the attitude among the Germans met by the Americans as they crossed the war-torn landscape in the spring of 1945 as a combination of 'desperation, defiance and desire' to rebuild the country.[7] However, it was not only the destruction of a considerate part of the basic conditions of life that the post-war planning officers were worried about. It was also an urgent matter to work out how to deal with a nation that had not only started a war twice in a quarter of a century but that was assumed to have a mindset of destructiveness, authoritarianism, anxiety, and aggression all at once.[8]

The core idea of occupational politics was to develop a programme of group-based learning experiences that would not only support the institutional development of democratic proceedings but also change the authoritarian (and submissive) aspects of the German national character which it was thought had led to the rise of National Socialism. Based on this concept, prominently developed by the exiled German psychologist Kurt Lewin (among others), a socio-anthropological approach led to a programme of educational reforms connecting the individual, social, and political spheres.[9] US government agencies, among them Civil Affairs Training Schools established through the War Department's Civil Affairs Division[10] at the beginning of the 1940s helped to pool psychologists', anthropologists' and political scientists' efforts to analyse the German national character and develop a programme for political reform. Spurred on by US progressive thinking and supported by the managerial resources of government officials, a network of scientific experts and staff were assembled to be deployed to Germany.

The network's foremost goal was to 're-educate' the people, by placing individual behaviour within a framework of public politics, that would connect family attitudes and virtues with behaviour towards the state, party politics, and democratic endeavour. These social scientists, anthropologists, media experts, and political scientists were all trained in psychology to observe and eventually engineer a change in German thoughts and actions that was called within US government circles, 'Operation on the German Mind'. In the years that were to follow, the reconstruction of political institutions and public administration clearly involved creating a context truly conducive for democratic thinking. As soon as they arrived on German soil, the US experts developed schemes to analyse and better comprehend the state of the German mind.[11] They developed means and ways to reach out to the individual. It was thought that Germans could be taught democratic behaviour by instilling new family values and modes of self-expression; and a mindset of individual responsibility. This was based on the assumption that individual and public education were decisive for character building, as was family structure, and these ultimately affected political behaviour.

Since socialisation within the family was considered the realm of female responsibility, American wartime planning was thus holding women responsible for the development of a democratic society. German women were therefore chosen as prime targets for launching this process of 'democratisation'. The American authorities regarded German women as family-centred, providing not only for a family's material needs but also forming the major part of their moral and social attitudes. At the same time, it was argued, German women were in turn shaped by underlying moral and social attitudes. German family structure not only cast women in very traditional roles, but this structure was also thought to have contributed to the overall authoritarianism of the German society. Since women had been, according to US perception, ousted involuntarily from public life by National Socialism, they would surely welcome the changes this new policy would herald.[12] This somewhat naïve assumption about German women's mentality and behaviour shaped the US approach towards German society. Initial encounters and surveys conducted by the US Military Psychological Warfare Division and the Information Control Division of the military administration in Germany seemed to reinforce this approach.

On 11 November 1945, a meeting took place in Heidelberg, set up by Marianne Weber – a respected German women's activist, former chair of the BDF (*Bund Deutscher Frauenvereine*/Federation of German Women's Organisations), and widow of the sociologist Max Weber, with American officers of the newly established 'Office for Military Government for Germany'. Robert Wolfe, a young publications control officer, took minutes of this gathering. In his summary, Wolfe made a number of hasty and ambiguous interpretations.

> Women in Germany today have to fight for their mere existence. They are tired, worried, uninformed and in danger of being proletarianized socially and mentally. While individual women stood up remarkably against the Nazis, the broad masses of women were the most Nazified segment of the population. Women were more opposed to the whole process of denazification than men, more critical towards Allied measures, less sympathetic in regard to former concentration camp inmates.

And the conclusion, that '[i]f properly led, their influence can be highly beneficial'[13], was rather stark and simplistic.

These superficial observations were subsequently given further credence by the evidence from public opinion surveys. The first survey results on the democratic attitudes of German women seemed to indicate that German women still followed a pattern of submissiveness to authoritarianism combined with an unwillingness to condemn Nazism and a reluctance to get involved in public activities.[14]

The US military authorities reacted in two ways. They set up a programme of leadership training, which selected a range of people who were considered not only untainted by Nazism[15] but also willing and able to take up new responsibilities; and they started channelling resources into building up tools and training for civic participation.

The first step was to initiate and support the establishment of different types of media: especially radio, magazines and newspapers. They selected German specialists to run these by setting up a system of licensing procedures, which allowed the occupying powers to control the development of media. By the end of 1945, there were three major radio stations in Stuttgart, Frankfurt, and Munich, and each had special programmes for women. Aired daily, they were a major tool for reaching out to a wider audience of women and raising awareness through open public debates. Magazines like *Regenbogen* (Rainbow) or *Die Welt der Frau* (Woman's World) grew into platforms for political debate and also later for networking among women's activists.

Educational training courses were at a later stage organised in cooperation with Women Affairs offices, set up in every state (*Land*) to be integral parts of the otherwise male-dominated administration structure of OMGUS (the Office of Military Government of Germany). Led by American women's activists (such as trade unionists, parliamentarians, and representatives of women's organisations like the League of Women Voters), they became centres for developing political strategies and exchange programmes between organisations in each country that intensified the level of cooperation among German and American women in the second half of the occupation. From 1948, select German personnel were invited on tours to the US to look at how the education system, political procedures and civic organisations worked over there.[16] These exchange programmes were instrumental in fostering a spirit of participation and democratic self-determination.

## Motherhood as a Political Argument

The ambiguous diagnosis of the US military officials not only characterised the American attitude towards the German population at the beginning of the occupation, but also reflected to some extent the self-perception of the Germans. With a mixture of self-indulgence, self-proclaimed victimhood (in the face of the devastation left by total warfare) and an unspoken undercurrent of shame and guilt, Germans were looking for ways to make some sense of the new post-war reality. For some, this meant political participation, and it could be argued that for many Germans under occupation (although there were other motivations) this reflected a widespread urge to assert a continuation of the German nation through a new definition of it.

The calls for German political engagement straight after the fall of the Third Reich can thus be read as an attempt to legitimise a German voice in the process of reconstruction. In a political setting where not only the nation state had ceased to exist (through unconditional surrender), but where everything German was now morally discredited, the political elites, among them the women described here, were aware that it would take great efforts to make their voices properly heard.

German women started to organise themselves locally at a grass-roots level immediately after the war had ended. They declared themselves ready to take on responsibilities related to securing the everyday survival of their community. However, in claiming this role of public responsibility they were not limiting themselves to the daily concerns of the *Trümmerfrauen* ('rubble women') and housewives. Their aspirations were certainly more far-reaching and it expanded the concept of politics itself. The rhetoric and strategy of the post-war women's movement were based on a concept of motherhood as a political argument, which allowed for a gender-based approach to the entire field of politics.[17] This idea of applying the particular feminine skills (which came from a gendered division of labour in family and society) to public affairs had been nascent in the bourgeois German women's movement since the Kaiserreich. In the concept of 'expanded or spiritual motherhood', this pre-Nazi women's movement had sought to redefine the realm of public politics by placing a new emphasis on traditionally 'female' concerns such as education, health and welfare. At the same time they were more generally promoting the notion of a *weibliche Kulturaufgabe* (a distinctively female approach to culture and politics). In the final stages of the Weimar Republic, this approach was transformed into a strategy which connected social reform and liberal democracy with national power politics[18] – the latter influenced by German thinkers such as Max Weber and Friedrich Naumann.

In May 1933, the executive board of the major women's umbrella organisation the Federation of German Women's Organisations had decided to dissolve itself than succumb to aligning itself with the new regime. This marked the end of an organised national women's movement in Germany. At the same time prominent members were either ousted from public life, developed strategies to survive within the boundaries of the system, or went into exile.

Thus the catastrophic conditions in 1945 proved fertile ground for ideas that had been present in the women's movement at the end of the Weimar Republic but had been banished for so long. Two motifs reappeared in the reasoning of German women after 1945: motherhood and femininity as a positive way to reconfigure the political sphere through a revindication of traditionally feminine responsibilities and competence.[19]

By rearticulating the ideas of the pre-1933 women's movement in the post-war context, women politicians claimed to uphold a tradition of the bourgeois feminist movement while at the same time distancing themselves from the recent past and experiences of Nazi Germany.

German women politicians after 1945 formulated a distinctive stance towards liberal democracy. One of their arguments was that women now formed a majority of the population, a fact they argued was decisive in a democracy. The other argument they used was that, as women, they had been 'naturally' opposed to the imperialist, militaristic, and masculine nature of National Socialism, even though German women were acknowledged to have been partly responsible for the fact that National Socialism had been able to function for such a long period of time. However, they argued, what women had endured had been entirely at odds with their 'womanly' nature. Based on this gender-based interpretation of National Socialism, women activists after the war reinvented motherhood as a social and political mission. Due to the conditions of defeat, destruction and devastated living conditions, women now had to take on special obligations. Since men had obviously failed, the traditional tasks of women gained a new public importance. If women were guilty because of their passivity under National Socialism, they would now make amends by taking up active responsibilities. Women were thus naturally the bearers of a 'national renaissance'. Their position as the 'natural' adversary of imperial power politics would also give women a pivotal position in the future of the nation.[20]

Thus at a very early stage after the war, the arguments made by German female politicians to justify their political engagement shifted away from the acknowledgment of a special responsibility towards a rhetorical strategy to undo individual and collective guilt in post-war German society. Femininity was described as peaceful, reconciliatory, pragmatic, and willing to take on responsibilities in contrast to whatever National Socialism had stood for. This argument not only allowed for self-empowerment, it also directed the debate concerning German guilt towards the more pressing pragmatic problems of post-war survival. The question of fair treatment by the occupation authorities and of the appropriate allocation of resources became a key issue for Germans across the political spectrum. For example, in Stuttgart, about 5000 women took to the streets at the beginning of 1946 to join in a women's 'walk of supplication' initiated by the women's local executive board to protest against an order from the American military authorities which was evicting them from their homes. They complained about the distress caused to their families and the social consequences that would ensue. Moreover, in their request for the order to be revoked, they referred to their perceived democratic rights, by pointing out that its implementation was impossible under conditions of distress, neglect, and misery. In the name of humanity, the women of Stuttgart particularly appealed to American women by asking them to express their solidarity with all women and mothers.[21] In 1946 and 1947, before the Moscow Foreign Ministers' conference between the Allied powers, several women's groups also spoke in public about trying to get the Allied powers to release German prisoners of war[22] with the argument that they were being prevented from taking part in the very important task of building up democracy.

The rhetoric of motherhood resulted in a twofold political strategy: it was argued that womanhood should be exculpated from all guilt in the *Männerstaat* of the recent Nazi past; and thus specifically 'female' virtues should justify participation in the new peaceful society that was to be constructed in post-war Germany. By using the rhetoric of motherhood and developing the idea of femininity as a specific social and political category, German female political activists could distance themselves from their discredited and defeated male counterparts. In a second step, as early as the end of 1945, women joined in the rhetoric of rebuilding a nation state, from the perspective that the nation should focus on the plight of a defined community of (German) victims. This narrative of national sacrifice was marked by references to timeless German values and an emotionally charged but conveniently vague notion of 'responsibility'.

## Reformulating Women's Politics

However, the idea of a distinctively female sphere of responsibility and a particular female perspective on politics, together with a gender-based interpretation of National Socialism, was not shared by all women active in redefining women's politics in post-war Germany. In a speech at the conference held at the Paulskirche in Frankfurt am Main, Gabriele Strecker rejected the rhetoric of motherhood as a 'facile glorification'.[23] However, it did provide the basis for a particular group of prominent activists who belonged to a generation that had been politically educated during the Weimar Republic.[24] In addition, some prominent representatives of the pre-1933 women's movement were involved and were influential in the debates on national reconstruction.

Marie Elisabeth Lüders was a prime example of this older generation. Her pronounced nationalism and self-confident reference to German traditions make her stand out from the often ambiguous attitudes of most other German women towards their own country. Lüders's popularity among her female compatriots owed a lot to her outspoken views on the occupying forces and her self-assured bearing towards them. In 1947, Elia Fay Hartshorne (an education and religious affairs officer with OMGUS in Berlin) gave a decidedly double-edged description of Lüders's performance at a women's conference in Bad Boll.

> She was a German Democratic Party member of the Reichstag under the Weimar Republic and is now, at 60 [Lüders at that time was 69 years old, MZ] a vivid personality who had evidently captured the hearts of the younger groups. She is tall, with short straight white hair and a square sharply chiseled face. She has something of the boyish eagerness of a terrier. She declared, as an economist and lawyer, that the youth should bear no guilt, that it was ridiculous to give them an amnesty, they would have been declared as not responsible, that she herself could admit no share in the guilt, since she fought against the Nazi regime.

Hartshorne then added that '[t]here was whispered comment that the youth would not be so enthusiastic for her if they had access to her newspaper articles of 1939 praising the War Services Work, among other things […]'[25].

Despite qualms like this occasionally being expressed, Lüders' stout nationalism did not prevent her from becoming one of the most popular liberal parliamentarians[26] in the West German Bundestag. One of her achievements was integrating key elements of western liberal ideas about citizenship into post-war women's politics with her insistence on democratic values, social justice, and the representation of women's interests at all levels in politics.

The German women who created the framework of women's politics under the auspices of the occupying powers were a group of middle-aged, middle-class, educated women with a pragmatic approach who wanted to influence public politics and play a role in rebuilding a German state. The common denominator linking them was that they defined women as an interest group, and agreed that women now formed the majority of the population, and that basic welfare and resource allocation issues should be the priority of any political agenda.

Already in the spring of 1945, ad hoc grass-roots movements, so-called Antifa (anti-fascist) committees, acted at the local level to regulate and allocate resources. After municipal administrations were established by the occupying powers, the Antifa committees continued to exist as advisory boards. At the same time, as early as possible after July 1945, the occupying powers issued directives that political parties could be founded.[27]

The women's initiatives, *Frauenausschüsse*, which were also set up in 1945, acted independently from the grass-roots Antifa movements and from the emerging structures of institutionalised politics.[28] Originating in local groups and working together with the intention of pooling local resources, these 'women's committees' grew into political interest groups, encouraged, supported and acknowledged by officials in the American military government. Over the next two years, they built well-organised networks at both the local and then the state level. While expanding from local initiatives into regional and then state-level institutions, they added their voices to public debates.

In their pragmatic reformulation of women's politics within the tradition of western liberalism, the activists of the local women's organisations saw social policy and democratic constitutionalism as fundamental elements of democracy, and women's traditional activities and areas of competence as part and parcel of it. They therefore tried to tie in the fight for equal rights and opportunities for women with a new political agenda. To that extent their ideas coincided with those of the military government officials responsible for creating an infrastructure for women's participation in the newly defined democracy. The fact that the women were already organised in opposition to the revival of institutionalised hierarchical party politics meant that they were soon seen by the US officials as the best means of instilling a true democratic spirit in West Germany. At the same time, they were viewed by the party rank and file on the German side as political competitors.

In her first account of the history of the German women's movement after 1945,[29] Gabriele Strecker, a former physician and from 1946 head of the women's programme broadcast by the radio station in Frankfurt, described how the movement had emerged in all the major cities in Germany, and what their goals were. They were based on voluntary effort, were independent from party politics, were explicitly anti-fascist, and were eager to assume political responsibility. These groups did not involve large numbers of women but had a remarkably high public profile. They formed, in Strecker's words, a 'unitary interest group for women that was free of class distinctions'. They were independent, based their agenda on the daily needs of the population, had low-key organisational structures, networked actively and worked together with other bodies such as trade unions and church groups.

The South German Women's Working Committee, the Frankfurt Women's Committee, and the Württemberg Women's Parliament were all led by professionals who used the tools of the newly established media to formulate an agenda of women's politics that extended from questions of supply and housing to the release of German prisoners of war, female representation in elected assemblies, and German reparations. In a series of conferences and meetings, of which the Frankfurt Paulskirchen Conference of May 1948 was one of the most remarkable, a public agenda was set out that referred to German traditions of liberal democracy. Balancing between interest politics, the quest for representation in a more conventional way through political parties and parliaments, and references to the democratic tradition of the German women's movement, these groups and organisations sought to define a strategy that preserved their independence from traditionally institutionalised politics. Non-partisan networking and lobbying were the characteristics of these first faltering steps for institutionalised women's politics.

For a short period of time, women conveyed the impression that they were not only a powerful but also decisive force; and the more the women's groups and organisations became politically involved in the years between 1946 and 1948, the more they simultaneously claimed to be independent from party politics. From their beginnings in 1945–1946, this 'broad church' approach had been adopted to allow for a wide spectrum of interests and competencies and so that the organisations would have multiple means to adapt to new challenges. At the same time, however, political parties were emerging across the country, and it culminated in conflicting opinions at meetings in Stuttgart and Frankfurt where members of the West German Social Democratic Party (SPD) began questioning the type of women's activism that sought to operate outside party politics. These conflicts were also spurred on by the higher echelons of the party, so they were not just at the local level. In a 1947 speech, Kurt Schumacher, the dominant figure of the SPD in the post-war era, accused women's activists of being either communists striving for influence or bourgeois women inspired by a sense of social superiority.[30] The SPD was at this time competing with other political forces to assert its status as the legitimate anti-Nazi force in Germany. It rejected the independent women's organisations as 'separatist', and accordingly the SPD women's bureau, headed by Herta Gotthelf, and under the control of the party leadership, dedicated most of its time to fighting them.

Ironically, the most powerful and outspoken activists and the most influential figures of the women's organisations happened to be members of the SPD: these included Lisa Albrecht and Else Reventlow in Bavaria, Helli Knoll in Hesse, and Anna Haag in Württemberg-Baden. By taking a stance against the party line's opposition to independent women's organisations, they either left the political arena or at a later stage compromised this with party politics.[31]

By 1952, when Strecker published her booklet on the history of the German women's movement since 1945,[32] local and state initiatives had been transformed into publicly funded, officially recognised, supra-regional associations. This survival was not least due to the favour shown them during the occupation by the American military government.

The US licensing measures were initially reluctant to allow the refounding of traditional political parties, seeing them as potentially hierarchical and undemocratic. While there are no indications that the debate on motherhood had any influence on the US military government's perception of the Germans, the establishment of women's political groups became a central issue. Within the framework of American re-education policy, group activities, civic education and democratic development from below were decisive. To this end, in July 1945, the US military government issued a directive for establishing political organisations and parties by stating that 'the development of local responsibility, with a view to the eventual reconstruction of German political life on a democratic basis'[33] was a major goal.

One prerequisite of American plans for democratisation was to identify members of a future political elite who would be trustworthy and seen as willing to cooperate with the military government, so interviews were conducted with individuals who were politically active. These interviews also served as a means for assessing the state of the 'German mind' and to promote the American concept of re-education and political reconstruction. Internal memoranda and policy papers stressed that political initiatives had to be initiated and conducted by the Germans, while the US authorities' job would be to guide and supervise.[34]

The American policy was initially characterised by a dilemma: its declared policy was to support the founding of initiatives and organisations by Germans, but American military government officials still regarded Germans and their democratic aspirations with a deep-seated mistrust. However, this perception on the part of the US military government changed over the course of the occupation period. The so-called punitive phase came to an end as tensions grew between the US and Britain on the one hand and the US and USSR on the other. In this nascent Cold War context, the German political elite came to be seen in a more favourable light, and as more of a potential asset.

These developments also shaped US policy towards women's organisations. Cooperation between military government officials and independent women's organisations intensified in the later period of the occupation. Margret M. Blewett, who became the director of the OMGUS Women's Affairs Office (Württemberg-Baden) in July 1948, was a prime example of an American official who actively supported women's campaigns. She started out with an assessment of the activities since the establishment of the military government in order to continue with a programme covering the period of its rule until 1949. She stated that German women should be educated 'to awaken [...] a sense of their responsibilities as citizens.'[35] In an internal paper, she also spelt out what motivated the Americans to foster and support the cooperation partners they had chosen.

Representing as they do an under-privileged group, their efforts are bent to loosening and liberalizing the bureaucratic hierarchy so that it will represent with some degree of equanimity the interests of all the people. As a political democracy can function only on the basis of political parties, it is important that they be encouraged to study political issues, reach political decisions and support the party of their choice.[36]

In her opinion, the independent women's organisations were breaking new ground by addressing social, legal, and political problems.[37] Blewett supported their efforts by organising supra-party roundtables, which reinforced the networking efforts that were already being made.[38] Not limiting her activities to Stuttgart, she sought to establish a close-knit network of women's organisations, maintaining those that already existed and bringing new initiatives into being for the whole region and the newly founded state of Württemberg-Baden.[39]

## Becoming an Active Citizen in the Cold War Context

Applying for a license for their journal in 1946, the representatives of the Heidelberg Women's Association argued that the responsibility for reconstructing Germany lay in the hands of its female population. As women were now the majority of the population, this was a golden opportunity for women to determine the shape of the new democratic order. In the application they argued that women not only had to learn to think and act politically but also to be prepared for their duties as citizens: be able to express their political will; equipped for participation in public life; recognised in their professional lives; and encouraged in their efforts to build international links with women abroad.[40]

In one of its first public announcements in December 1945, one of the leading figures of the women's initiative in Frankfurt, Helli Knoll, outlined that women's politics should consist of three major components: overcoming National Socialism by integrating all women into a concept of citizenship ('[t]he duty of women leaders is to enlighten all women about the civic tasks'); securing women's influence in the newly built institutions; and strengthening the responsibility felt towards rebuilding a German nation that would become internationally vindicated. Women's organisations in the second half of the occupation period were now pursuing a threefold strategy: preparing for citizenship in a political system that saw itself as the antithesis of National Socialism; claiming certain constitutional rights for women; and taking responsibility for the common good within the framework of a nation state.

The political break marked by the unconditional surrender of Germany in 1945 had not changed the constitutional framework as one might have thought. At least, the continuing existence of a German nation had certainly not been explicitly questioned at any point by the Allied powers. Indeed, the idea of a common German citizenship in all four occupied zones was still formally in existence,[41] so claiming democratic rights based on the idea of German citizenship (while under occupation) was not unrealistic. Democratisation would be based on the concept of constitutional and social rights, of civil liberties, and active civil participation. In claiming these rights, women activists were referring to a democratic tradition derived from the German state-building efforts of the previous century. Harking back to these state efforts, while simultaneously reaching forwards to the goal of citizenship within a modern democratic state became cornerstones in the endeavour to form a political identity in the western zones immediately after the war. Citizenship was a useful device for sustaining national continuity in a period of moral devastation and fragile reconstruction. A normatively based notion of citizenship seemed to be the integrating factor for an otherwise morally devastated society like Germany in 1945. Cultural traditions of national unity and universalist ideals (which could still accommodate the idea of the nation) were the vantage points for setting an agenda consisting of personal freedoms, the protection of human dignity against totalitarianism, and measures being taken to get everyone involved in a more active citizenship.

Women's insistence on their rights to participate, and their call (in the first two years of occupation) for a women's mission to overcome the harmful legacy of the 'masculine' Nazi state, became the rallying cry for women's campaigns in which it was not so much the moral rhetoric of 'motherliness' that was important, but pragmatic political action. From 1947 onwards, new organisations were founded by lobbying, and strategies were developed for ensuring that social justice at the local level would advance to the state level. The concept of re-education contributed to these forms of women's policymaking. In the first phase, the key priorities were independence from party politics and the insistence on formulating women's interests as a matter of public policy. To this cohort of women activists, it was clear that they were acting first and foremost as women, and not simply as 'neutral' citizens; at the same time, they had no qualms about entering traditionally male public spheres such as parliament or party politics.

In the second half of the occupation period, new developments took place: political parties were created, governmental administrative institutions on the state level, and state and communal parliaments were established, bringing about not only the concept of politics on the national and supra-zonal level but actually putting it into practice. Women's organisations were now an essential part of rebuilding political institutions. Thus grass-roots initiatives were transformed into state-subsidised lobbies and organisations.

Women were ready to answer questions about how to best allocate public means; about matters of everyday life; and interests particular to women as a whole. Responsibility towards the state and its institutions were tightly woven together in a fabric of argumentation that was capable of being extended from the local and regional level to state-oriented larger structures. By 1947, however, the Cold War had gained momentum, and women's politics were decisively influenced by the ideological schism it created. All four military governments supported conferences that brought women politicians together (and from each of the zones). Although these became a major tool for the visibility of women's politics, they were also a site for the escalation of Cold War tensions between the representatives of each of the women's organisations. It was in the Soviet zone that the first effective move took place to institutionalise women's politics at the 'national' level; and this, in turn triggered a response to counter this by the officials in the western zones.

This first conference in the Soviet sector of Berlin was in March 1947, at the Admiralspalast with 1,400 participants. At that meeting, the women's committees of the Soviet zone had united (with the support of the Soviet Military Administration of Germany) to form the *Demokratische Frauenbund Deutschlands* – the first supra-regional organisation. Its agenda was in line with what the Soviet administration required, and was dominated by the German communists.[42]

The western powers reacted quickly. From 20–23 May 1947, in Bad Boll, a little spa town south of Stuttgart, about two hundred women assembled, among them prominent exponents of the pre-Nazi women's movement like Dorothee von Velsen, Agnes Zahn-Harnack, and Marie-Elisabeth Lüders, together with younger leading figures in the western zones, to form a new organisation capable of uniting forces among the representatives of the western zones, particularly between the British and US zones. American military officials were present as observers. The agenda discussed during the two-day meeting included applied economics, civic responsibility, world peace, and reconciliation. The resolution stating that civic education should enable all women to participate in all areas of public life was supplemented by requests to the Allied powers to remedy living conditions, to improve the supply situation and to release German prisoners of war, as well as to reform the education system. The women's organisations saw themselves as getting Germany 'to open up to social issues and problems of our time'[43] as part of the effort to rebuild the nation. Theonolte Bähnisch, an official of the Niedersachsen state administration in Hannover, stated that women had to take on greater responsibilities due to their past passivity in the face of National Socialism; and so it would be necessary to make particular efforts to get women interested and involved in public life. Meanwhile Agnes Zahn-Harnack took an international perspective by requesting that there be 'a new international understanding combined with a new, alternative national sentiment, that would foster love and pride for a new and different Germany.'

By setting up institutions of adult education, organising conferences, and establishing international exchange programmes, the cooperation between American and German women reached new levels and provided the basis for a female voice from 1949 onwards in the newly founded Federal Republic. To acquire citizenship, to be an equal and responsible member of the community, the majority of women needed education or some kind of training. Women were encouraged and taught to express themselves in groups, organise campaigns, and learn how parliamentary democracy worked. Women's organisations in the western zones saw themselves as outposts of 'freedom versus dictatorship' which threatened from the east. They adapted themselves to institutionalised politics, centralised their associations and absorbed the ideological concepts of the divided post-war Germany. The Office for Civic Women's Activities, the news bulletin

*Informationen für die Frau,* and the German Women's Council became instruments for lobbying the concerns of women's rights over the years to come.

In 1948, a small group of middle-class women succeeded in focusing public awareness on the issue of women's rights by launching a campaign to get equal rights explicitly written into the draft constitution for the Federal Republic – the Basic Law. Elisabeth Selbert, a well-known social democratic lawyer and member of the Parliamentary Council that drafted the Basic Law, was the driving force behind an initiative that insisted a clause be included (article 4) which granted women equal rights and status unconditionally. This was one of the most notable results of the process by which women in the western occupied zones achieved a public voice.

## Conclusion

The women activists' described here are one example of the political elites who were not only willing but also able to put into practice western ideas of democracy. In the end, these activists and their organisations succeeded in developing a concept of politics that had a formative influence on West German women's politics for decades thereafter. They anticipated – individually and collectively – developments towards socio-political modernisation and liberalisation. They succeeded in integrating and mobilising a considerable number of women left not only among the physical rubble of their homes but also in the mental debris of their political convictions.

The US military administration had since its establishment in 1945 sought to be instrumental in creating a new responsible Germany. The officials found Germans ready to be converted to their cause, and by the end of the occupation, German politicians in the western zones realised that the Cold War ideological rivalry between the Allied powers was a chance for them to regain access to the international political community and to upgrade the status of the new West German state by becoming a key part of the western alliance. The common conviction of the political elites across the political spectrum in West Germany (with the exception of the Communist Party) was against the idea of communism and a belief in the effectiveness of parliamentary procedures.

By the end of the occupation, it had become clear that the concept of western democracy had been almost hijacked as an ideological formula for demarcating West from East Germany. The independence from party politics that had initially been a factor bestowing credibility on women's organisations now became a major obstacle in the rush to institutionalise. It can thus be argued that these German women activists in the US occupied zone did have an impact on political developments during the occupation, and that they would not have had the same impact without the support of the American women, who matched them in class, education and stamina. They gradually lost their influence, however, due to the revival of a party-centred and hierarchical public sphere and a society that was gender-based in a new and different way during the 1950s and 1960s. Their strategies were directed solely towards participation and were focused on the framework and the agenda of the nation state. As a result, they fell victim to the ideological contradictions of the Cold War in as far as they saw themselves as part of the political establishment. Therefore, in the end they failed to assert themselves as a unique political voice and, until the new women's movement emerged decades later, independent women's politics in West Germany took place at the (nearly) invisible level of civic associations and marginally influential lobby associations for over two decades.

NOTES

1  This chapter is based on my book: *Redefining Germany: Reeducation, Staatsbürgerschaft und Frauenpolitik im US-amerikanisch besetzten Nachkriegsdeutschland* (Göttingen: Vandenhoeck & Ruprecht, 2007). My special thanks go to Prof. Elizabeth Harvey, Nottingham, for her assistance.
2  On gender relations generally, see E. D. Heineman, *What Difference Does a Husband Make? Women and Marital Status in Nazi and Postwar Germany* (Berkeley: University of California Press, 1999); E. D. Heineman, 'The Hour of the Woman: Memories of Germany's "Crisis Years" and West German National Identity', in *American Historical Review* 101, no. 2 (1996), 354–394; on the correlation between race and gender in post-war Germany, see M. Höhn, *GIs and Fraeuleins: The German-American Encounter in the 1950s West Germany* (Chapel Hill: University of North Carolina Press, 2002); on the relations of personal encounters and their influence on American foreign policy towards Germany, see P. Goedde, *GIs and Germans: Culture, Gender and Foreign Relations, 1945–1949* (New Haven, CT: Yale University Press, 2002). See also A. Kuhn (ed.), *Frauen in der deutschen Nachkriegszeit* (Düsseldorf: Schwann, 1986); R. G. Moeller (ed.), *West Germany under Construction: Politics, Society, and Culture in the Adenauer Era* (Ann Arbor: University of Michigan Press, 1996); R. G. Moeller, *Protecting Motherhood: Women and Family in the Politics of Postwar West Germany* (Berkeley: University of California Press, 1993); R. G. Moeller, '"The Last Soldiers of the Great War" and Tales of Family Reunions in the Federal Republic of Germany', in *Signs: Journal of Women in Culture and Society* 24, no.1 (1998), 129–145; R. G. Moeller, 'War Stories: The Search for a Usable Past in the Federal Republic of Germany', in *American Historical Review* 101, no. 4 (1996),1008–1048; K. Naumann, ed., *Nachkrieg in Deutschland* (Hamburg: Hamburger Edition, 2001); W. Loth and B.-A. Rusinek (eds), *Verwandlungspolitik: NS–Eliten in der westdeutschen Nachkriegsgesellschaft* (Frankfurt am Main: Campus, 1998).
3  The chapter focuses on the middle class spectre of the Feminist Movement in Post-War Germany, based on the particular role they played in the American strategy of reconstructing a political elite in post-war Germany.
4  H.-J. Rupieper, 'Bringing Democracy to the Frauleins: Frauen als Zielgruppe der amerikanischen Demokratisierungspolitik in Deutschland 1945-1952', in *Geschichte und Gesellschaft* 17 (1991); D. Tscharntke, *Re-educating German Women: The Work of the Women's Affairs Section of the British Military Government 1946–1951* (Frankfurt am Main: Peter Lang, 2003); P. Grundhöfer, *Ausländerinnen reichen die Hand: Britische und amerikanische Frauenpolitik in Deutschland im Rahmen der demokratischen Re-education nach 1945* (Phil. diss., Universität Trier,

1995); R. Boehling, 'German Municipal Self-Government and the Personnel Polities of the Local US Military Government in Three Major Cities of the Zone of Occupation', in *Archiv für Sozialgeschichte* 25 (1985); R. Boehling, *A Question of Priorities: Democratic Reform and Economic Recovery in Postwar Germany; Frankfurt, Munich, and Stuttgart under U.S. Occupation 1945-1949* (Providence, RI: Berghahn, 1996).

5  As early as May 1945, special women's initiatives (*Frauenausschüsse*) at the community level were facilitating the allocation of resources to improve living conditions and developing strategies for political influence. For an example of this in Karlsruhe, see B. Guttmann, *Den weiblichen Einfluß geltend machen... Karlsruher Frauen in der Nachkriegszeit 1945-1955* (Karlsruhe: Badenia, 2000); for Berlin, see R. Genth and I. Schmidt-Harzbach, 'Die Frauenausschüsse: das halb gewollte, halb verordnete Netz', in R. Genth et al. (eds), *Frauenpolitik und politische Wirken von Frauen im Berlin der Nachkriegszeit 1945-1949* (Berlin: Trafo, 1996).

6  On how the German elite established their perception of the Holocaust, see J. Herf, *Divided Memory: The Nazi Past in the Two Germanys* (Cambridge, MA: Harvard University Press, 1997); J. Herf, 'Multiple Restorations: German Political Traditions and the Interpretations of Nazism, 1945-1946', in *Central European History* 26, no. 1 (1993), 21-55; K. H. Jarausch and M. Geyer, *Shattered Past: Reconstructing German Histories* (Princeton, NJ: Princeton University Press, 2003); K. H. Jarausch, *After Hitler: Recivilizing Germany 1945-1995* (New York: Oxford University Press, 2006).

7  D. Harsch, 'Public Continuity and Private Change? Women's Consciousness and Activity in Frankfurt, 1945-1955', in *Journal of Social History* 27, no. 1 (1993), 29-58.

8  H. Arendt, 'Besuch in Deutschland: Die Nachwirkungen des Naziregimes', in *Zur Zeit: Politische Essays*, ed. M. L. Knott (Hamburg: Rotbuch, 1999; originally published by the American Jewish Committee in 1950); D. V. McGranahan, 'A Comparison of Social Attitudes among American and German Youth', in *Journal of Abnormal and Social Psychology* 41, no. 1 (1946), 245-257; D. V. McGranahan and M. Janowitz, 'Studies of German Youth', in *Journal of Abnormal and Social Psychology* 41, no. 1 (1946), 3-14; S. K. Padover, *Experiment in Germany: The Story of an Intelligence Officer* (London: Phoenix House, 1946); J. K. Pollock, H. L. Bretten and J. H. Meisel, *Germany under Occupation: Illustrative Materials and Documents* (Ann Arbor: George Wahr Publishing, 1949).

9  K. Lewin, *Resolving Social Conflicts* (New York: Harper &Brothers, 1948); K. Lewin, 'Conduct Knowledge and the Acceptance of New Values' and 'Cultural Reconstruction', both in *Resolving Social Conflicts*; K. Lewin, 'The Special Case of Germany', *Public Opinion Quarterly* 7 (Winter 1943), 555-556; F. L. Neumann, 'Military Government and the Revival of Democracy in Germany', *Journal of International Affairs* 2 (1948); F. L. Neumann, 'Re-educating the Germans', in J. E. Johnsen (ed.), *The Dilemma of Postwar Germany* (New York: H.W. Wilson, 1948), 211-225.

10  K.-E. Bungenstab, 'Die Ausbildung der amerikanischen Offiziere für die Militärregierungen nach 1945', *Jahrbuch für Amerikastudien* 18 (1973); K.-E. Bungenstab, *Umerziehung zur Demokratie? Re-education-Politik im Bildungswesen der US-Zone 1945-1949* (Düsseldorf: Bertelsmann, 1970); P. Gulgowski, *The American Military Government of the United States Occupied Zone of post-war II Germany in relation to policies expressed by its Civilian Governmental Authorities at home during the course of 1944/45 through 1949* (Frankfurt am Main: Haag & Herchen, 1949); E. F. Ziemke, *The U.S. Army in the Occupation of Germany 1944-1946* (Washington, DC: Center of Military History, 1975).

11 A. J. Merrit and R. Merrit, *Public Opinion in Occupied Germany: The OMGUS Suryeys, 1945-1949* (Urbana: University of Illinois Press, 1970); R. Merrit, *Democracy Imposed: U.S. Occupation Policy and the German Public 1945-1949* (New Haven, CT: Yale University Press, 1995).
12 Report on a Conference on Germany after the War, April–June 1944, Institut für Zeitgeschichte (IfZ), München 5/297–1/1; Neumann, 'Military Government'.
13 ICD Report on Meeting in Heidelberg, 11 November 1945, IfZ 5/240–2/44.
14 'Influence of the women's vote upon Bavarian politics', in ICD, Intelligence Branch, 10 July 1946, Hauptstaatsarchiv (HASTA) München, OMGBY 10/110–3/19.
15 H. L. Wuermeling, *Die weiße Liste: Umbruch der politischen Kultur in Deutschland nach 1945* (Berlin: Ullstein, 1981).
16 K.-H. Füssl, *Deutsch-amerikanischer Kulturaustausch: Bildung – Wissenschaft – Politik* (Frankfurt am Main: Campus, 2004).
17 This seems to have been a paradoxical step, because one undisputed conclusion about Nazi society has been that it was gender-biased. Men and women were drawn into the system by state organisations based on gender segregation. The dissolution of the autonomous women's movement in 1933 did not mean the end of organisational life for girls and women; particular spaces were created by integrating the female population into the system of state-controlled organisations and ideologies like the *Bund deutscher Mädel* (BDM) and NS-*Frauenschaft*. Although women could often find an outlet for their aspirations and energies in such organisations, they essentially existed to propagate the regime's goals among women, rather than articulate their interests. These organisations mobilised women in the NS concept of the 'total state' to take part in its activities, as Nazism was able to adapt to the concept of developed modernity (Dagmar Reese), signified by the concept of equality in marriage, higher education for women, and striving for a professional career. Yet it was clearly limited by the mechanism of social (and physical) exclusion based on racism. Among the literature on national socialism, modernity, and women, see D. Reese (ed.), *Die BDM-Generation: Weibliche Jugendliche in Deutschland und Österreich im Nationalsozialismus* (Berlin: Verlag für Berlin-Brandenburg, 2008); D. Reese, *Growing up Female in Nazi Germany* (Ann Arbor: University of Michigan Press, 2006); R. Bavaj, *Die Ambivalenz der Moderne im Nationalsozialismus* (Munich: Oldenburg, 2004); M. Kater, *Hitler-Jugend* (Darmstadt: Wissenschaftliche Buchgesellschaft, 2005).
18 I. Stoehr, *Emanzipation zum Staat? Der Allgemeine Deutsche Frauenverein – Deutscher Staatsbürgerinnenverband (1893–1933)* (Pfaffenweiler: Centaurus, 1990).
19 C. Sachße, *Mütterlichkeit als Beruf: Sozialarbeit, Sozialreform und Frauenbewegung 1871–1929* (Frankfurt am Main: Suhrkamp, 1986).
20 Rosine Speicher, *Ruf der Mütter*, 1946.
21 *Frankfurter Rundschau*, 12 April 1946.
22 A. Haag, 'Appeal to Eleneor Roosevelt', *Neue Zeitung*, 8 March 1946; *Frauenwelt*, November 1946, on Lisa Albrecht; 'Kriegsgefangene, die Heimat ruft Euch!' in *Neue Presse*, 22 January 1947; *Frauenwelt*, November 1946, on the resolution of the *Landesarbeitsgemeinschaft für Kriegsgefangenenfrage*. See also R. G. Moeller on the national discourse of prisoners of war as victims, 'The Last Soldiers of the Great War', 129–145.
23 'Frauenkongreß in Frankfurt', *Frankfurter Rundschau*, 27 May 1948. Paradoxically, femininity in the following years became a central term in the discourse of the leftist women's peace movement. See I. Stoehr, 'Feministischer Antikommunismus and weibliche Staatsbürgerschaft in der Gründungsdekade der Bundesrepublik', in *Feministische Studien* 1 (1998); I. Stoehr, 'Der Mütterkonress fand nicht statt: Frauenbewegungen, Staatsmänner und Kalter Krieg 1950', in *Werkstatt Geschichte* 17 (1997).

24 I. Stoehr, 'Neue Frau und Alte Bewegung? Zum Generationenkonflikt in der Frauenbewegung der Weimarer Republik', in J. Dalhoff, U. Frey and I. Schöll (eds), *Frauenmacht in der Geschichte* (Düsseldorf: Schwann, 1986).

25 E. F. Hartshorne, 'Report on Women's Conference, Bad Boll, 20–23 May 1947', IfZ, OMGUS, 5/294-1/11-13.

26 In a radio commentary, Else Reventlow, the leading figure of the *Süddeutsche Frauenarbeitskreis*, characterised her as '[...] the leading figure of the former Bund Deutscher Frauenvereine' and *'die einzige Persönlichkeit, die dem Pyrmonter Kongreß für wenige Minuten das Gesicht eines ernsthaft zu nehmenden politischen Gremiums gab'*; E. Reventlow, 'Mittwochskommentar im Bayrischen Rundfunk', 12 October 1949. Similar: U. Illing in *Der Silberstreifen* 1, no. 10 (1947), 2–3.

27 SMAD (Soviet Military Administration of Germany) Befehl Nr. 2, 10 June 1945. The Western Allied Powers reacted to the Potsdam conference (17 July – 2 August 1945) by allowing all democratic political parties to be founded.

28 Boehling, 'German Municipal Self-Government', 380; M. Moskowitz, 'The Political Reeducation of the Germans: The Emergence of Parties and Politics in Württemberg-Baden (May 1945 – June 1946)', in *Political Science Quarterly* 61, no. 4, (1946), 535–561.

29 G. Strecker, *Überleben ist nicht genug: Frauen 1945–1950* (Freiburg im Breisgau: Herder, 1981).

30 A speech by Dr. Schumacher, Frankfurt am Main, 2 June 1947, Archiv der sozialen Demokratie (AdsD), PV SPD 0244A, Frauenbüro.

31 Some left the party, like for instance, Anna Haag in Stuttgart, or else they sought for careers outside the party like E. Reventlow who became a journalist on Bavarian radio.

32 G. Strecker, *Hundert Jahre Frauenbewegung in Deutschland* (Wiesbaden: Wiesbadener Graph. Betriebe, 1952).

33 Administration of Military Government in the US Zone in Germany, 27 August 1945, HASTA Stuttgart, OMGUS 12/187-2/13.

34 R. Boehling, 'Occupation and Grass Roots Democracy', in J. M. Diefendorf et al. (eds), *American Policy and the Reconstruction of West Germany, 1945–1955* (Washington, D.C.: German Historical Institute, 1993), 281–306; Boehling, *Question of Priorities*; H. Hurwitz, 'Antikommunismus und amerikanische Demokratisierungsvorhaben im Nachkriegsdeutschland', in 'Aus Politik und Zeitgeschichte' (a supplement to *Das Parlament*), 22 July 1978, 29f.

35 'Report on Women's Affairs', 17 November 1948, IfZ 12/89-2/10.

36 OMGUS, Community Education Branch Women's Affairs, 'Cumulative Report Covering the Period 30 April 1948 to 1 May 1949', IfZ 5/294-1/11-13.

37 'Meldung über die Gründung einer Heidelberger Frauenarbeitsgruppe', in *Stuttgarter Zeitung*, 10 October 1950.

38 *Die Welt der Frau*, 5/1948 (December).

39 M. M. Blewett, 'Women's Affairs Report',17 November 1948, IfZ 5/294-1/11-13.

40 An application to the military regime by the Heidelberg Women's Association, October 1946, NL Lüders.

41 D. Gosewinkel, *Einbürgern und Ausschließen: Die Nationalisierung der Staatsangehörigkeit vom Deutschen Bund bis zur Bundesrepublik Deutschland* (Göttingen: Vandenhoeck & Ruprecht 2001), 421.

42 R. Pawlowski, 'Der Demokratische Frauenbund Deutschlands (DFD)', in Genth et al., *Frauenpolitik und politisches Wirken*.

43 'Die Aufgeschlossenheit für die soziale Arbeit und für die Zeitprobleme', in R. Speicher, 'Interzonale Frauenkonferenz', *Frauenwelt* 12–13 (June–July 1947).

# Sources and Bibliography

## Archival sources

Archiv der sozialen Demokratie (AdsD)
PV SPD 0244A, Frauenbüro.

Hauptstaatsarchiv (HASTA), München
OMGBY 10/110–3/19.

Hauptstaatsarchiv (HASTA), Stuttgart
OMGUS 12/187-2/13.

Institut für Zeitgeschichte (IfZ), München
5/294-1/11-13
5/297–1/1
5/240–2/44
5/294-1/11-13
12/89-2/10

Soviet Military Administration of Germany (SMAD)
Befehl Nr. 2, 10 June 1945.

## Printed sources

*Die Welt der Frau*, 5/1948 (December)
*Frankfurter Rundschau*, 12 April 1946, 27 May 1948
*Frauenwelt*, November 1946, June–July 1947
*Neue Presse*, 22 January 1947
*Neue Zeitung*, 8 March 1946
*Stuttgarter Zeitung*, 10 October 1950

## Literature

Arendt, H., 'Besuch in Deutschland: Die Nachwirkungen des Naziregimes', in *Zur Zeit: Politische Essays*, ed. M. L. Knott. Hamburg: Rotbuch, 1999; originally published by the American Jewish Committee in 1950.

Bavaj, R., *Die Ambivalenz der Moderne im Nationalsozialismus*. Munich: Oldenburg, 2004.

Boehling, R., 'German Municipal Self-Government and the Personnel Polities of the Local US Military Government in Three Major Cities of the Zone of Occupation', in *Archiv für Sozialgeschichte* 25 (1985).

Boehling, R., 'Occupation and Grass Roots Democracy', in Diefendorf, J. M. et al. (eds), *American Policy and the Reconstruction of West Germany, 1945–1955*. Washington, D.C.: German Historical Institute, 1993.

Boehling, R., *A Question of Priorities: Democratic Reform and Economic Recovery in Postwar Germany; Frankfurt, Munich, and Stuttgart under U.S. Occupation 1945–1949*. Providence, RI: Berghahn, 1996.

Bungenstab, K.-E., *Umerziehung zur Demokratie? Re-education-Politik im Bildungswesen der US-Zone 1945–1949*. Düsseldorf: Bertelsmann, 1970.

Bungenstab, K.-E., 'Die Ausbildung der amerikanischen Offiziere für die Militärregierungen nach 1945', *Jahrbuch für Amerikastudien* 18 (1973).

Füssl, K.-H., *Deutsch-amerikanischer Kulturaustausch: Bildung – Wissenschaft – Politik*. Frankfurt am Main: Campus, 2004.

Genth, R. and Schmidt-Harzbach, I., 'Die Frauenausschüsse: das halb gewollte, halb verordnete Netz', in Genth R. et al. (eds), *Frauenpolitik und politische Wirken von Frauen im Berlin der Nachkriegszeit 1945–1949*. Berlin: Trafo, 1996.

Goedde, P., *GIs and Germans: Culture, Gender and Foreign Relations, 1945–1949*. New Haven, CT: Yale University Press, 2002.

Gosewinkel, D., *Einbürgern und Ausschließen: Die Nationalisierung der Staatsangehörigkeit vom Deutschen Bund bis zur Bundesrepublik Deutschland*. Göttingen: Vandenhoeck & Ruprecht 2001.

Grundhöfer, P., *Ausländerinnen reichen die Hand: Britische und amerikanische Frauenpolitik in Deutschland im Rahmen der demokratischen Re-education nach 1945*. Universität Trier, 1995 (Phil. diss.).

Gulgowski, P., *The American Military Government of the United States Occupied Zone of post-war II Germany in relation to policies expressed by its Civilian Governmental Authorities at home during the course of 1944/45 through 1949*. Frankfurt am Main: Haag & Herchen, 1949.

Guttmann, B., *Den weiblichen Einfluß geltend machen… Karlsruher Frauen in der Nachkriegszeit 1945–1955*. Karlsruhe: Badenia, 2000.

Harsch, D., 'Public Continuity and Private Change? Women's Consciousness and Activity in Frankfurt, 1945–1955', in *Journal of Social History* 27, no. 1 (1993).

Heineman, E.D., 'The Hour of the Woman: Memories of Germany's "Crisis Years" and West German National Identity', in *American Historical Review* 101, no. 2 (1996).

Heineman, E.D., *What Difference Does a Husband Make? Women and Marital Status in Nazi and Postwar Germany*. Berkeley: University of California Press, 1999.

Herf, J. 'Multiple Restorations: German Political Traditions and the Interpretations of Nazism, 1945–1946', in *Central European History* 26, no. 1 (1993).

Herf, J., *Divided Memory: The Nazi Past in the Two Germanys*. Cambridge, MA: Harvard University Press, 1997.

Hurwitz, H., 'Antikommunismus und amerikanische Demokratisierungsvorhaben im Nachkriegsdeutschland', in 'Aus Politik und Zeitgeschichte' (a supplement to *Das Parlament*), 22 July 1978.

Höhn, M., *GIs and Fraeuleins: The German-American Encounter in the 1950s West Germany*. Chapel Hill: University of North Carolina Press, 2002.

Jarausch, K.H., *After Hitler: Recivilizing Germany 1945–1995*. New York: Oxford University Press, 2006.

Jarausch, K.H. and Geyer, M., *Shattered Past: Reconstructing German Histories*. Princeton, NJ: Princeton University Press, 2003.

Kater, M., *Hitler-Jugend*. Darmstadt: Wissenschaftliche Buchgesellschaft, 2005.

Kuhn, A. (ed.), *Frauen in der deutschen Nachkriegszeit*. Düsseldorf: Schwann, 1986.

Lewin, K., 'The Special Case of Germany', in *Public Opinion Quarterly* 7 (Winter 1943).

Lewin, K., *Resolving Social Conflicts*. New York: Harper & Brothers, 1948.

Loth, W. and Rusinek, B.-A. (eds), *Verwandlungspolitik: NS–Eliten in der westdeutschen Nachkriegsgesellschaft*. Frankfurt am Main: Campus, 1998.

McGranahan, D.V., 'A Comparison of Social Attitudes among American and German Youth', in *Journal of Abnormal and Social Psychology* 41, no. 1 (1946).

McGranahan, D.V. and Janowitz, M., 'Studies of German Youth', in *Journal of Abnormal and Social Psychology* 41, no. 1 (1946).

Merrit, R., *Democracy Imposed: U.S. Occupation Policy and the German Public 1945–1949*. New Haven, CT: Yale University Press, 1995.

Merrit, A. J. and Merrit, R., *Public Opinion in Occupied Germany: The OMGUS Suryeys, 1945–1949*. Urbana: University of Illinois Press, 1970.

Moeller, R. G., *Protecting Motherhood: Women and Family in the Politics of Postwar West Germany*. Berkeley: University of California Press, 1993.

Moeller, R. G., 'War Stories: The Search for a Usable Past in the Federal Republic of Germany', in *American Historical Review* 101, no. 4 (1996).

Moeller, R. G., '"The Last Soldiers of the Great War" and Tales of Family Reunions in the Federal Republic of Germany', in *Signs: Journal of Women in Culture and Society* 24, no. 1 (1998).

Moeller, R. G. (ed.), *West Germany under Construction: Politics, Society, and Culture in the Adenauer Era*. Ann Arbor: University of Michigan Press, 1996.

Moskowitz, M., 'The Political Reeducation of the Germans: The Emergence of Parties and Politics in Württemberg-Baden (May 1945 – June 1946)', in *Political Science Quarterly* 61, no. 4 (1946).

Naumann, K. (ed.), *Nachkrieg in Deutschland*. Hamburg: Hamburger Edition, 2001.

Neumann, F. L., 'Military Government and the Revival of Democracy in Germany', *Journal of International Affairs* 2 (1948).

Neumann, F. L., 'Re-educating the Germans', in Johnsen, J. E. (ed.), *The Dilemma of Postwar Germany*. New York: H.W. Wilson, 1948.

Padover, S. K., *Experiment in Germany: The Story of an Intelligence Officer*. London: Phoenix House, 1946.

Pawlowski, R., 'Der Demokratische Frauenbund Deutschlands (DFD)', in Genth et al., *Frauenpolitik und politisches Wirken*.

Pollock, J. K. Bretten, H. L. and Meisel, J. H., *Germany under Occupation: Illustrative Materials and Documents*. Ann Arbor: George Wahr Publishing, 1949.

Reese, D., *Growing up Female in Nazi Germany*. Ann Arbor: University of Michigan Press, 2006.

Reese, D. (ed.), *Die BDM-Generation: Weibliche Jugendliche in Deutschland und Österreich im Nationalsozialismus*. Berlin: Verlag für Berlin-Brandenburg, 2008.

Rupieper, H.-J., 'Bringing Democracy to the Frauleins: Frauen als Zielgruppe der amerikanischen Demokratisierungspolitik in Deutschland 1945–1952', in *Geschichte und Gesellschaft* 17 (1991).

Sachße, C., *Mütterlichkeit als Beruf: Sozialarbeit, Sozialreform und Frauenbewegung 1871–1929*. Frankfurt am Main: Suhrkamp, 1986.

Stoehr, I., 'Neue Frau und Alte Bewegung? Zum Generationenkonflikt in der Frauenbewegung der Weimarer Republik', in Dalhoff, J., Frey U. and Schöll I. (eds), *Frauenmacht in der Geschichte*. Düsseldorf: Schwann, 1986.

Stoehr, I., *Emanzipation zum Staat? Der Allgemeine Deutsche Frauenverein – Deutscher Staatsbürgerinnenverband (1893–1933)*. Pfaffenweiler: Centaurus, 1990.

Stoehr, I., 'Der Mütterkonress fand nicht statt: Frauenbewegungen, Staatsmänner und Kalter Krieg 1950', in *Werkstatt Geschichte* 17 (1997).

Stoehr, I., 'Feministischer Antikommunismus and weibliche Staatsbürgerschaft in der Gründungsdekade der Bundesrepublik', in *Feministische Studien* 1 (1998).

Strecker, G., *Hundert Jahre Frauenbewegung in Deutschland*. Wiesbaden: Wiesbadener Graph. Betriebe, 1952.

Strecker, G., *Überleben ist nicht genug: Frauen 1945–1950*. Freiburg im Breisgau: Herder, 1981.

Tscharntke, D., *Re-educating German Women: The Work of the Women's Affairs Section of the British Military Government 1946–1951*. Frankfurt am Main: Peter Lang, 2003.

Wuermeling, H. L., *Die weiße Liste: Umbruch der politischen Kultur in Deutschland nach 1945*. Berlin: Ullstein, 1981.

Zepp, M., *Redefining Germany: Reeducation, Staatsbürgerschaft und Frauenpolitik im US-amerikanisch besetzten Nachkriegsdeutschland*. Göttingen: Vandenhoeck & Ruprecht, 2007.

Ziemke, E .F., *The U.S. Army in the Occupation of Germany 1944–1946*. Washington, DC: Center of Military History, 1975.

Maria Fritsche

## 4. Austrian Men 'Do Everything with Feeling!'[1]: Representations of Masculinity in Post-War Austrian Cinema (1946–1955)

Imperial Vienna under the reign of Kaiser Franz Joseph sets the scene for the historical costume film 'Die Deutschmeister' (*The Deutschmeister*, 1955) – one of the most popular films in Austrian cinema after the Second World War.[2] The film tells the love story between a young Viennese soldier called Jurek and a pretty country girl called Stanzi who comes to Vienna to work in her aunt's bakery. Stanzi first sets eyes on the dashing Jurek while watching a military parade in which he plays the drums; he, too, notices Stanzi and calls on her in the bakery shortly afterwards. As Jurek enters the shop he radiates an attractiveness that is almost feminine. The tightly cut, dark blue uniform draws attention to his delicate facial features and the smoothness of his cheeks. There is nothing hard about this military man; in fact, Stanzi tells him that she is not so much impressed by his brisk marching or the smartness of his uniform, as by the way he beats the drum 'with so much feeling', to which the young soldier replies zealously, 'I do everything with feeling!' Jurek then introduces himself as belonging to the well-respected Viennese Hoch-und Deutschmeister regiment and as being a talented and as yet unrecognised composer. The film presents the male lead Jurek as a man who combines the masculine norms of the Austro-Hungarian military with the sensitivity of an artist and the charm of a gentleman, in other words: a true Austrian.

Jurek thus represents an ideal of masculinity that is very different from the physically tough and emotionally restrained ideal of a man that was dominant in the western world in the first half of the twentieth century. In fact, Jurek embodies masculine characteristics which post-war Austrian cinema sought to promote as typically Austrian after the Second World War. It is important to note that popular cinema did not construct an entirely new ideal of masculinity, but rather remodelled older concepts to fit the desires and needs of a new era. These cinematic masculine role models were not one-dimensional, but came in many variations. In this chapter I want to analyse some dominant representations of masculinity in post-war Austrian cinema and discuss their function. My argument is that, in a period of major social and political upheavals following the Second World War, its enormous appeal gave Austrian cinema the power to intervene in and shape popular discourse. Popular cinema promoted gender role models that helped to stabilise troubled gender relations and, after a brief period of liberalisation, reinforce traditional gender order.

By addressing or avoiding specific issues and by offering imagery and narratives that affirmed, strengthened and sometimes also undermined traditional ideas about masculinity and femininity, cinematic discourse played an influential, albeit ambiguous role in the reconstruction of Austrian society. Films, as Douglas Gomery and Robert Allen have argued in their famous study on film history, 'derive their images and sounds, themes and stories ultimately from their social environment.'[3] While the medium of film cannot reflect social reality, it engages with it and can, in the words of Justin Smith, be considered 'the repository of currents of feeling' in a society.[4] By analysing film, we can thus gain unique insights into contemporary concerns and debates.

This chapter is based on the findings of a study of 140 feature films (out of a total of 212) that were produced in Austria between 1946 and 1955. The time frame was chosen because the period between 1945, when Austria as part of Nazi Germany suffered political and military defeat, and 1955, when Austria regained national independence, was formative for modern Austrian society in many ways. The decade following the war was a time marked by major changes, during which Austria made a quick economic recovery and became a stable democracy after many years of authoritarian rule.[5] It was also a period that saw a return to traditional gender relations after a brief period of female emancipation, as well as the growth of a strong Austrian identity, which, in this form, had not existed before.

In the following, I will analyse the concepts of masculinity that popular Austrian cinema promoted after the war, and discuss how these masculinities were constructed and which functions they fulfilled. My argument is that the representations of masculinity were varied, but aimed at the same goals: to provide positive role models for both men and women. These images fostered pride in the newly created Austrian nation, while at the same time subtly reinforcing traditional gender relations by cleansing Austrian men from any association with war-crimes and by softening their claim for power.

I will focus on three film genres that were particularly popular at the time. Comparing the visual representations of gender in different genres is a useful method for establishing the extent to which the representations therein are a result of generic convention, or of broader cinematic or social trends. By limiting audience expectations, a genre regulates what the audience gets to see, and how it sees a film.[6] This also means that representations of gender inevitably vary from genre to genre, as each caters to specific audience tastes and expectations. In this respect, a male protagonist in a comedy will usually have different looks, characteristics, mannerisms, and behaviour to one in a crime film or melodrama, even though some elements may be similar, depending on the type of cinema or time period in which the films were produced. My aim is to show in what way – and why – the representations of masculinity in postwar Austrian cinema are different or similar.

To understand these representations and their meanings in these films, however, it is important to examine them within the sociocultural and socio-historical context in which they were produced.[7]

## A Masculine Crisis in Post-War Austria?

The war and dictatorship, the military and political defeat and the subsequent occupation of Austria by the Allied Forces caused major upheavals in Austrian society. A large number of the men who eventually returned home were traumatised by their wartime experiences; many had suffered permanent physical or mental injuries. The veterans often found it difficult to adapt to civilian life after having lived a tightly regulated life in the military and in POW camps and their plight was heightened by the fact that the immediate post-war period was chaotic, food and living space was scarce, and unemployment was high.[8] While many men experienced a loss of social status post-1945, women had gained in power. They had become quite self-sufficient and expert in organising the survival of their family.[9] This growth in female independence that had begun already during the war and went hand-in-hand with a (temporary) decrease in male power, challenged traditional views on gender and undermined traditional gender order.[10]

While other countries also experienced strained gender relations in the wake of war, the feeling of loss was particularly pronounced among men in Austria and Germany. Richard Bessel argues that military defeat is often experienced as a crisis of individual masculinity, and not just national masculinity.[11] Austrian (and German) men had failed to defend their country and found their homeland – and their women – now occupied by their former enemies. Some scholars have suggested that what was clearly an enormous blow to these men's self-esteem was in fact a 'crisis of masculinity'.[12] However, we have to be careful with this notion of crisis which has gained traction in recent years and has been widely and often indiscriminately applied to describe almost any friction between men and masculine norms. If we acknowledge the plurality of masculinities at any given time, then we need to clarify *which* type of masculinity was 'in crisis' and how this so-called crisis then affected individual men.

The influential concept of 'hegemonic masculinity', which the sociologist R. W. Connell introduced, seeks to explain why some masculine ideals exert more influence than others. Connell's concept describes a complex hierarchical system in which not only men dominate over women, but also one in which different forms of masculinity compete for dominance and power.[13] The hegemonic ideal of masculinity refers to those 'masculine attributes which are most widely subscribed to – and least questioned – in a given social formation.'[14] The attributes that characterised this ideal in large parts of Europe and North America in the nineteenth and up to the first half of the twentieth century were physical strength, rationality, self-control, courage, and exclusive heterosexuality. The fascist ideal of the iron-willed and callous warrior built on and exaggerated these norms, but could never gain widespread influence.[15] The downfall of the Third Reich and the economic and social shifts which followed the end of the war not only brought the fascist ideal into disrepute, but also undermined the more traditional masculine norms.[16] This caused insecurity and confusion amongst many men who had (knowingly or unknowingly) striven for this standard of ideal manhood.

But the shake-up of Austrian society also opened up positive opportunities for innovation, and the immediate post-war period can also be seen as a time of liberalisation especially for women and children. Nevertheless, all efforts of the (predominantly male) elites went into trying to 'normalise' society by restoring some of the shattered pre-existing hierarchies. First and foremost it was the nuclear family that needed to be rehabilitated.[17] Men, who had lost their pre-war status as 'protectors, providers, and [...] procreators',[18] needed to get their former jobs back and return to being heads of households and providers for the family.[19]

But why did the efforts to reconstruct Austrian society focus chiefly on the empowerment of men and the restoration of the traditional patriarchal family, when clearly men still held the most important and influential positions at political, economic, and professional levels? Men were regarded as pillars of society and as embodiments of the nation. As they were benefiting from the 'patriarchal dividend',[20] most men, even those at the lower end of the hierarchical scale, did not feel inclined to change the gender order. Scholars have convincingly demonstrated the historical intertwining of citizenship, nation and masculinity by showing how the emergence of nation states went hand-in-hand with the exclusion of women from politics, linking the right to citizenship with compulsory military service.[21] Faced with widespread economic destruction and social chaos, the political, medical, and religious elites were convinced that the position of men had to be strengthened in order to secure the survival of society and the nation state. This seemed especially important in post-war Austria, where society was being rebuilt at the same time as a new national identity was being constructed. Last, but not least, many women, who were overworked and exhausted by the triple burden of earning a living, running a household, and securing food under the most difficult of circumstances, now longed for a return to a less strenuous and more secure 'normal' life.[22]

## The Quest for a New Austrian Identity

The collapse of the Third Reich forced the Austrians to reposition themselves ideologically as well as nationally. This was difficult because for decades many Austrians had identified themselves with being culturally German, even if they had described themselves as Austrian.[23] When the multiethnic Austro-Hungarian Empire disintegrated in 1918, people living in the German-speaking rump that was left behind found themselves in a significantly smaller Austrian state. Suffering severe economic difficulties, high unemployment, and political instability throughout the 1920s and

1930s, the majority of Austrians did not believe the country could survive as an independent state in the long run.[24] A considerable percentage of the population thus favoured unification with neighbouring Germany as the only means of survival.[25]

Interestingly, however, it was only after the *Anschluss* to Nazi Germany in 1938, which had been initially warmly welcomed, that Austrian national sentiment really awoke. In a united 'Greater Germany', Austrians often felt that they were treated as 'second-class Germans'. Especially the experience of war produced disillusionment and consequently a gradual dissociation from the Germans.[26] To fuel Austrian resistance against Nazi Germany, the British sought to foster a sense of independent Austrian national identity among the political groups in exile during the war.[27] And indeed, once the war was over, Austria's political elites started to distance the country from Germany and to promote a unique Austrian identity in a clear attempt to evade responsibility for the atrocities committed during the war. This was done by claiming that Austria had actually been the first victim of Germany's wartime aggression. The reasoning was that Austria could not be held responsible for Nazi crimes and deserved a better treatment from the Allies than Germany.[28] Austrian popular cinema played a crucial role in communicating this 'myth' of Austria's victimhood to the public through persuasive imagery and narratives. Both the elites and the wider public eagerly seized on these images that bolstered and illustrated their claim of an innocent Austrian nation.

Since popular cinema engages with the desires and fears of society, film can provide unique insights into the dominant concerns of that society. The majority of Austrian films produced in the first decade after the war painted the clichéd image of a nation with a unique culture, rich history and beautiful landscapes. The Austrians were stereotypically depicted as musical, culturally sophisticated, cheerful (*gemütlich*), and harmonious.[29] Post-war Austrian cinema used the cultural and cinematic repertoire of popular Viennese stereotypes, but often stripped them of their darker undertones. This, of course, begs the question as to why these images of Austria and Austrians were popular not only with audiences, but also with the government. The Austrian government was in no position to exert any pressure on the Austrian film industry; it lacked both the financial means and the power to issue directives. And nor does it seem that the occupying Allied Forces, who held supreme power in Austria at this time, interfered in national film production by censoring or banning any Austrian films.[30] Of course, there were pressures of a more subtle kind for Austrian filmmakers: having grown accustomed to very strict control under the Nazi dictatorship, they applied a certain amount of self-censorship to not offend the Allied Forces – which might partly explain the reluctance of filmmakers to touch on political issues.

Perhaps more significant, however, is the economic factor. We should keep in mind that film is first and foremost a commercial product, which means that production companies are chiefly driven by economic considerations and thus seek to cater to their audiences' taste. The representations of gender and national identity were thus most probably influenced to a large extent by what the producers felt would appeal to a mass audience. Those involved in film production were, to argue with Michel Foucault, as parts of society caught in the net of contemporary discourse which shaped and prescribed views on gender. Analyzing this cinematic discourse as part of the wider popular discourse in postwar Austria can give insights into which forms of masculinity or femininity were seen as 'valid', i.e, authentic and credible at the time.[31]

To analyse more closely how masculinity was depicted in post-war Austrian film, and why it was depicted in this particular way, I have chosen three film genres that were particularly popular at the time: historical costume film, *Heimatfilm* and tourist film.

Post-war Austrian cinema presents Austrian masculinity as white, heterosexual, and ideally monogamous. Male protagonists are predominantly middle class or, especially in period costume films, members of the aristocracy. The working class, in contrast, is clearly under-represented. As historian George Custen has noted, absences are as meaningful as presences because the 'patterns formed by both help cultivate specific assumptions about history.'[32] By omitting the lower classes, and setting the middle class up as the standard, Austrian cinema was promising material comfort and security, which must have held a strong appeal for people in the poverty-ridden post-war years. Furthermore, unifying everyone in an essentially apolitical middle class established harmony; it smoothed over the deep fractures in a society that had been terrorised first by violent class conflicts in the interwar period, and then the Nazi regime.

## The Demilitarisation of Austrian Men in Period Costume Films

The producers of Austrian period costume films – set in the historical past but not necessarily dealing with actual historical events or characters – seemed to have found the ideal formulae to attract mass audiences, both inside Austria and in neighbouring countries. The majority of these films were set in Imperial Vienna under the rule of Kaiser Franz Joseph.[33] They painted an idyllic and romanticised picture of the last decades of the Habsburg Empire and depicted a peaceful society in which war and privation were unknown, and a fatherly emperor watched kindly over his multiethnic subjects. The immense popularity of the period costume film genre in post-war Austria can only be understood in its historical context. These films obviously played to the desire for an uncomplicated, yet glamorous past. In this respect, neither the Nazi regime nor conflicts of the inter-war period offered a 'usable' past that the Austrians could be proud of, whereas the last decades of the Habsburg Empire were, in contrast, distant enough to be viewed with nostalgia.

The representations of masculinity in Austrian period costume film differ from their British and Hollywood counterparts of the 1950s, in that the latter, for instance, emphasised muscular strength and physical vitality, while the Austrian films highlighted male sensitivity and musicality.[34] Men in Austrian period costume film have a soft, almost feminine side. Musicality is presented as a deeply ingrained part of Austrian masculinity. Even though the films are populated with members of the Austro-Hungarian military, the men do not display what we would consider a military or hard-edged demeanour. They are presented as musical and hedonistic men who spend much of their time singing and dancing, and are chiefly interested in food, wine, and beautiful women. While such representations of military men are not unique to Austrian cinema, this specific mixture of ascribed attributes combined with narratives that emphasised Austrian innocence and (multiethnic) harmony in contrast to a German militaristic 'other', was clearly typical for post-war Austrian cinema.

Austrian men in these period costume films are neither tough nor very authoritative. The blue tunic the soldiers usually wear in these films radiates calmness and stability. Its tight cut and lack of embellishment accentuates the waist and draws attention to the face of the soldier, whose clean-shaven cheeks and wavy hair suggest a certain innocence. The body language, which is sedate and smooth, reinforces the idea that Austrian men are non-aggressive and cultured. Anything that might allude to violence, such as the display of weapons or battles, is confined to the 'other' – usually the figure of a Prussian officer, whose exaggerated militaristic behaviour serves to underline the claim on the distinct otherness of Austrian masculinity.

Another key factor in the conceptualisation of a national masculine ideal in period costume films is the treatment of Austria's multicultural heritage. The ethnic heterogeneity of the Habsburg Empire is presented as unproblematic and used to claim a cultural (and moral) superiority over the Germans. Also, in order to distance the Austrians from the Germans (and from the charge of having been complicit in Nazi crimes), the genre claims Hungarians and Czechs as 'fictional ancestors' to the Austrians. By emphasising the strong links between Hungarians, Czechs, and Austrians, the genre then uses traditional Austrian stereotypes of the Hungarian (passionate and musical) and the Czech (resentful of authority and subversive) to present them as being also Austrian traits.[35] In view of the political efforts to deny any responsibility for the Nazi crimes, the cinematic celebration of a multicultural past can also be read as an attempt to distance the Austrians from the racist policies of the Nazis. One could say that period costume films made in the post-war period thus put to good effect Austria's once despised Slav ancestry and turned it into a positive selling point.

However, while the claim of a distinct Austrian character is a dominant pattern in period costume film, it is by no means uncontested. A film such as the period costume comedy *Die Welt dreht sich verkehrt* (The World Turns Backwards, 1946/47) ironically comments on Austria's zealous attempts to depict itself in the most favourable light.[36] Furthermore, even though making fun of militaristic Germans is a recurring theme in Austrian period costume film, the mockery always remains light-hearted and ends with reconciliation between the Austrian and German, who eventually acknowledges Austrian cultural superiority. After all, the Austrian film industry could not risk offending German audiences, since West Germany remained the largest export market for Austrian film. In the same way, the Austrian confectioner Bachmaier mocks his customer, the Prussian captain

Krause, in *Kaiserwalzer* (The Emperor's Waltz, 1953) for not understanding the Austrian dialect, but at the end they both unite in a song about linguistic difficulties and share a glass of wine.[37]

The period costume genre fulfilled an important function in Austria's search for a national identity. Beautiful scenery and characterisations in that setting fuelled pride in Austrian history and granted audience satisfaction by inviting the spectator to relive a glorious and uncomplicated golden era. Through its imagery, the genre provided 'historical evidence' for the existence of Austrian traits that were distinct from German ones. By reviving the traditional stereotype of the Viennese *charmeur*, but stripping it of the darker ambiguities that the version from the 1930s often showed, the genre emphasised instead the harmless, sensitive side of Austrian masculinity. These characterisations of men as musical, charming, and cultured not only bolstered Austria's assertion of political innocence, but also made their higher status in the gender hierarchy more acceptable to the female audience.[38]

## Man as the Protector of the Heimat

The genre of *Heimatfilm* could broadly be described as a drama set in the idyllic countryside that promotes traditional values and the virtues of life in a rural community. While the *Heimatfilm* has been claimed to be uniquely German (in a cultural sense),[39] it shares analogies with other 'national' genres, such as the American Western. The *Heimatfilm* is different in so far as it feeds into a broader discourse of a traditional *Heimat* and thereby invokes sentiments of belonging. The term *Heimat* was popularised in the nineteenth century when growing industrialisation and urbanisation generated feelings of loss and alienation, and describes a feeling of belonging to a usually rural community (such as a shire) as well as to a nation.[40] However, the notion of *Heimat* itself is, as Celia Applegate pointed out correctly, 'slippery, infinitely malleable, capable of saying many things', which makes it difficult to pin down exactly.[41] The term's 'semantic flexibility' has meant that despite the use of *Heimat* in the cinema of the Third Reich, the motif remained politically acceptable, even in post-war cinema.[42] The popularity of *Heimatfilm* in post-war Austria and Germany is partly explained by the fact that the genre is intrinsically tied to the rural landscape which represents stability and eternity. Moreover, it defines an area of Germanic culture that goes beyond the confines of a nation state, which made it especially attractive to post-war audiences, many of whom had experienced the loss of their actual or ideological *Heimat*.

Even though films with *Heimat* themes had been produced from the early twentieth century, the actual breakthrough for *Heimatfilm* as a popular genre occurred in the early 1950s. The financial success of the German film *Schwarzwaldmädel* (Black Forest Girl, 1950) came as a surprise to its producers as much as anyone else. It sparked a boom in *Heimatfilm* productions both in West Germany and in Austria, reaching a peak with the Austrian release, *Echo der Berge* (Echo of the Mountains, 1954), better known under its German distribution title, *Der Förster vom Silberwald* (The Forester of the Silver Forest).[43] The Austrian film industry produced fifteen such films between 1946 and 1955. These frequently outsold more glamorous Hollywood productions at the box office despite their often inferior technical and aesthetic quality.[44] *Heimatfilm* obviously fed into the audiences' longing for stability in a time of rapid change and modernisation.

Although recent research has challenged the notion that *Heimatfilm* is intrinsically anti-modern by demonstrating how some West German *Heimatfilms* seek to negotiate between the conflicting needs to modernize and to preserve tradition,[45] the Austrian examples seem to remain essentially retrospective and anti-modern. Post-war Austrian *Heimatfilms* present urban spaces as turbulent and unsettling, contrasting them with an unspoilt, 'timeless' countryside that has not been tainted by war or modernism. In all other aspects, German and Austrian *Heimatfilms* from this period are very similar: they are often set in an indistinct Alpine setting and deliberately blur geographical and national boundaries, which creates the impression that the cinematic *Heimat* exists 'outside all national boundaries and historical determinants'.[46] Through its narrative and imagery, *Heimatfilm* endorses a patriarchal society, traditional gender roles, and unambiguous sexual identities. In a very archaic way, the genre defines masculinity predominantly through the act of hunting: the figure of the forester is a staple element of classic *Heimatfilm*. As a representative of the local community and guardian of the *Heimat*, he embodies the ideal masculine traits of discipline, rectitude, fairness, and humility. His traditional opponent is the poacher, in many ways equal to the forester, as he is positioned in the same landscape. Yet the poacher becomes a negative figure when he violates the rules of the community.

When analysing the meaning of different kinds of masculinity in *Heimatfilm*, it is important to examine the role and position of the male character within the landscape. Unlike women, who are not allowed to enter forests or mountains without a male chaperone and are bound to the house, men are free to move everywhere: they can enter forests, climb rocks, and stride across mountain pastures. Men – in their role as foresters – are presented as guardians of nature who police the *Heimat*. Their close connection to nature justifies their higher status and implies that nature itself legitimises a patriarchal social order.

The representations of masculinity in *Heimatfilm* differ quite markedly from those in period costume film. In this genre it is not charm, musicality, or sensitivity, but the traditional masculine attributes of physical strength, rationality, and righteousness that are championed. There is a remarkable stiffness about the men in these films: the male protagonists move in a very controlled manner and hardly gesticulate. The men are also noticeably unable to properly express their emotions. When, for instance, the character Liesl in *Echo der Berge* implores the forester Hubert to explain why he has begun to avoid her, he replies quite simply and abruptly, 'I cannot. It is just not possible.' Not only does he suppress his feelings for her, he also takes the blame for a poaching incident, in which Liesl's fiancé has shot a deer, to protect her reputation. Self-control and discipline are key elements in this traditional idea of masculinity which views the expression of emotions as unmanly. The men in *Heimatfilm* are thus, to a certain degree, ideal representatives of this normative standard. They are more likely to bite their lip than show any emotional reaction, and to suffer in silence rather than rebel against the injustices they experience, as this would identify them as weak and lacking in manliness. Whereas in the classic American Western this kind of taciturn behaviour might signify a certain 'coolness', in *Heimatfilm* the men are not allowed to be heroes quite so easily, and are instead forced into submission. The men have to exhibit patience until the course of nature, or the actions of other people, bring their innocence to light. For example, Michael, in *Das Siegel Gottes* (God's Signet, 1949) has to wait out two years in jail until he is set free by the deathbed confession of one of the arsonists for whose crime he has taken the blame.[47] It seems that the idealised world of the *Heimat* can only be sustained if the people and especially its male guardians adhere to strict rules.

But the way *Heimatfilm* deals with masculinity is much more ambiguous than it at first seems. On the one hand, it lauds physical strength, self-control, and virility as ideal masculine attributes; while on the other, it is also suspicious of traditional masculinity. In this post-war context, the genre seems to transmit a fear of men's aggression which is intrinsic to traditional masculinity; after all, the terrors of war had illustrated how much damage male aggression could do. Perhaps it is for this reason that *Heimatfilm* forces men into passive situations where they must test their masculine virtue to repress aggression. Thus, although *Heimatfilms* never directly address the war and the Nazi.[48] They loom like dark clouds on the horizon and cast a shadow on the men.

Post-war Austrian *Heimatfilm* only vaguely alludes to the men's guilt, never spelling out exactly what they are guilty of. At the same time, these representations leave no doubt that these men are first and foremost, victims. Hinting at a male past that remains largely shrouded in obscurity, we learn that Hubert in *Echo der Berge* had to flee his estate in the east after the war and start over as a humble forester in the 'silver forest' – a fictitious region in Austria. Similarly, in *Hoch vom Dachstein* (Dark Clouds over the Dachstein, 1952), it becomes clear that Hannes, who at the outset seems to be a local like any other, was in fact once 'Herr Khäls von Khälsberg', a minor aristocrat who had lost his estate for unknown reasons.[49] The men in these films suffer not only losses, but also injustices, and are wrongly accused of crimes. In the end, however, they are vindicated and invited back into the rural community. This narrative sent a powerful message to the Austrian and German audiences who similarly felt wrongly accused by the international community for crimes they felt they had nothing to do with. *Heimatfilm* thus had a twofold function which might explain its unexpected popularity in Austria and Germany in the decade following the war. Firstly, it offered the audience a means of escape from dreary everyday life through its powerful imagery of pristine landscapes, and visions of life in a community untouched by the conflict and turmoil of modernity. Secondly, it cleansed Austrian and German men and the nation from any association with war-crimes and instilled hope that the natural turn of events would eventually reveal the innocence of the wrongly accused. The unobtrusive heroism of the masculine ideal in *Heimatfilm*, with the idea that emotions had to be governed and personal happiness sacrificed for the greater good, made this concept of masculinity attractive to both men and women. Men were tested but emerged as morally virtuous. This, together with their intimate connection with nature, made men appear capable of rising above it all, and naturally superior.

## Modern Men in Tourist Film

Tourist film has often been considered to be a mere subcategory of *Heimatfilm*;[50] and yet, apart from their shared emphasis on landscape, these two genres have very little in common. Tourist films can be described as light-hearted comedies about people spending holidays in the countryside. The favourite settings for Austrian tourist films in this period were the Austrian lake districts of the Salzkammergut and Carinthia – which became the main tourist destinations for West German tourists from the beginning of the 1950s, when travel restrictions between the two countries had been removed and the economic boom had turned the West Germans once more into attractive customers for Austria's tourist industry.[51] While both tourist film and *Heimatfilm* aimed to sell the Austrian landscape to potential tourists, each of them also fulfilled specific and distinct functions. While *Heimatfilm* focused on the local rural community and was often anti-urban, city dwellers were the main protagonists in tourist film. Austrian tourist films were thus forward-looking, embraced modernity and progress and advertised the joy of mobility and work. Much of the attraction in tourist film lay in the positive mood it conveyed. Although only twelve tourist films were produced between 1945 and 1955 (approximately just 6% of total film production), they were very popular with audiences, particularly in the early post-war years. The tourist film, *Hofrat Geiger* (Privy Councillor Geiger, 1947), was one of the biggest box office hits in post-war Austria.[52]

The optimistic mood and light-hearted humour of this genre stood in stark contrast to the difficult post-war reality and thus fed escapist desires. However, it is safe to assume that the beautiful setting accounted as much for its success as anything else. Tourist films offered a kind of 'ersatz holiday' for many urban citizens who could not actually afford the change of scenery. Although travelling remained the preserve of the middle-class at the time, travelling for pleasure, not least as a result of the organised 'Joy through Strength'-holidays in Nazi Germany, was now, as Alon Confino has shown in his insightful analysis of tourist rhetoric in postwar West German, widely perceived as an established right 'that reflects the ability of the system to keep the promise of a better life'.[53]

Tourist film stand outs from the other post-war genres because of its relatively progressive representations of gender and gender relations. Men and women are presented as equals; they share the same work, the same space, display similar body language and behaviour, and they travel and have fun together. Particularly the earlier films feature energetic, self-confident women who are independent and deal with men as comrades rather than their lovers. The young men, too, are lively and practical; they sweep through the static countryside, bringing positive winds of change.[54]

Tourist film presents holidays as an imitation of paradise, in which everybody is equal.[55] Clothes are taken off and social boundaries are broken down. The fact that gender, nationality, and class differences lose significance in tourist film is illustrative of the genre's engagement with the post-war reality, where the joint experience of hardship diminished old distinctions of class. In these films, people move closer together, they share tables and cars, and they unite in their admiration of the unspoilt countryside and beautiful bodies on the beach. The imagery offers the vision of a homogenous society in which money and class are unimportant and, most importantly, the future is bright.

The leading men in tourist films are always kind-hearted, sanguine, and carefree. They resemble the cultured, non-aggressive masculine ideals of period costume films, although generic convention demands that the men in tourist film be sprightlier and more energetic. Being neither gutsy nor ambitious, they lack the attributes of hard-edged masculinity in *Heimatfilm*. Instead, tourist film shows men as empathic, harmonious, and striving for reconciliation. And even though the genre celebrates mobility, it presents men as more rooted than women, longing for stability and a home. This is illustrated by their appetite for marriage. Thus, the male protagonists in tourist film bear a strong resemblance to what Steven Cohan defined as the 'domesticated male', an ideal that dominated the public imagery in the US in the 1950s.[56]

The promotion of the domesticated male as a modern masculine ideal after the Second World War was a result of the concerns regarding men's experiences during the war, especially with regard to violence and homosexuality. Marriage and sexuality were intensely debated after the war in the western world. Not only had the war complicated relations between men and women, thus causing alarm among the political and professional elites, who saw the nuclear family and society as a whole endangered.[57] At the same time, anxieties grew about growing male homosexuality combined with a dangerous feminisation of society and consequent loss of male power.[58] As a consequence, the new ideal of modern masculinity that Hollywood started to promote softened the hard-edged attributes and emphasised equality, while nevertheless underlining the heterosexual orientation of the man. Unlike earlier ideals of masculinity, the modern 'domesticated man' was defined by 'object choice' and not so much by his 'masculine' behaviour.[59] Men were allowed to show effeminate body language or 'unmanly' conduct as long as there was no doubt that they were exclusively interested in the opposite sex. Austrian tourist film presents its own type of domesticated males; it allows men to carry handbags for their girlfriends, as in *Zwei in einem Auto* (Two in a Car, 1951),[60] or to work in the kitchen, as Bill Wokulek does in *Eva erbt das Paradies* (Eva Inherits Paradise, 1951).[61] However, such behaviour is only possible because the narrative continuously affirms the manliness of the protagonists: Georg is a dashing racing-car driver and a favourite with the women, while Bill is presented as a womaniser who likes to parade his muscular bare upper body in front of them.

Even though tourist films advertise gender equality, most men still have a higher status in them than women, both financially and professionally. This inequality is not challenged by the protagonists, but accepted as natural. In the film *Eva erbt das Paradies*, Eva has inherited a derelict hotel by a lakeside. She and her mostly female friends renovate the building and turn the newly named 'Hotel Paradise' into a prospering hotel business. Work is not allocated according to gender, but ability. The new acquaintance Bill, who is a musician, cooks for the hotel guests and plays the piano, while the young women paint and hammer. The theme of working together and combining efforts in the renovation project is a metaphor for the rebuilding of Austria. Any rifts the war had caused among the population, and especially between men and women, have been overcome for the greater good of making the country prosperous again. Differences are set aside, and equality reigns. However, this hotel is not newly built, but a renovation project. The fact that the façade has changed, but the foundations remain the same, can be read as an analogy to the state of Austrian society and its gender relations. While Austrian law had codified the equality of men and women, they were still regarded as different in their private lives, which is illustrated by the fact that women were legally responsible for running the household.[62] In this film, Eva manages her hotel business successfully, but when the debts weigh her down, it is her fiancé Hans who steps in with his assets and discreetly pays her electricity bills. The reward for his financial support is marriage and, as a predictable consequence, the reinstatement of patriarchal relations.

It might have been the combination of the promises of modernity with the security of the traditional, as presented in *Eva erbt das Paradies*, which appealed to the audiences. Tourist films' dominant *topoi* – landscape, road, mobility and modernity – reverberate in the masculinities the genre proposes. The landscape, traditionally an indicator of conservative values, is linked with modernity in tourist film, and it is through this connection between the countryside and modernity that the genders move closer together. Differences of gender and class are diminished, while similarities are emphasised instead. The road in tourist films denotes change, and it is in the representation of gender where this change becomes most visible.

## *Conclusion*

Antonio Gramsci famously argued that hegemonic power relies on cultural influence rather than the application of brute force. This brief essay on representations of masculinity in three popular film genres has sought to illustrate how post-war Austrian cinema intervened and shaped popular and political discourse on gender and national identity. The findings of the film analysis showed that masculinity is not one-dimensional and singular, but expressed through a number of forms, both in cinema and the social reality it depicts.

Yet although the representations of masculinity in post-war Austrian cinema are surprisingly varied, they share some traits, such as a love for harmony, musicality and sensitivity. The differences in the representations I have identified in this chapter are largely due to generic conventions. Each genre fulfils a function, caters for specific desires and is seeking to provide a source of identification for the audience.

The fact that *Heimatfilm* promotes a traditional and in many ways outdated concept of hard-edged masculinity can be explained with the emphasis that the genre places on traditional values, and the central role assigned to nature as a symbol of continuity. The aesthetic constraints of this genre do not permit a characterisation of masculinity that clashes with its themes. Tourist film, on the other hand, emphasises the similarities between the genders. In line with the genre's preoccupation with holiday, mobility and travel, tourist film drafts a modern ideal of masculinity that downplays any hard-edged masculine attributes, and instead presents the men as family-oriented and stable. The light-hearted, optimistic tone of tourist films from 1946–1955 eased anxieties about an uncertain future and embraced modernity by (at least ostensibly) celebrating gender equality. Period costume film fulfilled yet another important function in that it cleansed Austrian men from any association with violence, and provided 'historical proof' of the inherent Austrian qualities of charm, musicality, and a distaste for violence. Using visual references, these films inscribe ideal national traits onto the male body. The representations of Austrian masculinity in costume film as charming, placid men who prefer singing to shooting carried a strong message to contemporary audiences.

Hence, by presenting 'softer' characteristics such as sensitivity, musicality, or harmony as positive masculine traits, cinema supported the dominant discourse of Austria's victimhood during the war with effective imagery. Historians tend to question such an argument, asking for proof that the film industry actively supported the elites in this process of nation building. It has to be clarified that neither the Austrian film industry nor individual filmmakers intended their films to be put to this purpose, or to smooth troubled gender relations. Their prime interest was of a financial nature, and the goal was to attract large audiences. Still, post-war Austrian cinema participated in and fuelled popular discourse and thus played a key role in the stabilisation of Austrian society.[63]

## Notes

1. A quote from male protagonist Jurek in the period costume film *Die Deutschmeister*, directed by Ernst Marischka (Austria: Erma Filmproduktionsgesellschaft, 1955).
2. See Österreichisches Statistisches Zentralamt, *Beiträge zur österreichischen Statistik* (1959), 39, 145.
3. R. C. Allen and D. Gomery, *Film History: Theory and Practice* (New York: McGraw-Hill, 1985), 158.
4. J. Smith, 'Film History', the Institute of Historical Research website, http://www.history.ac.uk/makinghistory/resources/articles/film_history.html, retrieved 24 February 2009.

5  See, e.g., F. Weber, 'Wiederaufbau zwischen Ost und West', in R. Sieder, H. Steinert and E. Tálos (eds), *Österreich 1945-1995: Gesellschaft, Politik, Kultur* (Vienna: Verlag für Gesellschaftskritik, 1996), 68-79; E. Bruckmüller, 'Von der Unabhängigkeitserklärung zum zweiten Kontrollabkommen', in E. Bruckmüller (ed.), *Wiederaufbau in Österreich, 1945-1955: Rekonstruktion oder Neubeginn?* (Vienna: Verlag für Geschichte und Politik, 2006), 10-27.

6  S. Neale, *Genre* (London: BFI, 1980), 52-54.

7  Unfortunately, the sources on Austrian film production and distribution companies from that period are scarce; there are some statistical data on cinemas, film imports and domestic film productions, but no records of attendance figures or box office takings. I had to rely on information provided by trade journals, press coverage on Austrian film production, and film reviews.

8  As of yet, little research has been done on the lives of Austrian veterans after the Second World War. M. Maier, 'Defeated Masculinity: Transformations of Masculinity in the Narrated Life Histories of Two Former Austrian Wehrmacht Soldiers (1945-1960)', in A. Suppan and M. Graf (eds), *From the Austrian Empire to Communist East Central Europe* (Wien: LIT, 2010), 133-149. For post-war Germany see e.g., F. Biess, *Homecomings: Returning POWs and the Legacies of Defeat in Post-war Germany* (Princeton, NJ: Princeton University Press, 2006); R. G. Moeller, 'Heimkehr ins Vaterland: Die Remaskulierung Westdeutschlands in den fünfziger Jahren', *Militärgeschichtliche Zeitschrift* 60, no. 2 (2001), 404f.

9  See I. Bauer, 'Von den Tugenden der Weiblichkeit: Zur geschlechtsspezifischen Arbeitsteilung in der politischen Kultur', in T. Albrich et al. (eds), *Österreich in den Fünfzigern* (Innsbruck: Österreichischer Studien Verlag, 1995), 35-52; E. Langthaler, 'Ländliche Lebenswelten von 1945 bis 1950', in Sieder, Steinert and Tálos (eds), *Österreich 1945-1995*, 41-43.

10 For the strained gender relations in post-war Austria see specifically the excellent contributions in I. Bandhauer-Schöffmann and E. Hornung (eds), *Wiederaufbau Weiblich* (Vienna: Geyer-Ed., 1992); also E. Hornung and M. Sturm, 'Stadtleben: Alltag in Wien 1945 bis 1955', in Sieder, Steinert and Tálos (eds), *Österreich 1945-1995*, 54-67; Langthaler, 'Ländliche Lebenswelten', 41-43.

11 See R. Bessel, 'Was bleibt vom Krieg? Deutsche Nachkriegsgeschichte(n) aus geschlechtergeschichtlicher Perspektive', *Militärgeschichtliche Zeitschrift* 60, no. 2 (2001), 300.

12 See e.g., Biess, *Homecomings*; H. Fehrenbach, 'Rehabilitating Fatherland: Race and German Remasculinisation', *Signs* 24, no. 1 (1998), 107-127; R. G. Moeller, '"The Last Soldiers of the Great War" and Tales of Family Reunions in the Federal Republic of Germany', *Signs* 24, no. 1 (1998), 129-145; U. G. Poiger, 'Krise der Männlichkeit: Remaskulinisierung in beiden deutschen Nachkriegsgesellschaften', in K. Naumann (ed.), *Nachkrieg in Deutschland* (Hamburg: Hamburger Edition, 2001), 227-263.

13 See R. W. Connell, *Masculinities* (Cambridge: Polity Press, 1995), 76-81.

14 J. Tosh, 'Hegemonic Masculinity and the History of Gender', in S. Dudink, K. Hagemann and J. Tosh (eds), *Masculinities in Politics and War: Gendering Modern History* (Manchester: Manchester University Press, 2004), 47.

15 For the rise of 'modern hegemonic masculinity', see G. L. Mosse, *The Image of Man: The Creation of Modern Masculinity* (Oxford: Oxford University Press, 1998), 154-180; also W. Schmale, *Geschichte der Männlichkeit in Europa (1450-2000)* (Vienna: Böhlau, 2003), 192-203; E. Hanisch, *Männlichkeiten* (Vienna: Böhlau, 2005), 71-88; U. Frevert, '"Soldaten, Staatsbürger": Überlegungen zur historischen Konstruktion von Männlichkeit', in *Männergeschichte - Geschlechtergeschichte: Männlichkeit im Wandel der Moderne*, ed. T. Kühne (Frankfurt am Main: Campus, 1996), 69-87.

16 For the decline of this hegemonic ideal in post-war Austria, see Hanisch, *Männlichkeiten*, 99–110. For Germany see e.g. Kühne, *Männergeschichte – Geschlechtergeschichte*.
17 See A. Kuhn, 'Refamilialisierung versus Emanzipation? Kritische Überlegungen zur gegenwärtigen Forschungslage', in Bandhauer-Schöffmann and Hornung (eds), *Wiederaufbau Weiblich*, 153f.
18 Fehrenbach, 'Rehabilitating Fatherland', 109.
19 See S. Jeffords, 'The "Remasculinization" of Germany in the 1950s: Discussion', *Signs* 24, no. 1 (1998), 166; see also Fehrenbach, 'Rehabilitating Fatherland', 109. H. Schissler, '"Normalization" as Project: Some Thoughts on Gender Relations in West Germany during the 1950s', in H. Schissler (ed.), *The Miracle Years: A Cultural History of West Germany, 1949–1968* (Princeton, NJ: Princeton University Press, 2001), 364–365.
20 Connell, *Masculinities*, 80.
21 For example: E. Appelt, *Geschlecht – Staatsbürgerschaft – Nation: Politische Konstruktion der Geschlechterverhältnisse in Europa* (Frankfurt am Main: Suhrkamp, 1999); see also K. Hagemann, 'Venus und Mars: Reflexionen zu einer Geschlechtergeschichte von Militär und Krieg', in K. Hagemann and R. Pröve (eds), *Landsknechte, Soldatenfrauen und Nationalkrieger: Militär, Krieg und Geschlechterordnung im historischen Wandel* (Frankfurt am Main: Campus, 1998), 23–24.
22 I. Bandhauer-Schöffmann and E. Hornung, 'Trümmerfrauen – ein kurzes Heldinnenleben. Nachkriegsgesellschaft als Frauengesellschaft', in A. Graf (ed.), *Zur Politik des Weiblichen. Frauenmacht und -ohnmacht* (Wien: Verlag für Gesellschaftskritik, 1992), 116–117.
23 Even though Austria had existed for centuries, the Habsburg emperors never made any attempts to create an Austrian nation out of their multiethnic empire. See E. Hanisch, *Der lange Schatten des Staates: Österreichische Gesellschaftsgeschichte im 20. Jahrhundert* (Vienna: Ueberreuter, 1994), 155.
24 See K. R. Stadler, *Austria* (London: Benn, 1971), 106; see also Hanisch, *Lange Schatten des Staates*, 277–284.
25 Both the large Austrian Social Democratic Party who rejected the 'abhorred name Austria' and wanted it to be called Deutsch-Österreich (German-Austria) and the much smaller camp of the German nationalists favoured a union with Germany. See E. Bruckmüller, *Symbole österreichischer Identität zwischen 'Kakanien' und 'Europa'* (Vienna: Picus, 1997), 33. Stadler provides a concise analysis of the reasons behind the Social Democrats' support for a union with Germany. See Stadler, *Austria*, 107–112.
26 See Hanisch, *Lange Schatten des Staates*, 161–163. Already in 1940, the SS intelligence service SD reported that the antagonism between Austrians and Germans was growing, even within the Nazi party. See Bruckmüller, *Symbole österreichischer Identität*, 40. For the growth of anti-German sentiment and Austrian patriotism see also E. Bruckmüller, *Sozialgeschichte Österreichs* (Vienna: Herold, 1985), 518–520; Stadler, *Austria*, 181–199.
27 See P. Pirker, *Subversion deutscher Herrschaft. Der britische Kriegsgeheimdienst SOE und Österreich* (Wien: Vienna University Press, 2012).
28 The Austrian governments used the Declaration of the Four Nations on General Security, commonly known as the Moscow Declaration, signed by the Foreign Secretaries of the United States, Great Britain, and the Soviet Union on 30 October 1943, to support their claim that Austria had been the first victim of Nazi aggression. The resolution had declared the annexation of Austria by Nazi Germany as 'null and void', but also stated that the efforts of Austrians to free themselves from Nazi dictatorship would be crucial in reaching a decision about

29. the final status of Austria. 'Official Documents: Great Britain – Soviet Union – United States: Tripartite Conference in Moscow; November 1, 1943', *American Journal of International Law* 38, no. 1 (1944), 3–8.
30. These self-characterisations have been very successful and are still popular in Austria, as Karner has shown: Karner, K., 'The "Habsburg Dilemma" Today: Competing Discourses of National Identity in Contemporary Austria', *National Identities*. Volume 7: 4 (2005), 418.
31. See U. Halbritter, *Der Einfluss der Alliierten Besatzungsmächte auf die österreichische Filmwirtschaft und Spielfilmproduktion in den Jahren 1945 bis 1955* (unpublished Master's thesis, University of Vienna, 1993), 14; R. Wagnleitner, *Coca-Colonisation und Kalter Krieg: Die Kulturmission der USA in Österreich nach dem Zweiten Weltkrieg* (Vienna: Verlag für Gesellschaftskritik, 1991).
32. M. Foucault, *Archäologie des Wissens* (Frankfurt am Main: Suhrkamp, 1981), 42; also A. Landwehr, *Die Geschichte des Sagbaren: Einführung in die Historische Diskursanalyse* (Berlin: Edition Diskord, 2001), 7.
33. G. F. Custen, 'Making History', in M. Landy (ed.), *The Historical Film: History and Memory in Media* (New Brunswick, NJ: Rutgers University Press, 2001), 93.
34. Franz Joseph came to power after the Revolution in 1848 and remained Emperor of Austria until his death in 1916. Because of his long reign he is often mistaken to have been the last emperor of Austria; but his nephew Karl succeeded him to the throne in 1916, and was forced to abdicate in 1918.
35. See S. Harper, 'Bonnie Prince Charlie Revisited: British Costume Film in the 1950s', in R. Murphy (ed.), *The British Cinema Book* (London: BFI, 1999), 137.
36. While the Austrians have displayed great affinity towards the Hungarians, negative Czech stereotypes have remained strong throughout the twentieth century. See E. Bruckmüller, *The Austrian Nation: Cultural Consciousness and Socio-political Processes* (Riverside, CA: Ariadne Press, 2003), 135, 147–149, 151–152.
37. Director: Johannes Alexander Hübler-Kahla (Austria: Österreichische Wochenschau- und Produktions KG J. A. Hübler-Kahla & Co 1947).
38. Director: Franz Antel (Austria: Neusser Film, 1953).
39. Research has shown that period costume films were particularly popular with female audiences. See e.g. Harper, 'Bonnie Prince Charlie Revisited', 133.
40. See I. Reicher and S. Schachinger, 'Heimat Film and Mountain Films', in T. Elsaesser (ed.), *The BFI Companion to German Cinema* (London: BFI, 1999), 133–135; W. Kaschuba and D. Bahlinger, *Der deutsche Heimatfilm: Bildwelten und Weltbilder; Bilder, Texte, Analysen zu 70 Jahren deutscher Filmgeschichte* (Tübingen: Tübinger Vereinigung für Volkskunde, 1989), 9.
41. C. Applegate, *A Nation of Provincials: The German Idea of Heimat* (Berkeley: University of California Press, 1990), 4; J. von Moltke, *No Place Like Home: Locations of Heimat in German Cinema* (Berkeley: University of California Press, 2005), 9.
42. Applegate, *Nation of Provincials*, 5.
43. Moltke, *No Place Like Home*, 8.
44. Director: Alfons Stummer (Austria: Rondo-Film Vienna, 1954).
45. See Kaschuba and Bahlinger, *Deutsche Heimatfilm*, 7. Generally, Austrian and German audiences preferred national productions over Hollywood films until the mid-1950s. See H. Fehrenbach, *Cinema in Democratizing Germany: Reconstructing National Identity after Hitler* (Chapel Hill: University of North Carolina Press, 1995), 163.
46. See Moltke, *No Place like Home*, 117; T. Bergfelder, *International Adventures. German Popular Cinema and European Co-productions in the 1960s* (New York, Oxford: Berghahn, 2006), 42–43.
47. S. Hake, *German National Cinema* (London, New York: Routledge, 2008), 119.

47 *Director:* Alfred Stöger (Austria: Wiener Mundus Film, 1949).
48 See Kaschuba and Bahlinger, *Deutsche Heimatfilm*, 11.
49 *Director:* Anton Kutter (Austria/Germany: Telos Filmgesellschaft & Süddeutsche Film-Produktion, 1953).
50 See e.g., G. Steiner, *Die Heimat-Macher: Kino in Österreich 1946–1966* (Vienna: Verlag für Gesellschaftskritik, 1987).
51 See H. Spode, 'Deutsch-österreichischer Tourismus und nationale Identität', in *Verfreundete Nachbarn: Deutschland-Österreich*, ed. Stiftung Haus der Geschichte der Bundesrepublik Deutschland (Bielefeld: Kerber, 2005).
52 *Director:* Hans Wolff (Austria: Willi-Forst Film, 1947). According to *Film-Kunst*, the film attracted 2.9 million Austrian viewers between its opening in 1947 and spring 1950; by 1950 every third Austrian had seen the film; its theme song, 'Mariandl', became a musical hit in both Austria and Germany. See E. von Neusser, 'Die österreichischen Filmerfolge', *Film-Kunst: Zeitschrift für Filmkultur und Filmwissenschaft* 5 (1950), 253.
53 See A. Confino, 'Dissonance, Normality and the Historical Method: Why Did Some Germans Think of Tourism after May 8, 1945?', in R. Bessel and D. Schumann (eds), *Life after Death: Approaches to a Cultural and Social History of Europe during the 1940s and 1950s* (Washington: German Historical Institute, 2003), 331–333.
54 Towards the mid-1950s, the gap between the genders widens and the genre starts to curtail the women's free movement. See M. Fritsche 'Einer gleichberechtigteren Zukunft entgegen? Inszenierung von Geschlechterbeziehungen im österreichischen Tourismusfilm der Nachkriegszeit', in *L'Homme. Europäische Zeitschrift für feministische Geschichtswissenschaft*, 26/2 (2015), 49–66.
55 F. Inglis, *Delicious History of the Holiday* (London: Routledge, 2000), 11–12.
56 Steven Cohan analyses how Hollywood cinema promoted the normative standard of the American family man, while at the same warning of the effects of such a 'domestication' of men (e.g., physical illnesses or fears of impotency). See S. Cohan, *Masked Men: Masculinity and the Movies in the Fifties* (Bloomington: Indiana University Press, 1997), 49–61.
57 See D. Herzog, 'Desperately Seeking Normality. Sex and Marriage in the Wake of War', in Bessel and. Schumann (eds), 161–164; Cohan, *Masked Men*, 45–49.
58 See J. B. Gilbert, *Men in the Middle: Searching for Masculinity in the 1950s* (Chicago: University of Chicago Press, 2005), 67.
59 See Cohan, *Masked Men*, 49–61, xii.
60 Director: Ernst Marischka (Austria: Erma Filmproduktionsgesellschaft, 1951).
61 Director: Franz Antel (Austria: Alpenländische Filmproduktion, 1951).
62 As in West Germany, women were guaranteed equality in the constitution, but it was 'equality in difference'. See E. Carter, 'Alice in the Consumer Wonderland: West German Case Studies in Gender and Consumer Culture', in ed. R. G. Moeller (ed.), *West Germany under Construction: Politics, Society, and Culture in the Adenauer Era* (Ann Arbor: University of Michigan Press, 1997), 355. On the position of men and women in Austrian family law, see M. Mesner, 'Die "Neugestaltung des Ehe- und Familienrechts": Re-Definitionspotentiale im Geschlechterverhältnis der Aufbau-Zeit', *Zeitgeschichte* 24, 5–6 (1997), 186–210.
63 See M. Fritsche, *Homemade Men in Post-war Austrian Cinema: Nationhood, Genre and Masculinity* (Berghahn: New York, Oxford, 2013).

# Sources and Bibliography

## Audiovisual material

*Die Welt dreht sich verkehrt* (The World Turns Backwards), directed by Johannes Alexander Hübler-Kahla (Austria: Österreichische Wochenschau- und Produktions KG J. A. Hübler-Kahla & Co 1947).
*Hofrat Geiger* (Privy Councillor Geiger), director: Hans Wolff (Austria: Willi-Forst Film, 1947).
*Der Förster vom Silberwald* (The Forester of the Silver Forest), director: Alfred Stöger (Austria: Wiener Mundus Film, 1949).
*Das Siegel Gottes* (God's Signet), director: Alfred Stöger (Austria: Wiener Mundus Film, 1949).
*Zwei in einem Auto* (Two in a Car), director: Ernst Marischka (Austria: Erma Filmproduktionsgesellschaft, 1951).
*Eva erbt das Paradies* (Eva Inherits Paradise), director: Franz Antel (Austria: Alpenländische Filmproduktion, 1951).
*Kaiserwalzer* (The Emperor's Waltz), director: Franz Antel (Austria: Neusser Film, 1953).
*Hoch vom Dachstein* (Dark Clouds over the Dachstein), director: Anton Kutter (Austria/Germany: Telos Filmgesellschaft & Süddeutsche Film-Produktion, 1953).
*Echo der Berge* (Echo of the Mountains), director: Alfons Stummer (Austria: Rondo-Film Vienna, 1954).
*Die Deutschmeister*, a costume film directed by Ernst Marischka (Austria: Erma Filmproduktionsgesellschaft, 1955).

## Printed sources

*American Journal of International Law* 38, no. 1 (1944) ('Official Documents: Great Britain – Soviet Union – United States: Tripartite Conference in Moscow; November 1, 1943').
*Beiträge zur österreichischen Statistik*. Wien: Österreichisches Statistisches Zentralamt, 1959.
Neusser, E. von, 'Die österreichischen Filmerfolge', *Film-Kunst: Zeitschrift für Filmkultur und Filmwissenschaft* 5 (1950).

## Internet sources

Smith, J., 'Film History', the Institute of Historical Research website, http://www.history.ac.uk/makinghistory/resources/articles/film_history.html, retrieved 24 February 2009.

## Literature

Allen, R. C. and Gomery, D., *Film History: Theory and Practice*. New York: McGraw-Hill, 1985.
Appelt, E., *Geschlecht – Staatsbürgerschaft – Nation: Politische Konstruktion der Geschlechterverhältnisse in Europa*. Frankfurt am Main: Suhrkamp, 1999.
Applegate, C., *A Nation of Provincials: The German Idea of Heimat*. Berkeley: University of California Press, 1990.

Bandhauer-Schöffmann, I. and Hornung, E., 'Trümmerfrauen – ein kurzes Heldinnenleben. Nachkriegsgesellschaft als Frauengesellschaft', in Graf A. (ed.), *Zur Politik des Weiblichen. Frauenmacht und -ohnmacht.* Wien: Verlag für Gesellschaftskritik, 1992.

Bandhauer-Schöffmann I. and Hornung, E. (eds), *Wiederaufbau Weiblich.* Vienna: Geyer-Ed., 1992.

Bauer, I., 'Von den Tugenden der Weiblichkeit: Zur geschlechtsspezifischen Arbeitsteilung in der politischen Kultur', in Albrich, T. et al. (eds), *Österreich in den Fünfzigern.* Innsbruck: Österreichischer Studien Verlag, 1995.

Bergfelder, T., *International Adventures. German Popular Cinema and European Co-productions in the 1960s.* New York, Oxford: Berghahn, 2006.

Bessel, R., 'Was bleibt vom Krieg? Deutsche Nachkriegsgeschichte(n) aus geschlechtergeschichtlicher Perspektive', *Militärgeschichtliche Zeitschrift* 60, no. 2 (2001).

Biess, F., *Homecomings: Returning POWs and the Legacies of Defeat in Post-war Germany.* Princeton, NJ: Princeton University Press, 2006.

Bruckmüller, E., *Sozialgeschichte Österreichs.* Vienna: Herold, 1985.

Bruckmüller, E., *Symbole österreichischer Identität zwischen 'Kakanien' und 'Europa'.* Vienna: Picus, 1997.

Bruckmüller, E., *The Austrian Nation: Cultural Consciousness and Socio-political Processes.* Riverside, CA: Ariadne Press, 2003.

Bruckmüller, E., 'Von der Unabhängigkeitserklärung zum zweiten Kontrollabkommen', in Bruckmüller E. (ed.), *Wiederaufbau in Österreich, 1945–1955: Rekonstruktion oder Neubeginn?* Vienna: Verlag für Geschichte und Politik, 2006.

Carter, E., 'Alice in the Consumer Wonderland: West German Case Studies in Gender and Consumer Culture', in Moeller, R. G. (ed.), *West Germany under Construction: Politics, Society, and Culture in the Adenauer Era.* Ann Arbor: University of Michigan Press, 1997.

Cohan, S., *Masked Men: Masculinity and the Movies in the Fifties.* Bloomington: Indiana University Press, 1997.

Confino, A., 'Dissonance, Normality and the Historical Method: Why Did Some Germans Think of Tourism after May 8, 1945?', in Bessel, R. and Schumann, D. (eds), *Life after Death: Approaches to a Cultural and Social History of Europe during the 1940s and 1950s.* Washington: German Historical Institute, 2003.

Connell, R. W., *Masculinities.* Cambridge: Polity Press, 1995.

Custen, G. F., 'Making History', in Landy, M. (ed.), *The Historical Film: History and Memory in Media.* New Brunswick, NJ: Rutgers University Press, 2001.

Fehrenbach, H., *Cinema in Democratizing Germany: Reconstructing National Identity after Hitler.* Chapel Hill: University of North Carolina Press, 1995.

Fehrenbach, H., 'Rehabilitating Fatherland: Race and German Remasculinisation', *Signs* 24, no. 1 (1998).

Foucault, F., *Archäologie des Wissens.* Frankfurt am Main: Suhrkamp, 1981.

Frevert, U., '"Soldaten, Staatsbürger": Überlegungen zur historischen Konstruktion von Männlichkeit', in , Kühne, T. (ed.), *Männergeschichte – Geschlechtergeschichte: Männlichkeit im Wandel der Moderne.* Frankfurt am Main: Campus, 1996.

Fritsche, M., *Homemade Men in Post-war Austrian Cinema: Nationhood, Genre and Masculinity.* Berghahn: New York, Oxford, 2013.

Fritsche, M., 'Einer gleichberechtigteren Zukunft entgegen? Inszenierung von Geschlechterbeziehungen im österreichischen Tourismusfilm der Nachkriegszeit', in *L'Homme. Europäische Zeitschrift für feministische Geschichtswissenschaft,* 26/2 (2015).

Gilbert, J.B., *Men in the Middle: Searching for Masculinity in the 1950s.* Chicago: University of Chicago Press, 2005.

Hagemann, K., 'Venus und Mars: Reflexionen zu einer Geschlechtergeschichte von Militär und Krieg', in Hagemann, K. and Pröve, R. (eds), *Landsknechte, Soldatenfrauen und Nationalkrieger: Militär, Krieg und Geschlechterordnung im historischen Wandel*. Frankfurt am Main: Campus, 1998.

Hake, S., *German National Cinema*. London, New York: Routledge, 2008.

Halbritter, U., *Der Einfluss der Alliierten Besatzungsmächte auf die österreichische Filmwirtschaft und Spielfilmproduktion in den Jahren 1945 bis 1955* (unpublished Master's thesis, University of Vienna, 1993).

Hanisch, E., *Der lange Schatten des Staates: Österreichische Gesellschaftsgeschichte im 20. Jahrhundert*. Vienna: Ueberreuter, 1994.

Hanisch, E., *Männlichkeiten*. Vienna: Böhlau, 2005.

Harper, S., 'Bonnie Prince Charlie Revisited: British Costume Film in the 1950s', in Murphy, R. (ed.), *The British Cinema Book*. London: BFI, 1999.

Herzog, D., 'Desperately Seeking Normality. Sex and Marriage in the Wake of War', in Bessel and Schumann (eds).

Hornung, E. and Sturm, M., 'Stadtleben: Alltag in Wien 1945 bis 1955', in Sieder, Steinert and Tálos (eds), *Österreich 1945–1995*.

Inglis, F., *Delicious History of the Holiday*. London: Routledge, 2000.

Jeffords, S., 'The "Remasculinization" of Germany in the 1950s: Discussion', *Signs* 24, no. 1 (1998).

Karner, K., 'The "Habsburg Dilemma" Today: Competing Discourses of National Identity in Contemporary Austria', *National Identities*. Volume 7: 4 (2005).

Kaschuba, W. and Bahlinger, D., *Der deutsche Heimatfilm: Bildwelten und Weltbilder; Bilder, Texte, Analysen zu 70 Jahren deutscher Filmgeschichte*. Tübingen: Tübinger Vereinigung für Volkskunde, 1989.

Kuhn, A, 'Refamilialisierung versus Emanzipation? Kritische Überlegungen zur gegenwärtigen Forschungslage', in Bandhauer-Schöffmann and Hornung (eds), *Wiederaufbau Weiblich*.

Landwehr, A., *Die Geschichte des Sagbaren: Einführung in die Historische Diskursanalyse*. Berlin: Edition Diskord, 2001.

Langthaler, E. 'Ländliche Lebenswelten von 1945 bis 1950', in Sieder, Steinert and Tálos (eds), *Österreich 1945–1995*.

Maier, M., 'Defeated Masculinity: Transformations of Masculinity in the Narrated Life Histories of Two Former Austrian Wehrmacht Soldiers (1945–1960)', in Suppan A. and Graf, M. (eds), *From the Austrian Empire to Communist East Central Europe*. Wien: LIT, 2010.

Mesner, M., 'Die "Neugestaltung des Ehe- und Familienrechts": Re-Definitionspotentiale im Geschlechterverhältnis der Aufbau-Zeit', *Zeitgeschichte* 24, 5–6 (1997).

Moeller, R. G., '"The Last Soldiers of the Great War" and Tales of Family Reunions in the Federal Republic of Germany', *Signs* 24, no. 1 (1998).

Moeller, R. G., 'Heimkehr ins Vaterland: Die Remaskulierung Westdeutschlands in den fünfziger Jahren', *Militärgeschichtliche Zeitschrift* 60, no. 2 (2001).

Moltke, J. von, *No Place Like Home: Locations of Heimat in German Cinema*. Berkeley: University of California Press, 2005.

Mosse, G. L., *The Image of Man: The Creation of Modern Masculinity*. Oxford: Oxford University Press, 1998.

Neale, S., *Genre*. London: BFI, 1980.

Pirker, P., *Subversion deutscher Herrschaft. Der britische Kriegsgeheimdienst SOE und Österreich*. Wien: Vienna University Press, 2012.

Poiger, U. G., 'Krise der Männlichkeit: Remaskulinisierung in beiden deutschen Nachkriegsgesellschaften', in Naumann, K. (ed.), *Nachkrieg in Deutschland*. Hamburg: Hamburger Edition, 2001.

Reicher, I. and Schachinger, S., 'Heimat Film and Mountain Films', in Elsaesser, T. (ed.), *The BFI Companion to German Cinema*. London: BFI, 1999.

Schissler, H., '"Normalization" as Project: Some Thoughts on Gender Relations in West Germany during the 1950s', in Schissler, H. (ed.), *The Miracle Years: A Cultural History of West Germany, 1949–1968*. Princeton, NJ: Princeton University Press, 2001.

Schmale, W., *Geschichte der Männlichkeit in Europa (1450–2000)*. Vienna: Böhlau, 2003.

Spode, H., 'Deutsch-österreichischer Tourismus und nationale Identität', in *Verfreundete Nachbarn: Deutschland-Österreich*, ed. Stiftung Haus der Geschichte der Bundesrepublik Deutschland. Bielefeld: Kerber, 2005.

Stadler, K. R., *Austria*. London: Benn, 1971.

Steiner, G., *Die Heimat-Macher: Kino in Österreich 1946–1966*. Vienna: Verlag für Gesellschaftskritik, 1987.

Tosh, J., 'Hegemonic Masculinity and the History of Gender', in Dudink, S. Hagemann, K. and Tosh, J. (eds), *Masculinities in Politics and War: Gendering Modern History*. Manchester: Manchester University Press, 2004.

Wagnleitner, R., *Coca-Colonisation und Kalter Krieg: Die Kulturmission der USA in Österreich nach dem Zweiten Weltkrieg*. Vienna: Verlag für Gesellschaftskritik, 1991.

Weber, F., 'Wiederaufbau zwischen Ost und West', in Sieder, R., Steinert H. and Tálos, E. (eds), *Österreich 1945–1995: Gesellschaft, Politik, Kultur*. Vienna: Verlag für Gesellschaftskritik, 1996.

# III

Gendered Memories:
Finland and Hungary

Tiina Kinnunen

## 5. Fallen Angels, Fallen Nation?
Representations of Patriotic Women and Images of a Nation in Finland's Post-War Memory

This chapter focuses on Finland after the Second World War, and reveals how personal, public and official memories of the war were – and still are – intertwined in complex, often conflicting (re)negotiations and how these memories inform personal and collective identities.[1]

The following discussion draws on the idea that the past is a contested and unstable field because interpretations of the past and identity politics are intimately interwoven and, simultaneously, power relations influence knowledge production. Furthermore, knowledge of the past includes various treatments and, thus, is not limited to interpretations produced in academic historiography.

During the post-war decades, the Finns had to cope with the legacy of three wars that the nation had recently fought as part of the European theatre of war: the Winter War (1939–1940) and the Continuation War (1941–1944) against the USSR; and the Lapland War (1944–1945) against Germany, formerly the ally in 1941–1944. Differing in duration and intensity, these wars were experienced in distinctive ways.[2] On the official state-level, the memory of the wars had to be silenced so that foreign relations with the USSR, the former enemy, could be established on a new positive basis. In contrast to the official silence, the experiences and interpretations of the period 1939–1945 were thus only articulated in private circles but in some ways memories were also dealt with in the public sphere. In both the private and public realms, evacuees from the lost areas, orphans, widows and war invalids were living reminders of the wars.[3] The loss of family members and homes was mourned privately and also dealt with in literature. For instance, the traumas of the Finnish Karelian evacuees – altogether over 400,000 people – who were resettled after their home regions were annexed to the USSR, were dealt with in fiction, documentary literature and memoirs even if the loss of the area could not be officially discussed as a political issue.[4]

Public war-related commemoration focused on the sacrifices, especially of Finland's fallen soldiers. Still today, the commemoration of fallen soldiers is integrated into some national celebrations.[5] Within the male culture of war remembrance, in particular, emphasis was laid on action: individual and collective deeds were recounted and retold. For instance, one widely read magazine, published between 1956–1986, was called *A People at War*

– Told by the Men (*Kansa taisteli – miehet kertovat*). In contrast to this public treatment of male experiences, women's memories were bypassed and their wartime work met with silence. It took until the late twentieth century to redress the balance.[6]

In this chapter, the focus is on the politics of public memory[7] regarding the Second World War in Finland. My particular interest centres on how images of the war have shifted since the 1950s, and upon the processes of inclusion, exclusion, marginalisation and reappraisal. Special attention is paid to gender and how it operates in memory production and related national identity politics. In terms of national identity, the Second World War was and still is of great significance for Finns. In fact, the years after the collapse of the USSR ushered in a new nationalistic wave of war commemoration.[8] In this respect, Finland's memory culture shows some similarities with elsewhere in Eastern Europe, even though dependence upon the USSR was never quite as total. In a similar way to Eastern Europe, the end of the Cold War opened up a space for some suppressed and marginalised national and personal memories.[9] The Finnish memory culture of the Second World War was – and to some degree still is – characterised by its national orientation, which presupposes a homogeneous experience of war among Finns and the specificity of Finland's history.[10] This national orientation excludes the globalisation of war memory and of the Holocaust, for example, which is only marginally remembered. One essential element in Finland's war memory is the tenacious interpretation that in 1941–1944 Finland cooperated with Germany in such a way that the country had nothing to do with German warfare on any other fronts.[11]

Due to my focus on public memory here, personal remembrance and the processes of passing on war memories to the next generation in private are not examined. Instead, the field of popular war history – where war memories are recounted in novels, films, popular history books, and memoirs with representations of wartime experience – is scrutinised. My study starts in the early 1950s when the concept of Finnishness had to be renegotiated after the defeat of the armed forces and the loss of human lives and material resources. The debate was strongly influenced by the novel 'The Unknown Soldier' (*Tuntematon sotilas*) by Väinö Linna, published in 1954. After discussing this novel, I will briefly analyse the discourse surrounding war that took place in the 1960s and 1970s when the political and cultural climate became more radical. This legacy reverberates in the film *Tuntematon sotilas*, which is based on Linna's novel and was made in 1985. This chapter then concludes with an examination of the film *Lupaus* (Promise) from 2005.

These three examples of popular history capture the crucial features of the connection between war and national identity in post-war Finland. In addition, they allow an examination over a time period of fifty years. These examples are also suited for an analysis of how the nation is (re) imagined through gender. In the mid-1980s, Joan Scott astutely pointed to gender as being constitutive in power relations.[12] In Finland, as in other belligerent countries, the Second World War disturbed traditional gender orders, and after the men's homecoming, gendered power relations had to be renegotiated. The impact of war on gender equality is ambiguous. On the one hand, male identity was reconstructed at the expense of women when, for example, men were favoured in the labor market. On the other, even if women in many cases were faced with a backlash, they could draw on the empowering experiences of coping when they were at war and thus the discrimination did not necessarily damage their new self-reliance.[13]

The reconstruction of the nation and national identity after the war can also be analysed from a gendered perspective without focusing on women's factual agency. Instead, emphasis can be laid on symbolic representations. Concerning Finland, Johanna Valenius points out the constitutive element of gender in nineteenth-century national imagery: the purity and innocence of the emerging post-war Finnish nation, still within the Russian sphere of influence, is embodied by the Finnish maiden.[14] Drawing on this discourse, I will analyse how the Finnish nation was imagined and the national identity reconstructed in representations of war in the post-war decades and how gender operates in these treatments. Emphasis will, in particular, be laid upon representations of the Lottas, members of a patriotic, paramilitary women's organisation called the *Lotta Svärd*, in the above mentioned popular history treatments (the novel and the film *Tuntematon sotilas* and the film *Lupaus*).

According to my interpretation, the Lottas represent the central elements of Finland's war memory and the various shifts in national imagery that took place over a period of fifty years. The film *Lupaus* deals with the history of the *Lotta Svärd*, whereas it is argued that the Lottas play a marginal role in the novel *Tuntematon sotilas* and the film based on it. I argue, however, that the Lotta figure in the novel and its respective film nevertheless hold a strong symbolic position.

## *Contextualisation*

In order to clarify my interpretation, this chapter is introduced with a contextualisation that outlines the history of Finland in the twentieth century, intertwined with the history of the *Lotta Svärd*. Although Finnish narratives of the Second World War were influenced by tensions growing out of political life after 1944, they were rooted in the pre-war political culture. The 1918 civil war and its legacy affected Finnish society well into the post-war period. Finland, as an autonomous part of the Russian Empire since 1809, gained independence in December 1917. Soon after this, political and social tensions escalated, resulting in a civil war fought between the socialist Red Guard and the bourgeois White Guard from January to May 1918. The Reds were defeated and, as a result of the war, Finland was politically and socially torn apart by a deep clash between the victors and the defeated.[15]

The *Lotta Svärd* was founded in 1921 to safeguard Finland's newly won independence by women who had supported the White Guard during the Civil War. The female paramilitary *Lotta Svärd* and the male military Civil Guard, which the Lottas supported, continued the legacy of the White Guard. Thus, the patriotism of the Lottas was politically biased and class-bound even though the organisation formally stood beyond party politics. Anti-socialism, combined with Russophobia and anti-Soviet sentiments, was rooted in the Lotta ideology and in the Lottas' world view. Their social background varied from agrarian to bourgeois but they were united by their commitment to the values of so-called White Finland – 'home, religion, and fatherland'.[16]

The Lotta ideology was not only formed by class but also by gender. The *Lotta Svärd* propagated a gendered notion of women's citizenship, defined by its leader Fanni Luukkonen as being a 'social mother's love'. One of its essential elements was moral strength, as embodying the purity of the nation was seen as the specific responsibility of all Lottas. The conception of moral strength was closely linked to Christianity. In addition to practical, strictly unarmed work for the Civil Guard, the Lottas were to strive, in a Lutheran spirit, towards their own moral strength and the moral improvement of their male counterparts.[17]

During the Second World War the *Lotta Svärd* grew so rapidly that in 1944 it had over 200,000 members out of a population of less than 4 million people. Although conscription was not extended to women, they were obliged to carry out work for the nation's defence; and the *Lotta Svärd* organised an important part of this work. Lottas worked voluntarily and unarmed near the battlefields and on the home front caring for both soldiers and civilians. During the Continuation War (1941–1944) the solidarity among Finns experienced during the Winter War (1939–1940) gradually broke down, and this led to political radicalisation in post-war Finland. During the late 1940s, the Communist Party enjoyed significant popularity among voters. In the 1930s, it had been banned because of the perceived threat it presented to Finland's independence. In 1944, however, it was legalised again as part of the armistice agreement.[18] According to this peace agreement, the Finnish government was also forced to dissolve and forbid a number of organisations that were declared by the Soviets as anti-Soviet. Among these organisations was the *Lotta Svärd*. It was thus dissolved in November 1944.

In the following, the history of post-war Finland is told from two different, conflicting perspectives. These two perspectives are associated with different interpretations of the war and thus create a different image of the same nation. These interpretations of the war will then be discussed in more detail later on. The first nationally loaded narrative of 1944 and post-war Finland seems today, after the collapse of the USSR and the end of the Cold War, to be the 'natural' one. In September 1944, exhausted after three years of war against the USSR, Finns had to meet with the bitter reality that they must surrender. Following the massive offensive of the Red Army in June 1944, the Finnish government was forced to sign an armistice agreement that entailed heavy obligations. However, Finland was not occupied and could sustain its political system based on western democratic values.

One of the obligations of the armistice agreement was for Finland to flush out its former German ally stationed in the north, which led to a new war, the Lapland War, that finally ended in April 1945. In October 1944, the Allied Control Commission, dominated by the Soviets, came to Finland in order to supervise the fulfilment of the agreement. Finland was not occupied by the USSR, but its independence was conceived by wide circles of the population as fragile. The efforts of the Finnish communists to seize power were also strengthened by the Soviet influence.[19]

Public opinion of the Lottas, whose wartime work was valued, was that they were victims of political circumstance. Although the dissolution of the organisation was heartbreaking for many Lottas, it was accepted because the decision was seen as forced. And yet the post-war representations in literature were generally insulting, especially in two novels: Väinö Linna's *The Unknown Soldier* (*Tuntematon sotilas*), 1954, and Paavo Rintala's *The Commando Lieutenant* (*Sissiluutnantti*), 1963. The previous conception of the Lottas' moral strength and sexual purity was turned upside down in these works, and the dominant public image of the Lottas actually became one of sexually loose women. Meanwhile the communist newspapers depicted a hard-core group of the *Lotta Svärd* as fascists and thus unpatriotic.[20]

But *Tuntematon sotilas* conveys not only the hardships that the nation had to cope with, but also the successes in the face of hardship: Finland was not occupied and thus the outcome of the war was a kind of victory, called a defensive victory. In addition, the nation looked forward, rebuilt the country, and created a welfare state. The narrative also underlines the success of the resettlement of the Finnish Karelian evacuees and in doing so, excludes the othering that these people often experienced. In the 1960s and 1970s we should bear in mind that Finnish society was shaken by a left-wing cultural turn. Peculiarly, the baby boomers channelled their revolt into demands for a rapprochement with Moscow. This realignment, defined abroad as 'Finlandization', poisoned Finnish political culture in many ways, one of which was the continual defamation of the *Lotta Svärd* during these years. It was only after the collapse of the USSR that the years of 1939–1944 could be framed in any other way.[21]

*Tuntematon sotilas* thus takes a left-wing perspective. It sustained its credibility until the collapse of communism even though it never replaced the former narrative as the dominant one. Finland, which fought as an ally with the Third Reich and thus on the wrong side, was defeated, but this implied a new beginning for the nation that had been misled by its right-wing leadership. The dissolution of the *Lotta Svärd* was welcomed because the organisation was a reminder of the fascist legacy of the pre-war decades. The peace agreement suggested the promise of a more democratic and socially just future, since the Communist Party, which had been forbidden in the 1930s, was tolerated once more. In addition, the outcome of the war forced Finland to adopt a new course vis-à-vis the USSR. The new foreign policy promoted a mutual understanding and political as well as economic cooperation and thus prepared the way for a positive rethinking of the former enemy in Finland. The Allied Control Commission was a guarantee of this new era.

From this left-wing narrative's perspective, the 1990s memory culture of war was seen in a different way: the collapse of the USSR ushered in a new wave of patriotism which resonated with the militarism and anti-Soviet sentiments of the 1920s and 1930s.

## Representations of Nation and Gender in Tuntematon sotilas

As a result of the patriotic turn of the 1990s, representations of the *Lotta Svärd* increased substantially. During the last twenty-five years, personal testimonies of the Lottas have been collected and published as authentic accounts of women's experiences in wartime. This activity was fuelled by women historians' interest in the agency and experiences of women, which was now extended to wartime. In this chapter, contrary to the trend of recent years, the personal memories of the Lottas related to their war efforts is not discussed. Neither do I address their strategies of coping with a post-war life in politically new circumstances. This is not because I deny the importance of giving voice to the Lottas themselves or, to use another metaphor, of making them visible; on the contrary, but I call for a critical analysis of their testimonies and how they are used in the national imagery in post-Cold War Finland. In this chapter, I discuss the contested Lotta image in the novel *Tuntematon sotilas* (1954) by Väinö Linna. In post-war Finland, this novel is the point of reference for much heated debate on the *Lotta Svärd* and simultaneously on the nation at war.

> Some time later he passed a solitary Lotta standing beside the road. Raili Kotilainen had not found a husband on the campaign, but she had made up for this by taking an extraordinary number of lovers. It seemed years since the day the adjutant had taken a snapshot of her beside a captured Russian trench mortar in the early days of the war. Then Raili had still been a glowing maiden, but like everybody else she had been worn out by war.[22]

This description, beside some others within the work by Väinö Linna (1920–1992), which included critical comments about officers and Finland's political establishment of the pre-war and war period, caused a scandal and ignited a literary war in the mid-1950s. Linna's novel chronicles the experiences of a fictional machine gun company in the Continuation War. The debate was also fuelled by Linna's way of depicting ordinary Finnish soldiers. They did not fit into the traditional nineteenth-century nationalistic ideal of humbleness. Neither did they resemble the valiant fighters in most other contemporary books. They were insubordinate towards their superiors, sometimes scared and unheroic, sometimes outright cowardly. Linna's critics were also upset by the colourful language used by the soldiers. Almost the full range of swear words was to be found in the pages of the book.

Even if the novel by Linna is fictional, it was based on actual experiences and persons, for example, on the author's wartime acquaintances. The Lotta figure can thus be seen coherently as one reflection of reality. Raili Kotilainen, the only Lotta introduced by name in the novel, presents the opposite of the ideal Lotta (the decent middle class or farming woman), who was to embody the purity of the Finnish nation. During the war, in particular, the ideals painted by the *Lotta Svärd* leadership did not always correspond with the actual reality and they had to concede that some of their number 'lapsed' in their morals.[23] And neither did those Lottas who defended their collective honour in the mid-1950s deny this, but instead, together with their male supporters, they argued for a fairer description that would value their practical work above all else.

The ideology and everyday work of the *Lotta Svärd* was strongly based on collective strength. Thus, many of the Lottas felt they had collectively been let down and betrayed by Linna's depiction. However, I argue that this representation and the debate surrounding it did not only deal with Lottas' moral or sexual behaviour. If they had, the debate would not have been carried out with such intensity. To understand the explosive meaning of the representation, it needs to be analysed from the perspective of national (and, thus, political) symbolism. Raili, who had once been a 'glowing maiden', but who at the end of the war is 'like everybody else [...] worn out', is an allegory of the Finland of the 1920s, 1930s, and wartime. This Finland came under political and cultural attack after the war; and the change in political climate left room for alternative visions of Finnishness. For example, those defeated in the Civil War were gradually given a voice again and gained access to the public memory. Väinö Linna can thus be viewed as being a contributor to this context of cultural renegotiation.[24]

Gendered representations of body and sexuality are inscribed with varying, often conflicting political meanings. For example, in pre-revolutionary France the campaign against Marie Antoinette took on sexualised tones. According to Lynn Hunt's reading, these sexualised images served political purposes. The sexual decline of a leading woman symbolised the decadence of the political order.[25] In addition, Elizabeth Heinemann suggests that in West Germany, after the war, the moral degradation of the nation was articulated by the image of a German woman 'fraternizer' selling herself to an American soldier for cigarettes or stockings.[26] In the national imagery, there are also several counterbalances to these allegories of decadence, however. For example, Guido Vitiello points out the female allegories of moral renewal in post-war West German films.[27]

In my reading of the novel *Tuntematon sotilas*, Raili's body and sexuality have been instrumentalised for political purposes. The Lotta can be seen, in one respect, as an embodiment of the 'Old Regime' with the politics and values of White Finland, and in another, as an allegory for the whole nation. The Lottas saw themselves ideologically as the moral fibre of White Finland – the victorious side of the civil war – and they were politically active in the 1920s and 1930s in disseminating the ideology of White Finland. The Lotta as a morally fallen woman thus symbolises the political and moral degradation of the political hegemony that had existed before the war. The political order of the 'Old Regime' was symbolically humiliated and its bankruptcy demonstratively displayed. The political figure of a morally fallen Lotta had already been disseminated back in the 1920s in the communist press, but because the Left was marginalised at this time the image never penetrated any further into the public sphere.[28]

From the perspective of the whole nation, the figure of Raili Kotilainen can also be seen as representing the maiden of Finland (*Suomen neito*) which was how the country had been portrayed in the public imagination since the nineteenth century. However, this time the innocence and purity of the maiden were clearly lost, as she had taken 'an extraordinary number of lovers'. Linna was clearly also describing 'everybody else', i.e., the whole nation as being 'worn out by war', but although the image of an exhausted nation might seem to imply a sense of victimhood, this was not Linna's aim. Instead, he called for a politically responsible leadership, rather than the previous one that had been intoxicated with the fantasy of a Greater Finland incorporating Eastern Karelia. The war had been a needless waste of energy and human life.

The general interpretation of Finland as being a victim of the great powers was, however, largely accepted in the post-war period. In the public imagination, the trials of 1945–1946 and the sentences pronounced against the leading politicians for taking Finland to war in 1941 were seen as unjust. The accused were clearly victims of a political performance contrived by the Soviets and their Finnish communist cronies – indeed this was the interpretation supported by the historian Arvi Korhonen. In 1948, he internationally introduced his thesis of wartime Finland being a piece of 'driftwood' between the superpowers. He later based his thesis on finer details, where the aim was conspicuously to absolve the wartime political leadership of any responsibility with regard to the decisions made concerning, for example, cooperation with the Third Reich. This German-Finnish cooperation was defined during the war and afterwards, by Korhonen among others, from the perspective of national interests and as being somehow separate from the European theatre of war.[29] In this narrative, Finland, the small nation, was the victim of Soviet aggression and cooperation with Germany (as 'brothers in arms') was the only way to survive. This narrative of political inevitability excludes any questions being asked, for example, about whether an ideological acceptance of nazism was also part of this cooperation.

From the novel it seems that Linna's ordinary soldiers were critical of their leaders' dealings with the Germans. For Linna, it was a fiction that Finland was fighting a separate war.[30] In his novel, the way these soldiers are depicted criticise the commonly accepted interpretation that the outcome of war was, after all, a 'defensive victory' for Finland. One of them, for example, when the fight was over, 'buried his face in his hands and for a long time stared at the ground without moving. [...] His eyes grew wet with tears, and his shoulders began to twitch. Then he shook with the bitter violent weeping of a grown man. Between sobs he murmured over and over, gritting his teeth: "We heard…they told us… Finland is dead… and snow… hides her grave…"'[31]

Linna's description of the chaotically retreating Finnish army noticeably contradicts the defensive victory narrative, and the fallen figure of Raili Kotilainen adds to this contradiction. In the following description of the Finnish defeat, the author throws light once more on the class antagonism that characterised Finnish society after the civil war of 1918 and surfaced again after the Second World War. The ordinary soldiers' attitude towards the Lotta woman is one of contempt, whereas the officer sympathises with her.

Now her bicycle had broken down, and she was feeling tired and sorry for herself. The passing men did not bother to disguise their contempt, and she was forced to endure their scurrilous shouts. Then, seeing Korpela, she decided to beg for his aid feeling that a man as old as he might show some fatherly sympathy. With an attempt at a smile she approached him.
– Please, I can't ride this and I'm so tired. Won't you take me on your cart?
A Lotta in the front lines! Her effect on Korpela was that of a rag to a bull.
– I've never yet carted dung on Sunday. And sure as hell I'm not going to start now.
As luck would have it, Lammio overheard his words. Bidding the girl climb on the next cart, he screamed at the Landsturm man.
– Private Korpela!
– I hear you.
– What did you tell that girl just now?
– I said what I said. I've got enough of a load, without carting whores.
– Look out, Korpela! You'll go too far. One more word and it'll go badly for you.
– Don't worry that head of yours, you goddamned popinjay.[32]

Väinö Linna's novel *Tuntematon sotilas* is paradoxical because it immediately became a bestseller, perhaps irrespective of its political message. Indeed, over time it has now become a classic of Finnish literature. For example, Arvi Korhonen, who authoritatively contributed to the aforementioned view of an innocent Finland at war, which Väinö Linna refuted, actually cherished Linna's novel. For him, it was simply a realistic description of ordinary soldiers. Besides Korhonen, there were other readers from the cultural and political establishment who also did not take too seriously Linna's – or his characters' – criticism of their leaders. Instead they focused on Linna's descriptions, which in the language of ordinary soldiers, gave a true account of their experiences. One explanation for the novel's enormous popularity might be that it was read as an exhibition of male companionship and heroism – even if the figures were not exactly full-blooded heroes.[33]

Although Finland was not occupied, which would have radically altered the ideal of Finnish masculinity, neither did the outcome of the war exactly proclaim any ability on the part of Finnish soldiers to protect their women and children. In addition, the extension of women's activities during the war in Finland was met with some ambivalence by the men. In post-war Finland, there were no explicit campaigns to move women back from their workplaces to the home, but their new-found agency and increased competence perhaps called for at least some symbolic treatment. 'A Lotta in the front line!' in the above description points out the challenge, and possibly even threat, that women (represented by the Lottas) posed for male identity, as traditionally one would consider the front-line in a war to be the most masculine of preserves.[34]

Sexualising Raili draws attention from her work contribution as a Lotta. There are examples of similar cultural mechanisms through which women's wartime agency was marginalised elsewhere in the world. In the post-war USSR, the scandalisation of former Red Army women soldiers meant their contributions were concealed. Meanwhile, in post-war Norway, the important work women had carried out in the resistance movement was marginalised by pointing out the 'private' nature of this work. In many cases, women acted inside or from within their homes, and by 'domesticating' women in this way, both sexually and in other respects, the gender order was, at least symbolically, reestablished.[35]

## Critical Views of Finland's Wars

*Tuntematon sotilas* was filmed for the first time in 1955. This film, directed by Edvin Laine, was a great success and has over time turned into a much-loved classic. Still today, it belongs to the regular TV programs shown on Finland's Independence Day, 6 December. In this film, the morally fallen Lotta figure does not appear. Väinö Linna accepted her removal at the director's bidding. This detail shows how the film adjusted the novel's original critical tone so that it could fit with a more nationalistic interpretation. Instead, the film lays more emphasis on the small nation's gallant struggle against its powerful neighbour, which is strengthened by Jean Sibelius' *Finlandia* being played throughout.[36]

The film and its warm reception reveals how nationalistic interpretations were gaining ground in the 1950s. At the same time the communist threat, which had caused political tremors in the late 1940s, seemed to be receding. As part of this development, the wartime leaders were restored to their former positions of honour. For example, in 1956 Risto Ryti, the wartime president who in 1946 had been sentenced to ten years imprisonment but was released in 1949 due to his weak physical condition, was awarded the title of Doctor *Honoris Causa*. In addition, the students of the University of Helsinki started a cult of Marshal Mannerheim, the wartime commander of the Finnish army.[37]

The end of the 1960s, however, ushered in a radical political change, with the Left gaining control of the government after two decades in opposition. In the course of this radicalisation, the war was critically reviewed, and this urge to rewrite history was shared by the president at that time – Urho Kekkonen. From the communist point of view, the war was interpreted as a fascist crusade with Finland being held responsible for the deterioration of Finnish-Soviet relations towards the end of the 1930s, which then justified the Soviet attacks. In the course of the 1980s, this communist interpretation became less prevalent, although even in the mid-1980s there was a heated debate about a statue commemorating the *Lotta Svärd* erected in Lappeenranta, a town near the Soviet border, in 1985. Because of Soviet concerns, it was not possible to put the statue – of a young Lotta about to leave home for an uncertain future in the service of her nation – in the capital. The Finnish communists rejected the statue because, from their point of view, it symbolised the association with Nazi Germany and the White heritage of Finland's past and, thus, posed a threat to the carefully nurtured Finnish-Soviet relations since the end of the war.[38]

But it was not just the Left who wanted to reinterpret the past, as from the 1960s onwards pacifist voices also challenged the nationalistic memory of war. From the pacifist point of view, war was part of the degradation of humanity. Paavo Rintala's *The Commando Lieutenant* (*Sissiluutnantti*), published in 1963, expressed this perspective by going beyond the factual historical context. In this novel, which also provoked a heated debate, the debasement of human nature is particularly evoked by a young Lotta who has frenzied sex with the male protagonist, a commando lieutenant; and to his dismay, she is sexually hyperactive, even aggressive. Rintala's critics read his novel in the national context related to the years 1939–1944 and for them it was sacrilegious.[39]

These more radical interpretations of the war by the younger generation, whether left-wing or pacifist, seemed to ignore the personal hardships that their parents had evidently gone through, along with their struggle to receive health care and other forms of compensation after the war, and it embittered veterans. Indeed, this turned into a reaction when the second film version of *Tuntematon sotilas* came out in 1985, directed by Rauni Molberg. This version echoed Linna's intentions more faithfully than the one from 1955. First of all, the actors were younger and could thus more credibly embody the experience of a young generation depicted in the novel. Secondly, the critical tone of Linna reverberated throughout the film. Raili Kotilainen featured in this film and, once again, her portrayal caused a reaction. In one sequence, for example she washes an officer's back while naked herself; and when, at the end of the war, the chaotically retreating Finnish army are shown, Raili is there begging for a ride as in the novel. She, a fallen angel, very vividly embodies a fallen nation.[40]

## *Pure Lottas and the Neo-patriotic Interpretations of Finland at War*

As a whole, the 1985 film galvanised the veteran organisations into becoming more active, and this activism, together with the decline of the USSR, resulted in a decision by the government to establish a national veterans' day to be held every 27 April. With the eventual collapse of the USSR, the discourse regarding how the war should be remembered intensified, but representations had already begun to multiply after the mid-1980s, as the fiftieth anniversary of the outbreak of the Winter War (1939) approached.

By the 1990s the nationalistic tone was no longer hidden. Increasingly, the imagery was becoming dominated by the elements that, in the 1940s, Väinö Linna had originally targeted. Finland was, in spite of its defeat in the Continuation War, seen as the defensive winner because the country had avoided occupation. The Winter War especially was depicted as a fight between David and Goliath. This nationalistic turn allowed little space for criticisms that would conflict with this image of a pure nation fighting for its very existence against the demands of its giant neighbour.

In the discourse of the 1990s, veterans were openly honoured as heroes.[41] Compared to previous decades, more attention was also paid to women's wartime work and experiences. This can be seen as the welcome result of an upsurge in women's history since the 1980s.[42] As a result, the Lottas were cast favourably in the limelight of the nation's memories. The 1990s discourse was characterised by the argument that people were forced to be silent about the war for many decades after. This interpretation, however, only partially corresponds to the reality. As already pointed out, it was only the official memory related to the Second World that had to be adjusted, according to the *Realpolitik*, and the the result was official silence, even though the public discourse regarding the Winter and Continuation War very much thrived, as can be seen from the successful sale of many books on the war period, mostly written from a male perspective.[43]

Most indicative of this nationalist turn was in 1991, when a celebration to commemorate the *Lotta Svärd* was organised at Finlandia House in Helsinki. This event was honoured by the highest representatives of the state, and a homage was paid to the Lottas' wartime efforts by the then prime minister, Esko Aho. It was the first time since 1944 that the Lottas received an official acknowledgement for their contribution, as after its dissolution, the *Lotta Svärd* had disappeared from the official national narrative. In the 1990s, other groups that had also been excluded from the official national narrative due to the war were also honoured – such as the politicians who, in 1946, were held responsible for wrongly taking Finland to war in 1941.

Since the early 1990s, as a result of this official attention, public representations of the *Lotta Svärd* have increased substantially. The focus of these depictions is on the Lottas' wartime work near the battlefields, with less attention paid to their work on the home front. The history is recounted via memoirs, novels, theatre plays, documentary and fictional films, radio programs, and popular history books. Many of these representations, created by the Lottas themselves or like-minded writers, are based on personal testimonies that are seen as true reflections of the past and 'how it really was'.

The image in these non-academic representations is overwhelmingly positive, often idealised, in tone; the Lottas are depicted as hard-working, morally decent, and non-political women.[44] These representations should be seen primarily as a counter-narrative to the earlier negative ones that focused on the Lottas' political or moral decadency. Positive counter-images were also created during the period from the 1950s until the 1980s but they never became dominant. From the point of view of former Lottas, these new representations are of importance since they reevaluate their work. To a certain extent, we can empathise with the Lottas' urge to revise the dominant, negative public image of the post-war decades; but we also have to recognise how the new dominant image draws on pre-war representations to such an extent that the ideals of the 1920s and 1930s reverberate to this day, excluding the multivocality of Lotta experiences and faults that are human but do not suit political ends.[45] Indeed, there are critical voices among former Lottas who do not identify themselves with the idealistic new narrative.

The film *Lupaus* from 2005, directed by Ilkka Vanne, is an excellent example of this old image of the Lotta revisited. It depicts the history of the *Lotta Svärd* from the perspective of individual experiences. The protagonists, sisters Anna and Mona, come from a well-off middle-class family. Following in her sister's footsteps, Mona joins the *Lotta Svärd* during the Winter War. The film depicts the sisters' fates through the Winter and Continuation War and ends after Finland, in 1956, was given back the Porkkala area that the USSR took in 1944. From the point of view of the Lottas' work, the film gives a true account of the various tasks they were responsible for. In general, they mended soldiers' clothing, assisted at military hospitals and catered for soldiers in canteens. They were also responsible for office work and communication services and they reported aircraft sightings. One of the most demanding tasks was to prepare fallen soldiers to be sent back home from the battlefields. In addition, Lottas cared for civilians such as invalids, orphans and refugees. Apart from the communication services, the reporting of aircraft sightings and the preparing of fallen soldiers, the film highlights two relatively unknown areas of Lotta work: they also worked as horse keepers and managing the operation of searchlights. For the latter task they were trained to use guns, which otherwise was strictly forbidden.

Thus, Mona and Anna and their colleagues are decent and hard-working women who fulfill the demands imposed on every single member of the *Lotta Svärd*. *Lupaus* can be seen as a half-documentary film that depicts the Lottas' work. By doing this, it responds to the post-war representations that sullied their valuable contribution. The film is based on a play *Rakas Lotta* (Dear Lotta) by playwright Inkeri Kilpinen. It debuted in 1989 and, thus, contributed to the new patriotic wave. Her outspoken aim was to reevaluate the work the Lottas carried out during the years of war. However, the play and the film can also be seen from a more broad-ranging national perspective of self-evaluation. In this reading, the rehabilitated fallen angels represent a rehabilitated nation and thus fulfil the need among a great many Finns to have a positive national self-image.

The film *Lupaus* is one example of how women are becoming more active and visible as producers of popular history, particularly women's history.[46] The script for the film was written by a female team and the film was financed by a foundation with the aim to preserve the legacy of the *Lotta Svärd* and to promote women's social activism. The most well-known treatments in previous decades, particularly the controversial ones, were all produced by men. On the other hand, Lottas were also supported in these controversies by men, like the director of the film *Tuntematon sotilas*, Edvin Laine. I would argue that the controversies were more based on a generational and class-related conflict than a gendered one. Young women in the 1960s and 1970s often did not identify with their mothers' generation and their patriotic experiences.[47]

In my reading of the film, Anna and Mona embody two essential elements of the dominant Finnish narrative about the Second World War. This narrative was created during or immediately after the war and was never excluded from the collective memory even if it was challenged, especially in the 1960s and 1970s. In the 1990s, this narrative became dominant again in public representations. Firstly, Finland is seen as a victim in the theatre of war, and secondly, the outcome of the war is seen as a defensive victory. The third element of the dominant narrative is the interpretation that Finland was fighting independently of Germany in the Continuation War.[48]

The theme of victimhood[49] is especially embodied by the Lotta called Anna. During the Winter War, she is responsible for reporting aircraft sightings. On shift, close to the front, she is captured by Soviet soldiers.

She, the innocent victim of outward circumstances, is missed by her family and fiancé. Miraculously, however, she is released and gets married in the summer of 1940. When the Continuation War breaks out, she joins the communication services, but when she realises she is pregnant, she returns home. She is unable to talk about her experience in captivity during the Winter War but finally, when she miscarries, it becomes clear that she must have been raped then too. This interpretation is strengthened by our knowledge of the sexual atrocities of the Red Army soldiers in Eastern Europe and Germany in 1944 and 1945. After somewhat recovering, Anna signs up for a course to manage searchlight operations. Whilst on shift, on the very last day of the war, she is killed by a Soviet spy.

Through Anna, the narrative of Finland as a victim that fights alone against the aggressor is retold. This narrative draws, among other representations, upon the writings of Arvi Korhonen, who in the post-war decades defended Finland's wartime decision-makers. According to him, Finland was thrown into the theatre of war against its own wishes. This interpretation is underlined when the Winter and Continuation Wars are both integrated into the narrative. On the one hand, from the perspective of reevaluating the Lottas' work, it is well-grounded that both wars are depicted because after the Winter War the range of work they did was indeed much greater. On the other hand, Finland's victimhood was less clear during the Continuation War. In 1939, Finland was attacked by the USSR after the negotiations failed concerning the territorial demands of the latter that were 'to guarantee the security of Leningrad'. It is clearly easier for many to see that Finland was being threatened at this point than to agree with the discourse from the 1960s and 1970s which argued that Finland was the aggressor.[50]

However, contrary to the Winter War, the Continuation War was not merely defensive. After crossing what, before 1939, had been the original border between Finland and the USSR, Finnish troops turned into occupiers.[51] The ensuing occupation of Eastern Karelia from 1941–1944, and especially the internment camps for those who were not Finnic, meant that Finland was clearly no longer the innocent victim; unless one counted this as legitimate retaliation – hence the significance of the Winter War in the patriotic narrative. The explanation was that extending Finland's territory would provide safe borders against the 'eternal enemy'. Interestingly today, however, the occupation of Eastern Karelia has conveniently faded from the patriotic narrative.[52] In a similar vein, the aforementioned Lapland War is a sensitive topic and is, perhaps not surprisingly, excluded from the story of Anna and Mona.

In the film's narrative, Mona and her sister Anna clearly do not embody any of the negative sides of Finland's wars, only the pure qualities that the *Lotta Svärd* encouraged in all their members.[53] The raping of Soviet Karelian women, the plundering of the cultural heritage of Eastern Karelia, or the active racism that occurred in the occupied areas is not brought up here.[54] Instead, the theme of defensive victory is embodied by Mona. During both wars, she works as a horse keeper, where she eventually meets her husband-to-be. These scenes, in which her moral strength and sexual purity are underlined, the film presents the *Lotta Svärd* ideals as a wartime reality. And at the end of the film, together with her daughter and husband, Mona is able to return to her childhood home in Porkkala, which was returned to Finland in 1956. She then gives her daughter the necklace she got from her sister – symbolic of passing on the national heritage of a free country from one generation to another, as women are often portrayed as the cultivators of national heritage in such narratives. The defensive victory of her return home is then finally underlined by the fluttering Finnish flag at the end of the film.

The concept of a defensive victory that was developed soon after the Continuation War – which Väinö Linna in his *Tuntematon sotilas* so clearly rejected – is based on the fact that in the summer of 1944 Finnish troops managed to stop the Soviet offensive from penetrating any further than the border conceded in 1940. This was psychologically important as after the wars the nation was in need of a new self-confidence and the concept of victory, albeit a defensive one, helped. In the 1990s, in line with the new patriotic wave, the reassurance of a defensive victory dominated the public discourse, and the collapse of the USSR added to this.[55]

To reposition the nation among the 'winners' like this also made it possible for Finns to finally distance themselves from their former wartime ally, Germany. In reality, Finland was both economically and militarily dependent on German help in the Continuation War, and without it the Red Army would probably not have been stopped in 1944. The post-war distance was necessary for at least two reasons. It is psychologically understandable that after the horrors of the Nazi regime became internationally known, the Finns rejected having anything to do with the tragedy. Despite cooperating with the Third Reich, Finland did not practice anti-Semitism, but there were Jews among the Soviet prisoners-of-war who were delivered to the Germans. In addition, eight Jewish refugees from Central Europe were delivered.[56] Politically, in order to have peaceful relations with the USSR after the war, the Finnish leadership had to bury or marginalise any memory of cooperating with the Third Reich. Although it was not totally excluded from the public's memory, the Finnish wars were framed in national terms that were separate from the German wars on other fronts. This interpretation was being used already during the Continuation War and it continues to reverberate to this day.[57] Indeed, in *Lupaus* this is expressed when Anna and Mona's father notes after the outbreak of the Continuation War that Germany is going to help Finland regain the areas that it had lost in 1940. By linking the cooperation with Germany simply to the losses incurred after the Winter War it can be seen in the pure and simple terms of the nation's good. Otherwise, the memory of Germany is excluded from the film. In reality, the *Lotta Svärd* cooperated quite fully with German women's organisations and some Lottas were even enthusiastic about Hitler's Germany. In Finland, several Lottas worked for the German troops, which were stationed mostly in Lapland.

*Conclusion*

Since the 1950s, the years 1939–1945 have not only been studied within the field of Finnish academic historiography, but also abundantly recounted in the country's popular history. In this chapter I have demonstrated how, in some of these treatments of Finland's cultural memory, the figure of a Lotta holds a strong symbolic position. Through this figure, conflicting interpretations of Finland's pre-war and wartime policies are expressed. In the original novel of *Tuntematon sotilas* (1954) and vividly so in the film version of it from 1985, the Lotta figure is used to convey a sense of national bankruptcy, because the conventional pre-war and wartime image of her being the morally strong symbol of a pure nation was turned upside down in these works – a fallen angel representing a fallen nation.

By the 1990s, after the collapse of the USSR, there was a new wave of patriotism and the fallen angel was resurrected. The rehabilitated figure of the Lotta also became inscribed with political meanings, whereby Finland was seen once more as being a victim of great powers that had to be played off against one another. Not only was the country between the rock of Nazi Germany and a Soviet hard place, but the war of 1941–1944 was seen as a national one, separate from other German interests.

During recent years, the memories associated with the Second World War in Finland, especially in historiography, but also to some extent popular history have changed. The globalisation of war memories calls for a deconstruction of the various national meta-narratives and opens up space for more complex narratives and transnational encounters. In Finnish memory culture there is the legacy from the radical period of the 1960s and 1970s, which, to a certain extent, can be revitalised. However, this discourse seems to have been biased in terms of gender sensitivity. Also the Holocaust has been largely excluded from Finland's history in spite of the alliance with Nazi Germany.

My discussion of how Lottas are represented in post-war Finland shows how, as figures, they were instrumental in serving different political purposes, and how these portrayals reveal national biases. These ageing ladies clearly deserve to tell their own stories, and I suggest we truly give them the space to share the *variety* of their experiences, as this might well be the key to finally deconstructing the national orientation of Finnish memory culture related to the Second World War.

## Notes

1 Comp. with R. N. Lebow, 'The Memory of Politics in Postwar Europe', in R. N. Lebow, W. Kansteiner and C. Fogu (eds), *The Politics of Memory in Postwar Europe* (Durham and London: Duke University Press, 2006), 28–39. Claudia Lenz, for instance, discusses these complex and conflicting processes with attention to gender in her article on the Norwegian memory culture related to the German occupation of 1940–1945. C. Lenz, 'Unbequeme Gedächtnis-Stützen: Künstlerische Interventionen in das Field der Erinnerungskultur in Norwegen', in H. Schmid and J. Krzymianowska (eds), *Politische Erinnerung: Geschichte und kollektive Identitität* (Würzburg: Königshausen & Neumann, 2007), 223–242.

2 For an overview of the subject, see O. Vehviläinen, *Finland in the Second World War: Between Germany and Russia* (Basingstoke: Palgrave, 2002); T. Kinnunen and V. Kivimäki (eds), *Finland in World War II. History, Memory, Interpretations* (Leiden: Brill, 2012).

3 Out of a Finnish population of 3.7 million in 1939, over 90,000 soldiers fell; 94,000 were disabled for life; 55,000 children were orphaned, and 30,000 women widowed.

4 For example, J. Loipponen, *Telling Absence: War Widows, Loss and Memory* (PhD Thesis, University of Edinburgh, 2009); O. Fingerroos, 'Karelia Issue: The Politics and Memory of Karelia in Finland', in Kinnunen and Kivimäki (eds), *Finland in World War II*, 490–508.

5 P. Raivo, 'This Is Where They Fought: Finnish War Landscapes as a National Heritage', in T. G. Ashplant, G. Dawson and M. Roper (eds), *The Politics of War Memory and Commemoration* (New Brunswick, NJ: Routledge, 2004), 145–164.

6 T. Kinnunen and M. Jokisipilä, 'Shifting Images of "Our Wars": Finnish Memory Culture of World War II', in Kinnunen and Kivimäki (eds), *Finland in World War II*, 435–482.

7 I use the concept of public memory in order to describe the arena of published representations of the past, such as novels, films, and drama. Private (individual) and public (collective) memories are interrelated, but public memory encompasses representations that are in some form published and 'achieve centrality within the public domain'. See T. G. Ashplant, G. Dawson and M. Dawson, 'The Politics of War Memory and Commemoration: Contexts, Structures and Dynamics', in Ashplant, Dawson and Roper (eds), *The Politics of War Memory and Commemoration*, 12. In this chapter, I focus on the field of public memory and historical culture. Hence the oral tradition (for example among family members) is excluded. In the German discourse, these different forms of memories are, for instance, subdivided into the categories *kommunikatives Gedächtnis* and *kulturelles Gedächtnis*. A. Assman, *Der lange Schatten der Vergangenheit: Erinnerungskultur und Geschichtspolitik* (Munich: C.H. Beck, 2006), 21–61.

8 For an introduction to Finnish memory culture related to the Second World War, see H. Rautkallio, 'Politik und Volk – die zwei Seiten Finnlands', in M. Flacke (ed.), *Mythen der Nationen: 1945 Arena der Erinnerungen* (Berlin: Deutsches Historisches Museum, 2004), 203–226, and especially Kinnunen and Jokisipilä, *Finland in World War II*, 435–482. For a more general account of Finnish historical culture and interpretations related to central events for Finland in the twentieth century, see S. Ahonen, *Historiaton sukupolvi? Historian vastaanotto ja historiallisen identiteetin rakentuminen 1990-luvun nuorison keskuudessa* (Helsinki: SHS, 1998); P. Torsti, *Suomalaiset ja historia* (Helsinki: Gaudeamus, 2012).

9 E. François, 'Die Erinnerung an den Zweiten Weltkrieg zwischen Nationalisierung und Universalisierung', in Flacke (ed.), *Mythen der Nationen*, 23–24.

10 The national orientation has characterised not only popular history but, until recently, also most of scientific studies. An introduction into Finnish historiography

on Finland and the Second World War, see V. Kivimäki, 'Three Wars and Their Epitaphs: The Finnish History and Scholarship of World War II', in Kinnunen and Kivimäki (eds), *Finland in World War II*, 1–46.

11 Compare with e.g., François, 'Erinnerung an den Zweiten Weltkrieg', 19–22. Concerning the memory of the Holocaust in Finland, see e.g., A. Holmila, 'Varities of Silence: Collective Memory of the Holocaust in Finland', in Kinnunen and Kivimäki (eds), *Finland in World War II*, 519–560; S. Muir and H. Worthen (eds), *Finlands Holocaust: Silences of History* (Basingstoke: Palgrave Macmillan, 2013).

12 J. W. Scott, 'Gender: A Useful Category of Historical Analysis', in J. W. Scott (ed.), *Gender and the Politics of History* (New York: Columbia University Press, 1986/1999), 28–50.

13 For an introduction to this complex subject, see P. Summerfield, *Reconstructing Women's Wartime Lives: Discourse and Subjectivity in Oral Histories of the Second World War* (Manchester: Manchester University Press, 1998), 2–8.

14 J. Valenius, *Undressing the Maid: Gender, Sexuality and the Body in the Construction of the Finnish Nation* (Helsinki: SKS, 2004). See also M. Urponen, 'Kansainvälisiä mutta siveellisiä? "Hymyilyjä olympiavieraillemme, mutta ei liian läheltä"', in T. Pulkkinen and A. Sorainen (eds), *Siveellisyydestä seksuaalisuuteen. Poliittisen käsitteen historia* (Helsinki: SKS, 2011), 278–299.

15 A. Heimo and U.-M. Peltonen, 'Memories and Histories, Public and Private: After the Finnish Civil War', in K. Hodgkin and S. Radstone (eds), *Contested Pasts: The Politics of Memory* (London: Routledge, 2003), 42–56. For a general introduction to the Finnish political history, see D. Kirby, *A Concise History of Finland* (Cambridge: Cambridge University Press, 2006); O. Jussila, S. Hentilä and J. Nevakivi, *From Grand Duchy to Modern State: A Political History of Finland since 1809* (London: Hurst, 1995).

16 K. Sulamaa, *Lotta Svärd – uskonto ja isänmaa* (Helsinki: Helsinki University Press, 1999); A. Latva-Äijö, *Lotta Svärdin synty: Järjestö, armeija, naiseus 1918–1928* (Helsinki: Otava, 2004).

17 Sulamaa, *Lotta Svärd*.

18 On 19 September 1944 the terms of the armistice were agreed. The peace treaty came into force in September 1947.

19 Kirby, *Concise History of Finland*, 235–242.

20 T. Kinnunen, 'Gender and Politics: Patriotic Women in Finnish Public Memory after 1944', in S. Paletschek and S. Schraut (eds), *The Gender of Memory: Cultures of Remembrance in Nineteenth- and Twentieth-Century Europe* (Frankfurt am Main: Campus, 2008), 190–195.

21 For example, V. Vares, 'Kuitenkin me voitimme! Uuspatrioottiset tulkinnat talvi- ja jatkosodasta suomalaisissa populääriesityksissä', in M. Jokisipilä (ed.), *Sodan totuudet: Yksi suomalainen vastaa 5.7 ryssää* (Helsinki: Ajatus, 2007), 184–185.

22 V. Linna, *The Unknown Soldier* (Helsinki: WSOY, 1954/2008; English trans. 1957), 282.

23 P. Olsson, *Myytti ja kokemus: Lotta Svärd sodassa* (Helsinki: Otava, 2005), 135–146.

24 In his trilogy, *Here Under the Northern Star* (*Täällä Pohjantähden alla*, 1959, 1960, 1962) Linna paints a picture of the history of Finland from the 1880s until the post-war period. He rewrote national history by including in it those defeated in the 1918 Civil War.

25 L. Hunt, 'The Many Bodies of Marie Antoinette: Political Pornography and the Problem of the Feminine in the French Revolution', in L. Hunt (ed.), *Eroticism and the Body Politic* (Baltimore, MD: Johns Hopkins University Press, 1991), 108–130.

26 E. Heinemann, 'The Hour of the Woman: Memories of Germany's "Crisis Years" and West German National Identity', in *American Historical Review* 101, no. 2 (1996), 354–395.

27 G. Vitiello, 'Deutschland, bleiche Mutter: Allegories of Germany in Post-Nazi Cinema', in Paletschek and Schraut (eds), *Gender of Memory*, 147–157.
28 T. Kinnunen, *Kiitetyt ja parjatut: Lotat sotien jälkeen* (Helsinki: Otava, 2006), 150–154.
29 T. Soikkanen, 'Objekti vai subjekti: Taistelu jatkosodan synnystä', in Jokisipilä (ed.), *Sodan totuudet*, 102–112.
30 Y. Varpio, *Väinö Linnan elämä* (Helsinki: Otava, 2006), 315–316.
31 Linna, *Unknown Soldier*, 310.
32 Linna, *Unknown Soldier*, 282.
33 Varpio, *Väinö Linnan elämä*, 333.
34 Kinnunen, *Kiitetyt ja parjatut*, 154–157. In reality, women were not on the front line.
35 For example, S. O. Rose, 'Women's Rights, Women's Obligations: Contradictions of Citizenship in World War II Britain', *European Review of History* 7, no. 2 (2000), 277–289; M. Liljeström, 'Kokemukset ja kontekstit historiankirjoituksessa', in M. Liljeström (ed.), *Feministinen tietäminen: Keskustelua metodologiasta* (Tampere: Vastapaino, 2004), 162–164; C. Lenz, 'Flintenweiber? Patriotische Mütter! Geschlechtergrenzgänge in den Repräsentationen des Widerstandes am Beispiel der deutschen Besatzung Norwegens 1940–1945', in G. Boukrif, C. Bruns and K. Heinsohn (eds), *Geschlechtergeschichte des Politischen: Entwürfe von Geschlecht und Gemeinschaft im 19. und 20. Jahrhundert* (Münster: LIT, 2002), 175–205.
36 *Finlandia* was composed by Sibelius during the russification period in the early twentieth century, and thus it conveys a strong symbolic meaning related to Finland's independence.
37 M. Turtola, *Risto Ryti: Elämä isänmaan puolesta* (Helsinki: Otava, 1994), 14; L. Kolbe, *Sivistyneistön rooli: Helsingin Yliopiston ylioppilaskunta 1944–1959* (Helsinki: Otava, 1993), 167–168.
38 Kinnunen, *Kiitetyt ja parjatut*, 162–166.
39 Kinnunen, *Kiitetyt ja parjatut*, 153–154.
40 Cf. Floya Anthias and Nira Yuval-Davis, who underline the symbolic meaning attached to women and their bodies in national and ethnical discourses: a pure woman embodies a pure nation or a pure ethnic group. Consequently, a morally fallen woman signifies a corrupt nation or ethnic group. F. Anthias and N. Yuval-Davis, 'Introduction', in N. Yuval-Davis and F. Anthias (eds), *Woman – Nation – State* (Basingstoke: Macmillan, 1989).
41 Ahonen, *Historiaton sukupolvi?*, 73–89.
42 For an introduction to women and gender in Finnish historiography, see M. Kaarninen and T. Kinnunen, 'Hardly women at all? Finnish historiography revisited', *Storia della Storiografia* 46 (2004), 152–170.
43 For example, Kinnunen and Jokisipilä, 'Shifting Images of "Our Wars"', 442–446.
44 Also in academic historiography the *Lotta Svärd* was dealt with, but in these treatments the focus was more strongly on the 1920s and 1930s.
45 P. Olsson, 'To Toil and to Survive: Wartime Memories of Finnish Women', *Human Affairs: A Postdisciplinary Journal for Humanities and Social Sciences* 12, no. 2 (2002), 127–138.
46 The work of the director Taru Mäkelä is one example of this trend. In 1995 a documentary film on the *Lotta Svärd* (*Lotat*) was shown and it was followed in 1999 by a fictional film on wartime nurses (*Pikkusisar*).
47 On the generational conflict of post Second World War Finland, see M. Tuominen, *'Me ollaan kaikki sotilaitten lapsia': Sukupolvihegemonian kriisi* (Helsinki: Otava, 1991).
48 For an analysis of the film *Lupaus*, see T. Kinnunen, 'Muista menneitten sukupolvien työ. Lupaus-elokuva lottahistorian kuvauksena', in T. Kinnunen and V. Kivimäki

(eds), *Ihminen sodassa. Suomalaisten kokemuksia talvi- ja jatkosodasta* (Helsinki: Minerva, 2006), 313–328.
49 The theme of victimhood has been characteristic of many national master narratives related to the Second World War. See e.g., H. Uhl, 'Vom Opfermythos zur Mitantwortungsthese: Die Transformationen des österreichischen Gedächtnisses', in Flacke (ed.), *Mythen der Nationen*, 481–508.
50 Soikkanen, 'Objekti vai subjekti', in Jokisipilä (ed.), *Sodan totuudet*, 105–114.
51 Kirby, *Concise History of Finland*, 224–226.
52 O. Silvennoinen, 'Kumpujen yöhön eli kuinka historiallinen muisti vääristyi', in J. Kirves and S. Näre (eds), *Luvattu maa: Suur-Suomen unelma ja unohdus* (Helsinki: Johnny Kniga, 2014).
53 The narrative of purity has been characteristic of many national master narratives related to the Second World War. In Eastern Europe, the more sinister side, especially the treatment of Jews, have only recently penetrated the public sphere. See e.g., K. Ruchniewicz, 'Polen: Abschied von der Martyrologie', in Schmid and Krzymianowska (eds), *Politische Erinnerung*, 207–210. Involvement in the Holocaust has been a difficult issue also in Western Europe – see e.g., H. Rousso, 'Vom nationalen Vergessen zur kolletiven Wiedergutmachung', in Flacke (ed.), *Mythen der Nationen*, 242–243.
54 Negative aspects of Finnish warfare have been dealt with in research, but the knowledge only gradually penetrates the larger field of historical culture, and thus the knowledge of non-academic citizens. One example of the treatments of these aspects is an article by Ville Kivimäki, in which he discusses the sexual violence of Finnish soldiers against Soviet women soldiers. V. Kivimäki, 'Ryvetetty enkeli: Suomalaissotilaiden neuvostoliittolaisiin naissotilaisiin kohdistama seksuaalinen väkivalta ja sodan sukupuolittunut mielenmaisema', *Naistutkimus / Kvinnoforskning* 20, no. 3 (2007), 19–33. See also the work of Oula Silvennoinen, e.g., 'Limits of Intentionality: Soviet Prisoners-of-War and Civilian Internees in Finnish Custody', in Kinnunen and Kivimäki (eds), *Finland in World War II*, 355–394.
55 Ahonen, *Historiaton sukupolvi?*, 74–79.
56 Rautkallio, 'Politik und Volk', 214–218; O. Silvennoinen, *Salaiset aseveljet: Suomen ja Saksan turvallisuusyhteistyö 1933-1944* (Helsinki: Otava, 2008).
57 M. Jokisipilä, 'Kappas vaan, saksalaisia! Keskustelu Suomen jatkosodan 1941–1944 luonteesta', in Jokisipilä (ed.), *Sodan totuudet*, 153–181.

# Sources and Bibliography

*Printed sources*

Linna, V., *The Unknown Soldier*. Helsinki: WSOY, 1954/2008 (English trans. 1957).
Linna, V., *Täällä Pohjantähden alla*, 1959, 1960, 1962 (*Here Under the Northern Star*).

*Literature*

Ahonen, S., *Historiaton sukupolvi? Historian vastaanotto ja historiallisen identiteetin rakentuminen 1990-luvun nuorison keskuudessa*. Helsinki: SHS, 1998.
Anthias, F. and Yuval-Davis, N., 'Introduction', in N. Yuval-Davis and F. Anthias (eds), *Woman – Nation – State*. Basingstoke: Macmillan, 1989.

Ashplant, T. G., Dawson, G. and Roper, M., 'The Politics of War Memory and Commemoration: Contexts, Structures and Dynamics', in Ashplant, Dawson and Roper (eds), *The Politics of War Memory and Commemoration*. New Brunswick, NJ: Routledge, 2004.

Assman, A., *Der lange Schatten der Vergangenheit: Erinnerungskultur und Geschichtspolitik*. Munich: C.H. Beck, 2006.

Fingerroos, O., 'Karelia Issue: The Politics and Memory of Karelia in Finland', in Kinnunen and Kivimäki (eds), *Finland in World War II. History, Memory, Interpretations*. Leiden: Brill, 2012.

François, E., 'Die Erinnerung an den Zweiten Weltkrieg zwischen Nationalisierung und Universalisierung', in Flacke (ed.), *Mythen der Nationen: 1945 Arena der Erinnerungen*. Berlin: Deutsches Historisches Museum, 2004.

Heimo, A. and Peltonen, U.-M., 'Memories and Histories, Public and Private: After the Finnish Civil War', in Hodgkin, K. and Radstone, S. (eds), *Contested Pasts: The Politics of Memory*. London: Routledge, 2003.

Heinemann, E., 'The Hour of the Woman: Memories of Germany's "Crisis Years" and West German National Identity', in *American Historical Review* 101, no. 2 (1996).

Holmila, A., 'Varities of Silence: Collective Memory of the Holocaust in Finland', in Kinnunen and Kivimäki (eds), *Finland in World War II. History, Memory, Interpretations*. Leiden: Brill, 2012.

Hunt, L., 'The Many Bodies of Marie Antoinette: Political Pornography and the Problem of the Feminine in the French Revolution', in Hunt, L. (ed.), *Eroticism and the Body Politic*. Baltimore, MD: Johns Hopkins University Press, 1991.

Jokisipilä, M., 'Kappas vaan, saksalaisia! Keskustelu Suomen jatkosodan 1941–1944 luonteesta', in Jokisipilä, M. (ed.), *Sodan totuudet: Yksi suomalainen vastaa 5.7 ryssää*. Helsinki: Ajatus, 2007.

Jussila, O., Hentilä, S. and Nevakivi, J., *From Grand Duchy to Modern State: A Political History of Finland since 1809*. London: Hurst, 1995.

Kaarninen, M. and Kinnunen, T., 'Hardly women at all? Finnish historiography revisited', *Storia della Storiografia* 46 (2004).

Kinnunen, T., *Kiitetyt ja parjatut: Lotat sotien jälkeen*. Helsinki: Otava, 2006.

Kinnunen, T., 'Muista menneitten sukupolvien työ. Lupaus-elokuva lottahistorian kuvauksena', in Kinnunen T. and Kivimäki, V. (eds), *Ihminen sodassa. Suomalaisten kokemuksia talvi- ja jatkosodasta*. Helsinki: Minerva, 2006.

Kinnunen, T., 'Gender and Politics: Patriotic Women in Finnish Public Memory after 1944', in Paletschek, S. and Schraut, S. (eds), *The Gender of Memory: Cultures of Remembrance in Nineteenth- and Twentieth-Century Europe*. Frankfurt am Main: Campus, 2008.

Kinnunen, T. and Jokisipilä, M., 'Shifting Images of "Our Wars": Finnish Memory Culture of World War II', in Kinnunen and Kivimäki (eds), *Finland in World War II. History, Memory, Interpretations*. Leiden: Brill, 2012.

Kinnunen, T. and Kivimäki, V. (eds), *Finland in World War II. History, Memory, Interpretations*. Leiden: Brill, 2012.

Kirby, D., *A Concise History of Finland*. Cambridge: Cambridge University Press, 2006.

Kivimäki, V., 'Ryvetetty enkeli: Suomalaissotilaiden neuvostoliittolaisiin naissotilaisiin kohdistama seksuaalinen väkivalta ja sodan sukupuolittunut mielenmaisema', *Naistutkimus / Kvinnoforskning* 20, no. 3 (2007).

Kivimäki, V., 'Three Wars and Their Epitaphs: The Finnish History and Scholarship of World War II', in Kinnunen and Kivimäki (eds), *Finland in World War II. History, Memory, Interpretations*. Leiden: Brill, 2012.

Kolbe, L., *Sivistyneistön rooli: Helsingin Yliopiston ylioppilaskunta 1944–1959*. Helsinki: Otava, 1993.

Latva-Äijö, A., *Lotta Svärdin synty: Järjestö, armeija, naiseus 1918–1928*. Helsinki: Otava, 2004.

Lebow, R. N., 'The Memory of Politics in Postwar Europe', in Lebow, R. N., Kansteiner, W. and Fogu, C. (eds), *The Politics of Memory in Postwar Europe*. Durham and London: Duke University Press, 2006.

Lenz, C., 'Flintenweiber? Patriotische Mütter! Geschlechtergrenzgänge in den Repräsentationen des Widerstandes am Beispiel der deutschen Besatzung Norwegens 1940–1945', in Boukrif, G., Bruns. C. and Heinsohn, K. (eds), *Geschlechtergeschichte des Politischen: Entwürfe von Geschlecht und Gemeinschaft im 19. und 20. Jahrhundert*. Münster: LIT, 2002.

Lenz, C., 'Unbequeme Gedächtnis-Stützen: Künstlerische Interventionen in das Field der Erinnerungskultur in Norwegen', in Schmid, H. and Krzymianowska, J. (eds), *Politische Erinnerung: Geschichte und kollektive Identitität*. Würzburg: Königshausen & Neumann, 2007.

Liljeström, M., 'Kokemukset ja kontekstit historiankirjoituksessa', in Liljeström, M. (ed.), *Feministinen tietäminen: Keskustelua metodologiasta*. Tampere: Vastapaino, 2004.

Loipponen, J., *Telling Absence: War Widows, Loss and Memory* (PhD Thesis, University of Edinburgh, 2009).

Muir, S. and Worthen, H. (eds), *Finlands Holocaust: Silences of History*. Basingstoke: Palgrave Macmillan, 2013.

Olsson, P., 'To Toil and to Survive: Wartime Memories of Finnish Women', *Human Affairs: A Postdisciplinary Journal for Humanities and Social Sciences* 12, no. 2 (2002).

Olsson, P., *Myytti ja kokemus: Lotta Svärd sodassa*. Helsinki: Otava, 2005.

Raivo, P., 'This Is Where They Fought: Finnish War Landscapes as a National Heritage', in Ashplant, T. G., Dawson, G. and Roper, M. (eds), *The Politics of War Memory and Commemoration*. New Brunswick, NJ: Routledge, 2004.

Rautkallio, H., 'Politik und Volk – die zwei Seiten Finnlands', in Flacke, M. (ed.), *Mythen der Nationen: 1945 Arena der Erinnerungen*. Berlin: Deutsches Historisches Museum, 2004.

Rose, S. O., 'Women's Rights, Women's Obligations: Contradictions of Citizenship in World War II Britain', *European Review of History* 7, no. 2 (2000).

Rousso, H., 'Vom nationalen Vergessen zur kolletiven Wiedergutmachung', in Flacke (ed.), *Mythen der Nationen: 1945 Arena der Erinnerungen*. Berlin: Deutsches Historisches Museum, 2004.

Ruchniewicz, K., 'Polen: Abschied von der Martyrologie', in Schmid, H. and Krzymianowska, J. (eds), *Politische Erinnerung: Geschichte und kollektive Identitität*. Würzburg: Königshausen & Neumann, 2007.

Scott, J. W., 'Gender: A Useful Category of Historical Analysis', in Scott, J. W. (ed.), *Gender and the Politics of History*. New York: Columbia University Press, 1986/1999.

Silvennoinen, O., *Salaiset aseveljet: Suomen ja Saksan turvallisuusyhteistyö 1933–1944*. Helsinki: Otava, 2008.

Silvennoinen, O., 'Limits of Intentionality: Soviet Prisoners-of-War and Civilian Internees in Finnish Custody', in Kinnunen and Kivimäki (eds), *Finland in World War II. History, Memory, Interpretations*. Leiden: Brill, 2012.

Silvennoinen, O., 'Kumpujen yöhön eli kuinka historiallinen muisti vääristyi', in Kirves, J. and Näre, S. (eds), *Luvattu maa: Suur-Suomen unelma ja unohdus*. Helsinki: Johnny Kniga, 2014.

Soikkanen, T., 'Objekti vai subjekti: Taistelu jatkosodan synnystä', in Jokisipilä, M. (ed.), *Sodan totuudet: Yksi suomalainen vastaa 5.7 ryssää*. Helsinki: Ajatus, 2007.

Sulamaa, K., *Lotta Svärd – uskonto ja isänmaa*. Helsinki: Helsinki University Press, 1999.

Summerfield, P., *Reconstructing Women's Wartime Lives: Discourse and Subjectivity in Oral Histories of the Second World War*. Manchester: Manchester University Press, 1998.

Torsti, P., *Suomalaiset ja historia*. Helsinki: Gaudeamus, 2012.

Tuominen, M., *'Me ollaan kaikki sotilaitten lapsia': Sukupolvihegemonian kriisi*. Helsinki: Otava, 1991.

Turtola, M., *Risto Ryti: Elämä isänmaan puolesta*. Helsinki: Otava, 1994.

Uhl, H., 'Vom Opfermythos zur Mitantwortungsthese: Die Transformationen des österreichischen Gedächtnisses', in Flacke (ed.), *Mythen der Nationen: 1945 Arena der Erinnerungen*. Berlin: Deutsches Historisches Museum, 2004.

Urponen, M., 'Kansainvälisiä mutta siveellisiä? "Hymyilyjä olympiavieraillemme, mutta ei liian läheltä"', in Pulkkinen, T. and Sorainen, A. (eds), *Siveellisyydestä seksuaalisuuteen. Poliittisen käsitteen historia*. Helsinki: SKS, 2011.

Valenius, J., *Undressing the Maid: Gender, Sexuality and the Body in the Construction of the Finnish Nation*. Helsinki: SKS, 2004.

Vares, V., 'Kuitenkin me voitimme! Uuspatrioottiset tulkinnat talvi- ja jatkosodasta suomalaisissa populääriesityksissä', in Jokisipilä, M. (ed.), *Sodan totuudet: Yksi suomalainen vastaa 5.7 ryssää*. Helsinki: Ajatus, 2007.

Varpio, Y., *Väinö Linnan elämä*. Helsinki: Otava, 2006.

Vehviläinen, O., *Finland in the Second World War: Between Germany and Russia*. Basingstoke: Palgrave, 2002.

Vitiello, G., 'Deutschland, bleiche Mutter: Allegories of Germany in Post-Nazi Cinema', in Paletschek, S. and Schraut, S. (eds), *The Gender of Memory: Cultures of Remembrance in Nineteenth- and Twentieth-Century Europe*. Frankfurt am Main: Campus, 2008.

Andrea Pető
http://orcid.org/0000-0002-7525-2582

# Silencing and Unsilencing Sexual Violence in Hungary[1]

Researching wartime rape is exceptionally difficult because the phenomenon is surrounded by a 'conspiracy of silence'.[2] The silence has also been reinforced by practically all those involved, whether they be the perpetrators, rape victims, or witnesses as they all share the interest to keep what has happened silenced. The wartime rape cases which we hear about should be handled with some methodological precaution. In recent mainstream literature the definition of rape has also noticeably shifted from being an exceptional occurrence, solely linked to the deviant attitude of an individual perpetrator. Recent research in Hungary has unleashed a public discourse that sometimes oversimplifies the analysis of rape, by explaining it away as a weapon of war. This treats rape as if it were a weapon in the hand of military leaders or politicians, and wielded to punish particular groups of people on purpose. This can be described as an 'intentionalist' interpretation, which ethnicises rape and associates it with a particular group of people. However, a 'structuralist' interpretation considers rape to be a foundational tool in the power relationship between genders and defined by patriarchy.

In Hungary, the publication in 2013 of a collected volume of archival sources edited by Tamás Krausz and Éva Varga, documented rapes committed by the occupying Hungarian army in the Soviet Union.[3] Despite its numerous methodological issues this volume nevertheless sheds light on how Hungarian soldiers implicated themselves in the culture of rape as occupiers. No matter how flawed, this is how research into this subject must begin, by breaking the conspiracy of silence and talking about wartime rape, it is now acknowledged as a valid topic of research. This is then be followed up by finer more detailed work, which should be professionally established, methodologically impeccable, and in accordance with research ethics.

Rapes committed by Soviet soldiers have remained unpunished. To date, we have little knowledge about the administrative mechanisms of justice within the Red Army, or even whether such mechanisms existed at all. Both these factors strengthened and perpetuated a culture of violence. For many years, I have tried to get permission to research Russian military sources to find out more about this, but without success. I will therefore analyse accessible online sources after first detailing the methodology. This analysis is critical because rapes committed by Soviet soldiers are presently becoming key tropes of Second World War historiographical research in Hungary, but if rape committed by Soviet soldiers is subject to analysis while rape committed by the Hungarian army's soldiers is not, then an intentionalist discourse of simplified victimhood will be produced, according to which 'the Russians raped Hungarian women'. In this chapter, based on a comparison of the rapes committed by German and Soviet troops in Hungary, I therefore aim to redress this balance. We need to emphasise early on that the topic of rape typically caters to certain simplifications such as this, where the woman's individual tragedy is supposed to represent the whole nation. Soviet soldiers raped Hungarian women, and Japanese soldiers raped Korean women, but this obscures other structural power relations inherent in the phenomenon. The intentionalist discourse can thus be misleading in two ways. First, it confounds rape's structural essence with any other kind of violence experienced in war, all the while enabling a one-sided collective remembrance that excludes all others. Second, the intentionalist discourse does not create a social space within which rape victims are given the chance to process the violent acts they suffered with dignity and so that they can have a better vision for the future.

In this chapter I am therefore going to undertake three tasks:

1. I will review the questions that emerge when we compare rapes committed by German and Soviet troops respectively, ignoring in this instance the equally cruel acts of the Hungarian troops when they were an occupation force. I will then examine how a simplified discourse is produced to explain the overall phenomenon.
2. I argue that the intentionalist politics of remembrance – based on victimhood and monopolising the historical truth – in the long run hinders the establishment of a critical view of history. I also suggest ways in which this conflict between intentionalist and structuralist interpretations be resolved.
3. I will examine whether the Russian sources available online might nuance the image of the 'raping Russian horde.' I do this to clarify the link between a lack of visual representation of rapes committed by Soviet soldiers, and the possibility of consequently reinterpreting the frame of remembrance. Again, I use this to argue for a reconciliation of intentionalist and structuralist approaches.

## Comparison

The German army was stationed in Hungary for only a short while. The two countries were officially allies, and so when German troops entered the territory on 19 March 1944, they were met with hardly any resistance. These two factors: the brevity of their stay, and that the fact the countries were allies defined how rapes committed by German soldiers in Hungary were remembered. If we rely on collective memories, including two letters I received after my lectures, then it appears that German soldiers did not rape Hungarian women; in direct contrast to Soviet soldiers, whom 'everyone knows' committed acts of mass rape against Hungarians, Jewish women in hiding, Germans, Poles, Slovaks, and so on. Although the Red Army eventually won bloody battles to finally defeat German and Hungarian troops that supported lethal fascist ideologies, they nevertheless lost the political battle of remembrance from the moment the country was 'liberated'.

If we are trying to analyse the rapes committed by German and Soviet soldiers more closely, the first question is: what kinds of sources are accessible? This accessibility has defined how the discourse has developed, and how rape is remembered. As noted above, the phenomenon is surrounded by a conspiracy of silence. When discussed, it is done within a restricted vocabulary and tight narrative framework, because of the multiple taboos attached to it. This posits a specific methodological and theoretical challenge for historians, and raises moral questions for researchers of gender. In my conclusion I will therefore argue the possibilities for an alternative discourse.

In Hungary the atrocities committed by Soviet soldiers against civilians were for a long time a taboo subject. Because of the wartime circumstances, only a small amount of written documents recorded the deeds of Soviet soldiers in Hungarian territories. Indirect sources had to be consulted as well.[4] For the longest time, and for manifold reasons, no one spoke publicly about the rapes committed against women – neither the victims themselves, the bureaucrats, the police, nor the perpetrators. Related documents are scarce and often incidental to something else. In principle, one could rely on military, medical, criminal, administrative, and foreign affairs sources for a comparative overview of rape cases. However, in Russia, access to the Red Army's relevant military and medical material is denied. Pioneering, critical and innovative archival research has just recently started.[5] In the Hungarian National Archives, among the era's documents related to foreign affairs, one can find individual letters of complaint from various parts of the country detailing atrocities against civilians. Hungarian administrative reports, and the *főispán*[6] reports made to the state, also mention some isolated cases, but these would seem to be insufficient to get an idea of the bigger picture. On those territories, which were on the frontline, and therefore first occupied by one army, and then another, the returning 'Arrow Cross'[7] men reported on the brutality of Soviet forces stationed previously in the area. The reports circulated, but the source value of these documents preserved among Arrow Cross files is low. Likewise, one should treat with caution the verdicts of the People's Courts, which charged people for standing up to the looting and pillaging of Soviet troops with the same crime as civilians who killed or informed on Jews during the war. The files of the chief medical officer and hospitals preserved at the Budapest Municipal Archive provide an incomplete view of the consequences of rape such as sexually transmitted diseases or abortion statistics. Meanwhile, orphanage and adoption files are not accessible due to privacy protection. Ecclesiastical sources, such as the materials kept at the Primate's Archives in Esztergom, testify that priests and pastors were complaining about the dire situation they had encountered when having to advise religious women who had been raped, impregnated, and needed an abortion.

Literary and cinematographic interpretations of the rapes committed by Soviet soldiers should also be mentioned. Alaine Polcz wrote about her own personal experiences in *One Woman in the War: Hungary 1944–1945* (*Asszony a fronton*, 1991), and György Konrád offered a fictional adaptation in his novel *A cinkos* (*The Loser*, 1982). These works juxtaposed the authenticity of personal experiences with what was then the 'official' history. Sándor Sára did this with his film *The Prosecution* (*A vád* – 1996). A more recent publication is Judit Kováts's fictional documentary *Denied* (*Megtagadva* – 2012), while Fruzsina Skrabski's *Silenced Shame* (*Elhallgatott gyalázat* – 2013) introduced historical facts to a wider audience, generating a significant public debate. These latest interpretations prove that fictional approaches and quasi-documentary novels using oral histories, interviews and contemporary interpretations as their primary sources are perhaps the most plausible means of narrating this historical fact. Importantly, speakers of these quasi-documentaries are witnesses – never the victims – of the atrocities. Hence we must bear in mind that they are not the ones who actually felt and experienced the rape. Because of the time lag too, there is an ever-slimmer chance that rape survivors will speak out. However, more and more people will discuss what they think happened based on what they saw or heard; or they will voice what they think they are supposed to remember and say. Remembrance is always the result of a ceaseless negotiation between past, present, and future.

The comparison of the Wehrmacht and Red Army posits the dilemma of *jus in bello* (justice in war) versus *jus ad bellum* (justice of war), as hypothesised by Michael Walzer.[8] The Wehrmacht was the executive force of the Nazi regime, which rode on the myth that they had nothing to do with civilian brutality, killing only on the battlefields consistent with successfully maintained self-imposed military rules. If we read memoirs from the Second World War, the occupying German soldiers are remembered as always acting in as disciplined and regulated manner as their their impeccably ironed uniforms. It was not until the 1998 Wehrmacht exhibition, that this military professionalism and stainless reputation was thrown into doubt.[9]

The statement of General Field Marshal Erich von Manstein, as well as those of other military leaders, reinforced the idea that German soldiers committed no rape, and that if they did, it was a singular occurrence which received punishment as an example to others. These statements remained unquestioned for decades on the western side of the Iron Curtain. Meanwhile, in the Soviet Union, despite the official policy of gender equality, a system of hegemonic masculinity remained. In the anti-fascist discourse, rape was represented as part and parcel of the Nazi (and thus also Hungarian) atrocities of occupation against civilians. The victim's position was thus morally fortified within an internationalist and anti-fascist framework, but not in a violent power-based military framework, as this would have challenged the hegemonic patriarchy.

But were Manstein and others (especially military historians) right when they claimed that German soldiers committed no rape, except for individual punishable cases? Most recently, research by Regina Mühlhäuser, Monika Flaschka, Birgit Beck and others scrutinised the so-called Manstein myth of an exemplary and disciplined Nazi German army.[10] Based on archival materials and memoirs, they also investigated how this myth of the well-disciplined soldier was in fact probably more to do with the strict sanctions against 'racial defilement' (*Rassenschande*), which according to Nazi ideology was a law that forbade sexual relations between 'Aryans' and 'non-Aryans'. Their research examined the veracity of these claims that German soldiers did not have any sexual relations with Slavic and Jewish women. On the Eastern Front approximately 10 million uniformed German men fought and worked. Military regulations were issued enforcing article 5a of the Wartime Penal Code on rape (*Notzucht*) and article 2 on racial defilement (*Blutschutzgesetz*), but in practice these laws were logistically ineffective. Nevertheless, remembrance of the German army is marked by the denial of sexual violence, similarly to the sporadic yet ever-present Hungarian myth, which equally denies that rape was committed by the Hungarian army when occupying Soviet territory. For the German military leaders, maintaining racial purity laws as well as military order and discipline were clearly of the utmost importance. Violating these compromised the Nazi ideal of masculinity and sex for reproductive purposes only; indeed, as Annette Timm puts it, 'male sexuality was not a source of individual pleasure, but a manifestation of the nation's military power'.[11]

Women who were raped by German soldiers on the Eastern Front received no legal compensation, whereas on the Western Front effective local administration permitted women to report offences. In the East there was mass rape despite every form of military discipline, regulation, and law, so such a right was unimaginable, with the exception of Hungary. Following German occupation from 19 March 1944, the Hungarian administration remained in place (paradoxically to facilitate the mass deportation of Hungarian Jews), but this cooperation between the Hungarian administration and German occupying forces also had the side effect of (on paper at least) protecting Hungarian women from mass rape. However, many personal accounts show that the Hungarian state's very own uniformed representatives raped Hungarian women citizens, particularly of Jewish origin.[12]

It is important to emphasise that the German military narrative portraying soldiers acting in accordance with the laws and orders of their superiors was never seriously disputed by the Allied powers. Although the Soviets submitted supplementary testimonies in the Nuremberg Trials, about rape committed by German, Hungarian, and other occupying soldiers on Soviet territory, these did not make it into the main narrative mostly because Soviet troops had also committed mass rape as an occupying ('liberating') force. I use the term 'mass' because – as I argued in a 1999 study in the *Történelmi Szemle* – calculating numbers is both scientifically as well as morally problematic. For example, if a woman is raped multiple times in one night, should each rape be counted or is that level of 'precision' missing the point and making things worse?[13] This is exactly why Skrabski's abovementioned documentary received much justified criticism, because in it the numbers of Hungarian rape cases shift between 80,000 and 800,000, without any reflection on what effect these calculations may have on those who were raped, nor the significance of the historical and factual impossibility of ascertaining the actual number of rapes with any certainty.

## Intentionalist politics of remembrance and its consequences

An intentionalist politics of remembrance, founded on victimhood and on a monopolisation of historical truth, in the long run hinders the establishment of a critical view of history. The history of rapes committed by Soviet soldiers in Hungary has been fully documented, though without the chance to analyse Russian archival materials, which I will come back to later. Almost uniquely in historiography, one may venture the statement that the entirety of Hungarian archival sources listed in the previous section were processed. Further micro-historical research may contribute to the deepening of local knowledge. Here I return to my opening statement: the discourse which is currently evolving in Hungary about the rapes committed by Soviet soldiers, though breaking the 'conspiracy of silence', at the same time simplifies the narrative by creating a victimised ethnic group whose members have all been punished equally. It is worrying that new, local historical researchers prompted by Skrabski's film among others, may well strengthen this simplistic perspective that it was all about the war between the Soviets and Hungarians, and the rape of women will be sidelined and instead used as a tool in the battle of male hegemonic memory politics.

To get away from this unhelpful frame of reference, I suggest two further sources that are becoming increasingly more available be included in the historical analysis. These are internet-based sources and visual representations, and they could potentially open up a new theoretical trajectory beyond the current intentionalist versus structuralist debate. These sources can be used in three ways against silencing: (i) *showcasing*, when contemporaries speak up as witnesses, victims, and perpetrators; (ii) *restructuring the narrative*, by lobbying for a law to ban simplistic attempts to ethnicise the issue of rape committed by the Red Army from the present international perspective of the Ukrainian crisis; and finally (iii) *legal confrontation*, in which court-martial decisions are made public. This latter point would show that there was in fact an institutional retribution for rape, at the same time doing away with the Red Army's image of being an 'uncivilised Asiatic horde'. This might be the most difficult but most promising strategy of the three to pull off, because it has the simultaneous potential of being a critique of militarism. All three strategies are, nevertheless, very much dependent on the decisions of political actors – in terms of what and how information is made available.

Based on the dates that online Russian sources became available, one can trace a clear paradigm shift. While in the early 2000s, self-examination and *showcasing* was at least somewhat possible, based on my limited web survey, the situation has shifted a lot. With the conflicts unfolding in the Crimea and Eastern Ukraine, there is increased interest in the rapes committed by Soviet soldiers, so we can expect there will be more discussion of this topic in the future. However, the mode and framing of these future discussions will be critical, and in this respect, the *restructuring of the narrative* has shifted more towards ethnicising rapes committed by Soviet soldiers, so that the narrative can be used in the language of everyday political fights. Meanwhile, although some documents have made it onto the web, Soviet military archives are still inaccessible, and due to their contingency, they can only provide rudimentary support for *legal confrontation*.

The exploration of internet-based sources requires a particular methodology sensitive to issues of selectivity, temporality, and representativeness – especially in Russia, where there are clearly attempts to exercise state censorship over the internet. Documents may make it onto the internet randomly, and no general conclusion can be directly drawn from these. Because of the way Russian archives function, it seems that individual users may offer online access to documents in selective ways that would not withstand scientific scrutiny. And the documents available online have a special inner temporality: sometimes it is impossible to know when the text was actually posted, and it is never certain either for how long it will remain accessible. Webpages that this paper references, for example, may quite clearly not be available in the future. This leads to the fundamental question of how representative are an active commentator's posts if they are using an alias? One possibility could be that identities are hiding the fact that some contributors might be working for powerful political actors.

Digitalisation has reached Russian archives too, though not without being scarred by the battles of memory politics. Priority is clearly given to preserving the memory of Second World War heroes. In September 2012, a user named 'allin' uploaded several documents from the 'OBD Memorial' (*Obschestvennaya Baza Dannyh Memorial*) – a public collection run by the Russian Federation's Ministry of Defence.[14]

The documents include material from the 26th Army's Third Court Martial of 19 April 1945, and its original is preserved in the Fifth Section of the Russian Federation's Ministry of Defence's Central Archive.[15] In principle, similar documents should already be a part of the OBD Memorial webpage, but are not (yet) accessible. In the Central Archive, such documents proved to be accessible only if one could prove to be a blood-relation. Unfortunately, this protection of privacy entirely disables research as this makes it difficult to obtain the soldiers' names. Furthermore, even if one did acquire the names of all those court-martialled, not all the soldiers who committed crimes were tried this way. Among the documents uploaded by 'allin', some are connected to the atrocities against Hungarian women: among other things, there are two verdicts. One is the case of the rape of a nine year-old Hungarian girl. The other is the case of a Hungarian woman's murder.[16] At any rate the document negates the previously prevalent opinion that rapists were either shot on the spot or got away with impunity. The document testifies that there was in effect an inner control mechanism in the Red Army. Those soldiers who transgressed the wartime penal code were put before a court martial, but who were these people precisely, and why were they tried? Why and for whom was this uploaded top secret document put together? To what extent was this strict verdict typical of the Red Army as a whole? Was the verdict actually carried out? There will be answers to these questions only when systematic research of the archives of extant Soviet military documents is made possible. The uploaded document, which is a summary that must have been attached to individual trial documents, shows that rape was reported, and it was punishable with ten years of imprisonment. However, without systematic research of Soviet military archives we can only have assumptions about the inner workings of the Soviet army and the lives of the soldiers in it. Only when those sources become available, can the narrative truly change.

## *Visual presentations*

There is a source, which has received little attention thus far from researchers of wartime rape.[17] That is visual representation. If there were pictures taken, they were of dead women – taking pictures of the act was out of the question. Concerning the dead women in the pictures, one can assume or the police have retrospectively concluded – and stated in writing – that the dead victims were raped. It is only very recently that women who survived wartime rape have identified themselves and told their story. This would not be happening were it not for the cracks appearing globally in the conspiracy of silence, driven by the emergence of supportive women's movements and organisations.

In light of the debate sparked off by Skrabski's movie, how, if at all, should rape be represented though? How should we build monuments, if at all, for the victims? In the film's black-and-white inserts based on the story of a survivor, rape was reconstructed and re-enacted with actors. The immediacy of these images is in sharp contrast with the paucity of photographic documentation in my research on the same topic over the past twenty years. Below are four visual documents, which support my statement that the visualisation and representation of rape has ties to the potential for articulating a hegemonic or normative historical truth.

The first picture is a police photograph made in the Viennese Prater, one of the many preserved in the police section of the City and Provincial Archives of Vienna. The corpse was found in the morning; so the police visited the scene, took pictures of it and, from the medical report attached to the picture, the doctor had judged the Austrian woman to have been raped then killed. Although it was not known who did it, the assumption was that one, or a number of Soviet soldiers were involved. As the barracks of the Soviet army were not under the auspices of the Austrian judiciary system, there was investigation possible. Case closed.

I found the second picture while deciding on an illustration for my paper on rapes committed by Soviet soldiers, that was going to be published in the journal and popular historical magazine *Rubicon*.[18] The picture was taken in Budapest by Yevgeny Khaldei (1917–1997), the well-known Soviet military photographer, who made many images that later became iconic, among them the picture of the Soviet flag on top of the Reichstag. His picture from Budapest was most probably made between March and April of 1945, because by mid-April, Khaldei was already taking pictures in Vienna. Árpád Rácz (editor-in-chief of *Rubicon*) had telephoned me to ask whether in my opinion those women in the picture were raped. If so, he asked whether he could publish the picture. Without hesitation I answered no. It would not be ethical because of the victims, and the picture had never been published. Since that time I have often wondered why such a picture has not, when the Khaldei collection has been used by so many for such a range of purposes?

The third picture is of a private (or at least an 'unauthorised public') monument by Polish artist Jerzy Szumczyk in Gdańsk, which caused some outrage last year. The sculpture was called *Komm Frau!* and showed a Soviet soldier raping a pregnant woman at gunpoint. It was eventually removed due to public protests and the lack of necessary permits.

The fourth, a monument in remembrance of Korean sex slaves ('comfort women'), or the *Pyeonghwa-bi* ('Peace Monument') was installed in Glendale, California in January 2014 despite the Japanese government's official protest. Here an empty chair reminds us of the woman killed by Japanese soldiers, and the commemorator, who could sit by the woman to listen to her story. This monument is a copy of the one erected in front of the Japanese Embassy in Seoul in 2011 to commemorate the one thousandth weekly protest held there every Wednesday since 1992. I would not undertake the risky, thankless task of suggesting the establishment of a monument for Hungarian women raped by Soviet soldiers the way quite a few people had did after Skrabski's film. Recent monuments in Hungary lack any sort of prior social consensus, articulating one-sided conceptualisations of memory politics and justifiably causing a storm.[19] However, if we carefully contemplate how to talk about and remember a historical event that lacks prior visual representation, we may come up with two strategies.

First, according to Susan Sontag, there should be no visual memorialisation, because looking at the picture representing violence not only recreates the visual culture of it, but by marvelling at the picture from the outside, the gaze itself repeats the violent act as well.[20] This was one of the arguments justifying the removal of the Gdańsk monument, and the one that made me refuse to let the Khaldei photograph be published with my article in Rubicon. This is also why Skrabski's film, despite its thorough consideration of ethical issues, contributed to the perpetuation of the violence-cycle and its visual culture through rape re-enactments.

But perhaps the unease and embarrassment we feel when looking at these images can contribute to critical self-reflection. Maybe such a regard can facilitate a way of moving beyond the structuralist vs. intentionalist debate while at the same time creating space for the victims: a space for self-expression and a space for deliberately chosen silence if that is wanted. When looking at pictures we can be aware that we interpret them through information made available after the rape had been committed. This interpretation, like an artwork's iconography, is not independent of the iconography of survivor and victim narratives. The making of *Komm Frau!* was indeed deeply influenced by stories of rape survivors.

I discussed two photographic representations of rape. Both are necessarily clichés, because suffering can be represented only within existing iconographical frameworks. The picture of the woman killed in the Prater is reminiscent of the iconography of Christian martyrdom, while in Khaldei's picture from Budapest, the man who mourns his female family members becomes the 'real' victim. Inevitably, in both cases the woman gets objectified. Meanwhile, the indifferent iconographical bluntness of the private ('unauthorized public') monument in Gdańsk, and the other extreme of the overly sentimental, idealised character of the Korean sex slave monument both fortify the victimised position of women. The monuments are based on narratives of the survivors, and the only narrative framework available to them is that of victimhood. If we subscribe to the intentionalist interpretation, which simply interprets rape as a weapon of war in the hands of military leaders or politicians that intentionally punish groups of people, we lose sight of the complexity and structural features arising from a proper analysis. In Hungary today, the discourse on rapes committed by Soviet soldiers is shifting towards such an intentionalist interpretation. Instead, our analysis should be looking more at the normative masculinity which is a foundational feature of militarism, and in this way we could confront the power-interests that underlie rape culture.

## Conclusions

However, if we only apply a structuralist interpretational framework, by focusing on the victims of rape and dismissing the context to be of little importance, we assume that the culture of rape is structurally supra-national, which simplifies matters by denying us the opportunity of understanding more about how someone becomes a perpetrator; the reasons and consequences of rape, and the victims.

It is wrong to consider the Soviet rapist soldier as that because he is Soviet, as this ignores the fact that both Hungarian, German, and Soviet armies had the same military culture which prompted or allowed rapes committed by soldiers. But it would be equally wrong if we observed the perpetrator simply as a man (not to mention that by doing so we would also render invisible male rape victims), without taking into consideration the complex system of reasons and consequences, which enabled a particular soldier to commit rape and go unpunished. The task of complex understanding is our moral and professional duty towards the dignity of millions of victims. This chapter asks whether visual iconography might be the first step in helping us confront our self-created limitations and memory deficiencies.

### Notes

1   For my other writings on the same theme, see 'A II. világháborús nemi erőszak történetírása Magyarországon', in *Mandiner* 31/3/2015, http://mandiner.hu/cikk/20150331_peto_andrea_a_ii_vilaghaborus_nemi_eroszak_tortenetirasa_magyarorszagon; 'Szovjet katonák és nemi erőszak- az orosz internetetes források tükrében', in *Mandiner* 11/7/2015 http://m.mandiner.hu/cikk/20150708_peto_andrea_szovjet_katonak_es_a_nemi_eroszak_orosz_internetes_forrasok_tukreben; and 'Miten lukea seksuaalisen väkivallan historiankirjoitusta?',

in S. Karkulehto and L-M Rossi (eds), *Sukupuoli ja väkivalta – lukemisen etiikkaa ja politiikkaa* (Helsinki: SKS, forthcoming).

2   See on this A. Pető, 'Memory and the Narrative of Rape in Budapest and Vienna', in R. Bessel and D. Schumann (eds), *Life after Death: Approaches to a Cultural and Social History of Europe during the 1940s and 1950s* (Cambridge: Cambridge UP, 2003), 129–149.

3   T. Krausz & E. M. Varga, *A magyar megszálló csapatok a Szovjetunióban – Levéltári dokumentumok 1941–1947* (Budapest: L'Harmattan Kiadó, 2013).

4   On the Hungarian archival sources of Soviet occupation, see L. Balogh Béni (ed.), *'Törvényes' megszállás: Szovjet csapatok Magyarországon 1944–1947*, [*'Lawful' occupation: Soviet troops in Hungary 1944–1947*, with English summaries], (Budapest: Magyar Nemzeti Levéltár, 2015).

5   K. Bischl, 'Telling stories: Gender relationships and masculinity in the Red Army 1941–45', in M. Röger and R. Leiserowitz (eds), *Women and Men at War – A Gender Perspective on World War II and its Aftermath in Central and Eastern Europe* (Osnabrück: Fibre, 2012), 117–135.

6   The *főispán* or 'county sheriff' was an administrative position in Hungary, abolished in 1950.

7   The Arrow Cross men belonged to the fascist National Socialist Party that ruled Hungary from 15 October 1944 to 28 March 1945.

8   M. Walzer, *Just and Unjust Wars: A Moral Argument with Historical Illustrations* (New York: Basic Books, 1977).

9   The exhibition (1995–1999), prepared by Hannes Heer and Gerd Hankel, was the first to present the German Army as perpetrators of war crimes.

10  R. Mühlhäuser, 'The Historicity of Denial: Sexual Violence against Jewish Women during the War of Annihilation, 1941–1945' in A. G. Altınay and A. Pető (eds), *Gendered Memories, Gendered Wars* (London: Routledge, 2016), 29–55; B. Beck, *Wehrmacht und sexuelle Gewalt: Sexualverbrechen vor deutschen Militärgerichten 1939–1945* (Paderborn: Schöningh, 2004); B. Beck, 'Rape: The Military Trials of Sexual Crimes Committed by Soldiers in the Wehrmacht, 1939–1944', in K. Hagemann and S. Schüler-Springorum (eds), *Home/Front: the Military, War and Gender in Twentieth Century Germany* (Oxford: Berg, 2002), 255–274; M. Flaschka, *Race, Rape and Gender in Nazi Occupied Territories*, doctoral dissertation (Kent State University, 2009).

11  A. Timm, 'Sex with a Purpose: Prostitution, Venereal Disease, and Militarized Masculinity in the Third Reich', *Journal of the History of Sexuality* 11, no. 1–2 (2002), 253.

12  S. M. Hedgepeth and R. G. Saidel (eds), *Sexual Violence against Jewish Women during the Holocaust* (Hanover: UP of New England, 2010); S. T. Katz, 'Thoughts on the Intersection of Rape and *Rassen[s]chande* during the Holocaust', in *Modern Judaism* 32, no. 3 (2012), 293–322; H. Sinnreich, '"And It Was Something We Didn't Talk about": Rape of Jewish Women During the Holocaust', *Holocaust Studies* 14, no. 2 (2008), 1–22.

13  A. Pető, 'Átvonuló hadsereg, maradandó trauma. Az 1945-ös budapesti erőszakesetek emlékezete', in *Történelmi Szemle* 1–2 (1999), 85–107.

14  http://www.obd-memorial.ru/html/default.htm

15  http://www.obd-memorial.ru/html/info.htm?id=4388906&page=3

16  http://allin777.livejournal.com/166277.html

17  A. Pető, 'Death and the Picture: Representation of War Criminals and Construction of Divided Memory about WWII in Hungary,' in A. Pető and K. Schrijvers (eds), *Faces of Death. Visualizing History* (Pisa: Edizioni Plus / Pisa University Press, 2009), 39–57.

18 A. Pető, 'Az elmondhatatlan emlékezet. A szovjet katonák által elkövetett nemi erőszak Magyarországon', in *Rubicon* 2/2014, 44–49.
19 More on the monument-debate: A. Pető, '"Hungary 70": Non-remembering the Holocaust in Hungary', in *Culture and History Digital Journal* 3, no. 2 (2014), e016 eISSN 2253-797Xdoi: http://dx.doi.org/10.3989/chdj.2014.016
20 S. Sontag, *Regarding the Pain of Others* (New York: Farrar, Straus & Giroux, 2003).

# Sources and Bibliography

## Printed sources

L. Balogh Béni (ed.), *'Törvényes' megszállás: Szovjet csapatok Magyarországon 1944–1947* Budapest: Magyar Nemzeti Levéltár, 2015 [*'Lawful' occupation: Soviet troops in Hungary 1944–1947*, with English summaries].

Krausz, T. and Varga, E. M., *A magyar megszálló csapatok a Szovjetunióban – Levéltári dokumentumok 1941–1947*. Budapest: L'Harmattan Kiadó, 2013.

## Internet sources

http://www.obd-memorial.ru/html/default.htm
http://www.obd-memorial.ru/html/info.htm?id=4388906&page=3
http://allin777.livejournal.com/166277.html

## Literature

Beck, B., 'Rape: The Military Trials of Sexual Crimes Committed by Soldiers in the Wehrmacht, 1939–1944', in Hagemann, K. and Schüler-Springorum, S. (eds), *Home/Front: the Military, War and Gender in Twentieth Century Germany*. Oxford: Berg, 2002.

Beck, B., *Wehrmacht und sexuelle Gewalt: Sexualverbrechen vor deutschen Militärgerichten 1939–1945*. Paderborn: Schöningh, 2004.

Bischl, K., 'Telling stories: Gender relationships and masculinity in the Red Army 1941–45', in Röger, M. and Leiserowitz, R. (eds), *Women and Men at War – A Gender Perspective on World War II and its Aftermath in Central and Eastern Europe*. Osnabrück: Fibre, 2012.

Flaschka, M., *Race, Rape and Gender in Nazi Occupied Territories*, doctoral dissertation (Kent State University, 2009).

Hedgepeth, S. M. and Saidel, R. G. (eds), *Sexual Violence against Jewish Women during the Holocaust*. Hanover: UP of New England, 2010.

Katz, S. T., 'Thoughts on the Intersection of Rape and *Rassen[s]chande* during the Holocaust', in *Modern Judaism* 32, no. 3 (2012).

Pető, A. 'Memory and the Narrative of Rape in Budapest and Vienna', in Bessel, R. and Schumann, D. (eds), *Life after Death: Approaches to a Cultural and Social History of Europe during the 1940s and 1950s*. Cambridge: Cambridge UP, 2003.

Mühlhäuser, R., 'The Historicity of Denial: Sexual Violence against Jewish Women during the War of Annihilation, 1941–1945', in Altınay, A. G. and Pető, A., *Gendered Memories, Gendered Wars*. London: Routledge, 2016.

Pető, A., 'Átvonuló hadsereg, maradandó trauma. Az 1945-ös budapesti erőszakesetek emlékezete', in *Történelmi Szemle* 1-2 (1999).

Pető, A., 'Death and the Picture: Representation of War Criminals and Construction of Divided Memory about WWII in Hungary', in Pető, A. and Schrijvers, K. (eds), *Faces of Death. Visualizing History*. Pisa: Edizioni Plus / Pisa University Press, 2009.

Pető, A., 'Az elmondhatatlan emlékezet. A szovjet katonák által elkövetett nemi erőszak Magyarországon', in *Rubicon* 2/2014.

Pető, A., '"Hungary 70": Non-remembering the Holocaust in Hungary', in *Culture and History Digital Journal* 3, no. 2 (2014), e016 eISSN 2253-797Xdoi: http://dx.doi.org/10.3989/chdj.2014.016

Pető, A., 'A II. világháborús nemi erőszak történetírása Magyarországon', in *Mandiner* 31/3/2015, http://mandiner.hu/cikk/20150331_peto_andrea_a_ii_vilaghaborus_nemi_eroszak_tortenetirasa_magyarorszagon.

Pető, A., 'Szovjet katonák és nemi erőszak- az orosz internetetes források tükrében', in *Mandiner* 11/7/2015 http://m.mandiner.hu/cikk/20150708_peto_andrea_szovjet_katonak_es_a_nemi_eroszak_orosz_internetes_forrasok_tukreben

Pető, A., 'Miten lukea seksuaalisen väkivallan historiankirjoitusta?', in Karkulehto S. and Rossi, L-M. (eds), *Sukupuoli ja väkivalta – lukemisen etiikkaa ja politiikkaa*. Helsinki: SKS, forthcoming.

Sinnreich, H., '"And It Was Something We Didn't Talk about": Rape of Jewish Women During the Holocaust', *Holocaust Studies* 14, no. 2 (2008).

Sontag, S., *Regarding the Pain of Others*. New York: Farrar, Straus & Giroux, 2003.

Timm, A., 'Sex with a Purpose: Prostitution, Venereal Disease, and Militarized Masculinity in the Third Reich', *Journal of the History of Sexuality* 11, no. 1–2 (2002).

Walzer, M., *Just and Unjust Wars: A Moral Argument with Historical Illustrations*. New York: Basic Books, 1977.

# List of Authors

Dr. Maria Fritsche is an historian and film scholar at the Norwegian University of Science and Technology, Trondheim. In her monograph *Homemade Men in Postwar Austrian Cinema: Nationhood, Genre and Masculinity* (Berghahn 2013) she analysed the role of popular cinema in rebuilding Austrian society after the Second World War. The transatlantic relations between the United States and Europe are the theme of her newest book *The American Marshall Plan Film Campaign and the Europeans: A Captive Audience?* (Bloomsbury 2017), which discusses the strategies of the US government to transfer American liberal-capitalist ideals to the Europeans through the medium of film. In her current project she returns to the theme of war and military justice and investigates German efforts to enforce consensus and discipline in Norwegian society by analysing court files of Wehrmacht military courts.

Dr. Petri Karonen (http://orcid.org/0000-0001-6090-5504) is a professor of Finnish History at the University of Jyväskylä. He has studied, e.g., the Swedish state building process during the early modern period, political and financial management of warfare, and the societal history of post-war crises from the sixteenth century to the post-1945 era. Karonen is the vice leader of the steering committee of the Finnish Center of Excellence in Historical Research, 'History of Society: Re-thinking Finland 1400–2000'. He is currently leading a research group in a Finnish-Swedish research project 'Demokratins drivkrafter: Kontext och särdrag i Finlands och Sveriges demokratier 1890–2020' (Driving Forces of Democracy: Patterns of Democratization in Finland and Sweden, 1890–2020). He has also written an overview of the history of Sweden and Finland in 1521–1809, *Pohjoinen suurvalta*, the fourth revised edition published in 2014.

Dr. Tiina Kinnunen is a professor of Finnish and Northern European History at the University of Oulu, Finland. She has published widely on the history of European feminism, history of historiography, and social and cultural history of war. She is currently working, e.g., on a comparative biography of the feminists Ellen Key and Alexandra Gripenberg. Among her publications in English are *Finland in World War II: History, Memory, Interpretations*, edited by Tiina Kinnunen & Ville Kivimäki (Brill 2012) and 'The Post-

Cold War Memory Culture of the Civil-War: Old-New Patterns and New Approaches', in *The Finnish Civil War 1918: History, Memory, Legacy* (Brill 2014). Kinnunen's most recent publication is *Biography, Gender, and History: Nordic Perspectives*, edited by Erla Hulda Halldorsdottir, Tiina Kinnunen, Maarit Leskelä-Kärki & Birgitte Possing (University of Turku 2016).

Dr. Ville Kivimäki is an historian and postdoctoral researcher at the University of Tampere, Finland. In his PhD thesis *Battled Nerves: Finnish Soldiers' War Experience, Trauma, and Military Psychiatry, 1941–44* (Åbo Akademi 2013), Kivimäki studied the emergence of 'war neuroses' and their treatment and conceptualizations in wartime Finland. His current research project is 'Trauma before Trauma: Finnish War Veterans and the Posttraumatic Stress, 1945–55'. Beyond the questions of war trauma, Kivimäki has focused on the social and cultural history of war, on the history of masculinities, experiences, and emotions, and on the history of mentalities in the postwar era. For publications in English, see *Finland in World War II: History, Memory, Interpretations*, edited by Tiina Kinnunen & Ville Kivimäki (Brill 2012), for instance.

Dr. Anu Mai Kõll is an historian and professor emeritus of Baltic History, Culture, and Society. She has worked at the Economic History Department and at the History Department of Stockholm University, and finally as the director of the Centre of Baltic and East European Studies (CBEES) at Södertörn University. Her works include Swedish agrarian history and the history of Estonian inter-war land reform and economic policy. She has also participated in a broader project on the history of communism launched by the Swedish Research Council after the collapse of the Soviet Union, with a local study of collectivization and dekulakization. After retirement, the fate of refugees and displaced persons after the Second World War has become her new research focus.

Dr. Marta Kurkowska-Budzan is an historian and an assistant professor at Jagiellonian University in Kraków, Poland. Her areas of expertise are interdisciplinary studies on the representations of the past in contemporary culture, Holocaust studies, oral history, and methodology of history. Her recent research concerns the cultural anthropology of sport and leisure in Poland 1945–1989. Over the past few years, she has been engaged in the following projects: 'Oral Sources Re-visited' (2016–), 'National Armed Underground in Białystok Region, 1942–1957: Memory Discourses' (2006–2009); 'Little Township, 1945–1989: Goniądz in Community Memory' (2008). She has held postdoctoral fellowships at the United States Holocaust Memorial Museum in Washington, DC, (2002) and at the Remarque Institute, New York University (2001).

Dr. Andrea Pető (http://orcid.org/0000-0002-7525-2582) is a professor at the Department of Gender Studies at the Central European University in Budapest, Hungary, and a Doctor of Science of the Hungarian Academy of Sciences. She has edited fifteen volumes in English, seven volumes in

Hungarian, and two in Russian, and her works have appeared in 15 different languages. She has also been a guest professor at the universities of Toronto, Buenos Aires, Novi Sad, Stockholm, and Frankfurt. Her books include: *Women in Hungarian Politics 1945–1951* (Columbia University Press 2003), *Geschlecht, Politik und Stalinismus in Ungarn: Eine Biographie von Júlia Rajk* (Gabriele Schäfer Verlag 2007), and together with Ildikó Barna, *Political Justice in Budapest after WWII / Politikai igazságszolgáltatás a II. világháború utáni Budapesten* (Gondolat 2012 and CEU Press 2015). Her recent book is co-edited with Ayse Gül Altinay: *Gendered Wars, Gendered Memories: Feminist Conversations on War, Genocide and Political Violence* (Routledge 2016). She serves as an associate editor for the *European Journal of Women's Studies*. In 2005, she was awarded the Officer's Cross, Order of Merit of the Republic of Hungary, by the President of the Hungarian Republic and the Bolyai Prize by the Hungarian Academy of Sciences in 2006. At the moment, she is working on gendered memory of the Second World War and political extremisms.

Dr. Marianne Zepp is a historian who received her PhD at the Technische Universität in Berlin with a thesis *Redefining Germany: Reeducation, Staatsbürgerschaft und Frauenpolitik im US- amerikanisch besetzten Nachkriegsdeutschland* (Vandenhoeck & Ruprecht 2007). She is the head of the Contemporary History Department at the Heinrich Böll Foundation in Berlin. Her work and research is focused on post-war Germany's democratization processes, politics of memory, and social movements. Her latest publication is 'Rationality of Fear: The Intellectual Foundations of the Peace Movement', in Christoph Becker-Schaum, Philipp Gassert, Wilfried Mausbach, Martin A. Klimke & Marianne Zepp (eds), *The Nuclear Crisis: The Arms Race, Cold War Anxiety, and the German Peace Movement of the 1980s* (Berghahn 2016).

# Abstract

## Continued Violence and Troublesome Pasts
Post-war Europe between the Victors after the Second World War

Edited by Ville Kivimäki & Petri Karonen

In most European countries, the horrific legacy of 1939–45 has made it quite difficult to remember the war with much glory. Despite the Anglo-American memory narrative of saving democracy from totalitarianism and the Soviet epic of the Great Patriotic War, the fundamental experience of war for so many Europeans was that of immense personal losses and often meaningless hardships. The anthology at hand focuses on these histories between the victors: on the cases of Hungary, Estonia, Poland, Austria, Finland, and Germany and on the respective, often gendered experiences of defeat. The book's chapters underline the asynchronous transition to peace in individual experiences, when compared to the smooth timelines of national and international historiographies. Furthermore, it is important to note that instead of a linear chronology, both personal and collective histories tend to return back to the moments of violence and loss, thus forming continuous cycles of remembrance and forgetting. Several of the authors also pay specific attention to the constructed and contested nature of national histories in these cycles. The role of these 'in-between' countries – and even more their peoples' multifaceted experiences – will add to the widening European history of the aftermath, thereby challenging the conventional dichotomies and periodisations. In the aftermath of the seventieth anniversary of 1945, it is still too early to regard the post-war period as mere history; the memory politics and rhetoric of the Second World War and its aftermath are again being used and abused to serve contemporary power politics in Europe.

# Index

Anti-communism 13–14, 32–33, 44–57, 72, 77, 112–113

Children 9, 17, 53–57, 88, 109, 117, 121, 125, 134
Cinema 14, 46, 85–98, 110–111, 115, 118–124, 135–139
Citizenship 13, 40, 63–65, 69–77, 88, 112

Demobilisation 7, 9, 36–37
Democracy 12, 14, 47–48, 54, 63–78, 86, 112–113
Deportations 8, 11, 14, 30–33, 35, 39, 49, 51, 136

Economy 7, 11, 56, 64, 76, 86, 88–90, 95, 113, 123

Fascism 8, 15, 29, 46–47, 50, 71, 87–88, 113, 118, 134–135

Gender 10–11, 13–15, 64, 68–70, 78, 80, 85–98, 102, 110–112, 113–115, 118, 121, 124, 132, 134–135
Germany 7–11, 13–15, 29–33, 35–38, 40, 44, 48–49, 51, 55, 63–78, 86–89, 91–95, 109–110, 112, 115–116, 118, 121–124, 133–136, 141
Great Britain 12, 73, 76, 89–90, 101

Holocaust 7–8, 11–12, 15, 32, 110, 124, 134, 136

Identity 7, 10, 14–15, 44, 46, 75, 86, 88–94, 97–98, 109–111, 117

Literature 46, 109–111, 113–120, 124–125, 135

Masculinity (crisis of) 10–11, 14–15, 68–69, 75, 85–98, 109–111, 117, 135–137, 141
Morality 8, 11, 14, 51, 54, 63–64, 66, 68, 75, 91, 95, 112–115, 118, 120, 122, 124, 134–136, 141
Motherhood 67–70, 73, 75, 112, 121

National socialism 8–10, 12–14, 16, 39, 64–70, 72, 74–76, 80, 86, 89–91, 94, 101, 116, 118, 123–124, 135–136

Occupation 8–16, 29–40, 44, 47–49, 55, 59, 63–77, 87, 89, 112–113, 119, 122, 132–136
Oral history 13, 45–47, 49–57, 125, 135

Prisoners of war 9–10, 13, 19, 37–38, 69, 72, 76, 87, 121–123
Punishment (legal and informal) 8, 11, 29–34, 38–39, 40, 52–53, 116, 118, 132, 134–138, 139, 141

Red Army 9, 12, 14–15, 29–31, 33, 36–37, 44, 48, 52, 55–56, 112, 117, 121–123, 132–135, 137–141
'Re-education' 8, 14, 64–65, 73, 75
Remembrance 7, 9, 11–12, 14–16, 44–46, 57, 109–125, 133–141
Resistance movements 13, 29, 33–34, 44–57, 89, 117–118

Sexual violence 9, 14–15, 122, 128, 132–141
Sexuality 14, 87, 90, 93, 96, 113, 114–119, 122, 136
Soviet Union (Russia) 7–10, 12–15, 29–40, 47, 49, 51, 55–57, 76, 101, 109–113, 116–124, 132–141

United States 9, 63–67, 69, 71, 73–77, 87, 92, 94, 96, 101, 115

Victimhood 9–12, 14–15, 30, 67, 70, 89, 98, 101, 116, 121–122, 124, 133–135, 137, 139–141

War veterans 9–10, 45–47, 50, 52, 58, 87, 119
Women's organisations 10–11, 13–14, 32, 63–78, 111–124, 139

'Zero Hour' 8, 16

## Studia Fennica Ethnologica

**Memories of My Town**
*The Identities of Town Dwellers and Their Places in Three Finnish Towns*
Edited by Anna-Maria Åström, Pirjo Korkiakangas & Pia Olsson
Studia Fennica Ethnologica 8
2004

**Passages Westward**
Edited by Maria Lähteenmäki & Hanna Snellman
Studia Fennica Ethnologica 9
2006

**Defining Self**
*Essays on emergent identities in Russia Seventeenth to Nineteenth Centuries*
Edited by Michael Branch
Studia Fennica Ethnologica 10
2009

**Touching Things**
*Ethnological Aspects of Modern Material Culture*
Edited by Pirjo Korkiakangas, Tiina-Riitta Lappi & Heli Niskanen
Studia Fennica Ethnologica 11
2008

**Gendered Rural Spaces**
Edited by Pia Olsson & Helena Ruotsala
Studia Fennica Ethnologica 12
2009

LAURA STARK
**The Limits of Patriarchy**
*How Female Networks of Pilfering and Gossip Sparked the First Debates on Rural Gender Rights in the 19th-century Finnish-Language Press*
Studia Fennica Ethnologica 13
2011

**Where is the Field?**
*The Experience of Migration Viewed through the Prism of Ethnographic Fieldwork*
Edited by Laura Hirvi & Hanna Snellman
Studia Fennica Ethnologica 14
2012

LAURA HIRVI
**Identities in Practice**
*A Trans-Atlantic Ethnography of Sikh Immigrants in Finland and in California*
Studia Fennica Ethnologica 15
2013

EERIKA KOSKINEN-KOIVISTO
**Her Own Worth**
*Negotiations of Subjectivity in the Life Narrative of a Female Labourer*
Studia Fennica Ethnologica 16
2014

## Studia Fennica Folkloristica

**Narrating, Doing, Experiencing**
*Nordic Folkloristic Perspectives*
Edited by Annikki Kaivola-Bregenhøj, Barbro Klein & Ulf Palmenfelt
Studia Fennica Folkloristica 16
2006

MÍCHEÁL BRIODY
**The Irish Folklore Commission 1935–1970**
*History, ideology, methodology*
Studia Fennica Folkloristica 17
2008

VENLA SYKÄRI
**Words as Events**
*Cretan Mantinádes in Performance and Composition*
Studia Fennica Folkloristica 18
2011

**Hidden Rituals and Public Performances**
*Traditions and Belonging among the Post-Soviet Khanty, Komi and Udmurts*
Edited by Anna-Leena Siikala & Oleg Ulyashev
Studia Fennica Folkloristica 19
2011

**Mythic Discourses**
*Studies in Uralic Traditions*
Edited by Frog, Anna-Leena Siikala & Eila Stepanova
Studia Fennica Folkloristica 20
2012

CORNELIUS HASSELBLATT
**Kalevipoeg Studies**
*The Creation and Reception of an Epic*
Studia Fennica Folkloristica 21
2016

**Genre – Text – Interpretation**
*Multidisciplinary Perspectives on Folklore and Beyond*
Edited by Kaarina Koski, Frog & Ulla Savolainen
Studia Fennica Folkloristica 22
2016

## Studia Fennica Historica

**Moving in the USSR**
*Western anomalies and Northern wilderness*
Edited by Pekka Hakamies
Studia Fennica Historica 10
2005

Derek Fewster
**Visions of Past Glory**
*Nationalism and the Construction of Early Finnish History*
Studia Fennica Historica 11
2006

**Modernisation in Russia since 1900**
Edited by Markku Kangaspuro & Jeremy Smith
Studia Fennica Historica 12
2006

Seija-Riitta Laakso
**Across the Oceans**
*Development of Overseas Business Information Transmission 1815–1875*
Studia Fennica Historica 13
2007

**Industry and Modernism**
*Companies, Architecture and Identity in the Nordic and Baltic Countries during the High-Industrial Period*
Edited by Anja Kervanto Nevanlinna
Studia Fennica Historica 14
2007

Charlotta Wolff
**Noble conceptions of politics in eighteenth-century Sweden (ca 1740–1790)**
Studia Fennica Historica 15
2008

**Sport, Recreation and Green Space in the European City**
Edited by Peter Clark, Marjaana Niemi & Jari Niemelä
Studia Fennica Historica 16
2009

**Rhetorics of Nordic Democracy**
Edited by Jussi Kurunmäki & Johan Strang
Studia Fennica Historica 17
2010

**Fibula, Fabula, Fact**
*The Viking Age in Finland*
Edited by Joonas Ahola & Frog with Clive Tolley
Studia Fennica Historica 18
2014

**Novels, Histories, Novel Nations**
*Historical Fiction and Cultural Memory in Finland and Estonia*
Edited by Linda Kaljundi, Eneken Laanes & Ilona Pikkanen
Studia Fennica Historica 19
2015

Jukka Gronow & Sergey Zhuravlev
**Fashion Meets Socialism**
*Fashion industry in the Soviet Union after the Second World War*
Studia Fennica Historica 20
2015

Sofia Kotilainen
**Literacy Skills as Local Intangible Capital**
*The History of a Rural Lending Library c. 1860–1920*
Studia Fennica Historica 21
2016

**Continued Violence and Troublesome Pasts**
*Post-war Europe between the Victors after the Second World War*
Edited by Ville Kivimäki and Petri Karonen
Studia Fennica Historica 22
2017

## Studia Fennica Anthropologica

**On Foreign Ground**
*Moving between Countries and Categories*
Edited by Marie-Louise Karttunen & Minna Ruckenstein
Studia Fennica Anthropologica 1
2007

**Beyond the Horizon**
*Essays on Myth, History, Travel and Society*
Edited by Clifford Sather & Timo Kaartinen
Studia Fennica Anthropologica 2
2008

Timo Kallinen
**Divine Rulers in a Secular State**
Studia Fennica Anthropologica 3
2016

## Studia Fennica Linguistica

**Minimal reference**
*The use of pronouns in Finnish and Estonian discourse*
Edited by Ritva Laury
Studia Fennica Linguistica 12
2005

Antti Leino
**On Toponymic Constructions as an Alternative to Naming Patterns in Describing Finnish Lake Names**
Studia Fennica Linguistica 13
2007

**Talk in interaction**
*Comparative dimensions*
Edited by Markku Haakana, Minna Laakso & Jan Lindström
Studia Fennica Linguistica 14
2009

**Planning a new standard language**
*Finnic minority languages meet the new millennium*
Edited by Helena Sulkala & Harri Mantila
Studia Fennica Linguistica 15
2010

Lotta Weckström
**Representations of Finnishness in Sweden**
Studia Fennica Linguistica 16
2011

Terhi Ainiala, Minna Saarelma & Paula Sjöblom
**Names in Focus**
*An Introduction to Finnish Onomastics*
Studia Fennica Linguistica 17
2012

**Registers of Communication**
Edited by Asif Agha & Frog
Studia Fennica Linguistica 18
2015

Kaisa Häkkinen
**Spreading the Written Word**
*Mikael Agricola and the Birth of Literary Finnish*
Studia Fennica Linguistica 19
2015

**Linking Clauses and Actions in Social Interaction**
Edited by Ritva Laury, Marja Etelämäki, Elizabeth Couper-Kuhlen
Studia Fennica Linquistica 20
2017

## Studia Fennica Litteraria

**Metaliterary Layers in Finnish Literature**
Edited by Samuli Hägg, Erkki Sevänen & Risto Turunen
Studia Fennica Litteraria 3
2008

**Aino Kallas**
*Negotiations with Modernity*
Edited by Leena Kurvet-Käosaar & Lea Rojola
Studia Fennica Litteraria 4
2011

**The Emergence of Finnish Book and Reading Culture in the 1700s**
Edited by Cecilia af Forselles & Tuija Laine
Studia Fennica Litteraria 5
2011

**Nodes of Contemporary Finnish Literature**
Edited by Leena Kirstinä
Studia Fennica Litteraria 6
2012

**White Field, Black Seeds**
*Nordic Literacy Practices in the Long Nineteenth Century*
Edited by Anna Kuismin & M. J. Driscoll
Studia Fennica Litteraria 7
2013

Lieven Ameel
**Helsinki in Early Twentieth-Century Literature**
*Urban Experiences in Finnish Prose Fiction 1890–1940*
Studia Fennica Litteraria 8
2014

**Novel Districts**
*Critical Readings of Monika Fagerholm*
Edited by Kristina Malmio & Mia Österlund
Studia Fennica Litteraria 9
2016

www.ingramcontent.com/pod-product-compliance
Lightning Source LLC
Chambersburg PA
CBHW080807300426
44114CB00020B/2861